INTRODUCTION TO
EARLY CHURCH HISTORY

INTRODUCTION TO EARLY CHURCH HISTORY

The First 500 Years

Perry Edwards

FOREWORD BY David Daniels

WIPF & STOCK · Eugene, Oregon

INTRODUCTION TO EARLY CHURCH HISTORY
The First 500 Years

Wipf & Stock
An Imprint of Wipf and Stock Publishers
199 W. 8th Ave., Suite 3
Eugene, OR 97401

www.wipfandstock.com

PAPERBACK ISBN: 978-1-6667-5520-6
HARDCOVER ISBN: 978-1-6667-5521-3
EBOOK ISBN: 978-1-6667-5522-0

To my wife, Karen

Table of Contents

Foreword

ONE OF MY FIRST memories of Perry Edwards is of him seated at a desk in a Toronto hotel room poring over Hebrew grammar for a course he was taking at Toronto Baptist Seminary. It is memorable because we were attending the annual conference of the Fellowship of Evangelical Baptist Churches in Canada, the family of churches in which we were both serving as senior pastors. These annual conferences were times for reconnecting with friends and colleagues, for fun and fellowship, as well as conducting the business of our denomination. But here was Pastor Edwards, alone in his room, studying. It is a memory that has proven to be indicative of the man he has become—a lifelong learner with a passion to pour into the lives of others what God is teaching him.

Over the course of our twenty-plus year friendship, Perry has been a diligent student of biblical studies, theology, and the history of the Christian church. And in addition to faithfully shepherding congregations in the Canadian provinces of Ontario and New Brunswick, he has taught both experienced and fledgling pastors in several countries of the majority world through the Carey International Pastoral Training program of Carey Outreach Ministries.

This book you hold in your hands is the culmination of years of personal study, reflection, and teaching on the first five centuries of the Christian church. Written primarily as a text for his course in early church history, this book is a valuable resource for anyone desiring to understand how the first five hundred years of the New Testament church's development informs and influences the church of today.

Regrettably, many Christians think that all they need for effective Christian living is the Bible alone. Pastor Edwards confronts that thinking in the opening paragraphs of the book, reminding readers that while "the Bible is our final source of faith and practice, it is impossible to adequately understand Christian theology and Christian experience if we are ignorant of our Christian heritage." He provides six reasons why every Christian should be aware of the history of the Christian church. Don't skip the introduction!

Early church history is filled with fascinating accounts of both strong and weak personalities. You will witness lively theological debate, along with political intrigue. Through it all you will see the mystery of God's providence at work, defeating Satan's destructive attacks and preserving the church through the centuries. You will discover the roots of early creeds and confessions and come to recognize that contemporary expressions of faulty theology have their roots in ancient heresies. You will learn how doctrines like the trinity, the deity of Christ, and the inspiration of Scripture were developed.

As you see God's hand at work, preserving and guiding his church in ancient times, you will be encouraged to emulate the faithful and courageous lives of those who came before us. You will grow in appreciation for the rich and glorious heritage you have in the universal church of our Lord and Savior, Jesus Christ.

It was my privilege to read early drafts of each chapter and to see the finished manuscript before publication. Indeed, this is a text for all Christians.

David Daniels
Whitby, Ontario
May 26, 2022

Introduction

It has been rightly said, "The recording of history is to tell the story of the human family."[1] If we apply this definition to the Christian church, we could say that "the recording of (church) history is to tell the story of the (Christian) family." Just as a person needs to understand the history of the world if he is to comprehend the present state of the world, the Christian must understand the church's history if they are to comprehend the present state of the church. While it is true, as Christians, that the Bible is our final source of faith and practice, it is impossible to understand Christian theology and Christian experience if we are ignorant of our Christian heritage. Several years ago, a man told me that he sold his entire library and was only going to read the Bible from that point on. He told me that he didn't need anything but the Bible and that other books would only influence his understanding of the Bible's teaching. While I appreciate the man's sentiment, there are several reasons why I strongly disagree with his decision.

First, the Bible says, "So Christ himself gave the apostles, the prophets, the evangelists, the pastors and teachers, to equip his people for works of service, so that the body of Christ may be built up until we all reach unity in the faith and the knowledge of the Son of God and become mature, attaining to the whole measure of the fullness of Christ."[2] This passage tells us that teachers are appointed by God. They are his gifts to the church. For two thousand years, God has been gifting the church with great preachers and teachers, and to ignore their teaching just because they are dead is a denial of this wonderful truth. If my friend's opinion were pushed to its logical conclusion, he would have to stop listening

1. Dowley, *Eerdmans' Handbook to the History of Christianity*, 2.

2. Eph 4:11, 12 (English Standard Version used throughout unless otherwise stated).

to living preachers as well, because their teaching influences his understanding of the Bible. A failure to recognize the need to listen to the voices of teachers who have gone before us is to negate the very teaching of the Scriptures we are devoted to understanding.

Second, our understanding of Christian doctrine and the language we use to express it was determined by those who came before us. Terms like the Trinity; one God and three persons; the dual nature of Christ; the same substance; etc., did not just appear, but were introduced to help clarify biblical doctrine. Much of this theological language was established during the first five hundred years of the church's history and has been handed down to us through the centuries. There is no need to reinvent new theological language when our forebears provided language that was strong and concise. Certainly, further clarification on the doctrines of Scripture can be obtained by additional reflection upon the text, thus strengthening our understanding, but it must be acknowledged that we stand on the theological shoulders of those who have come before us and do not need to start our theological reflection as though we were born in the first century.

Third, knowing church history equips us to identify, expose, and combat heresy in the present-day church. Ecclesiastes 1:9 says, "What has been will be again, what has been done will be done again; there is nothing new under the sun." This truth applies to heretical teaching as well. There are very few, if any, new heresies today. Virtually all the so-called "modern heresies" find their parallel in the early church. Studying the church's response to these various heresies is vital as we combat them in the present day, both so we can emulate their success and avoid their errors.

Fourth, church history contains many terrible yet wonderful stories of men, women, and even children who remained faithful in the face of violent and merciless persecution. We find men and women who lived out the Christian faith, providing good models for us to follow. We are confronted by men who willingly gave up fortunes to follow Jesus; young mothers who gave up their infants rather than deny their Saviour; pastors who longed for martyrdom that they might receive a more glorious entrance into the kingdom of heaven; men and women who endured unimaginable suffering and yet remained faithful to death; Christian leaders who chose exile over compromising their faith, and many other heroic examples of vibrant Christian faith being lived out in the midst of a cruel and wicked world. Reading these stories will not only encourage our wavering hearts but will help to increase our resolve to stand true in the face of whatever persecution we might experience in our day.

Fifth, studying church history encourages humility in our lives. It reminds us that we are but one person in a long line of hundreds of millions of believers who have lived over the centuries. We tend to be myopic in our vision and church history helps to broaden our vision to see more clearly. As we read about the lives of those who have gone before us, our self-importance becomes smaller in the light of this great multitude who have already lived and died in Christ. As we examine these lives, we are inspired to live humbly before God, devoting our lives to sacrificial service to others.

Sixth, and most importantly, church history is the study of God's dealing with his people in the world. God has been working in the lives of people for thousands of years, and it is most delightful to see his hidden hand working in the lives of those who have gone before us. Church history is a treasure-house filled with priceless stories of God's lavish grace manifesting itself in the lives of ordinary people. As we see the hand of God guiding and directing the events of history, we can be encouraged to know that he continues to work tirelessly in our day as well.

First Century

While this introduction to early church history does not cover all the events in the book of Acts, it must be recognized that the beginning of the New Testament church is found in Jesus Christ and his choice of twelve men to become his apostles. The original twelve disciples, except for Judas, who was replaced by Matthias, would become the foundational leaders for the church of Jesus Christ. Through them, and others who were saved through their preaching, the church would grow rapidly. On the day of Pentecost, when Peter preached the first New Testament sermon, three thousand people were added to the church. Shortly thereafter another two thousand were added. Acts 2:47 describes what was happening quite succinctly, "And the Lord added to their number day by day those who were being saved." Through the preaching of Peter, Philip, Paul, and others, growing churches were planted throughout the Mediterranean world. By the time one reaches the end of the book of Acts, about thirty years after Jesus ascended into heaven, there were likely tens of thousands of people who had professed faith in Jesus Christ. The rapid growth of the church did not come without challenges that needed to be addressed by the pastors and theologians of the church. These challenges included doctrinal disputes revolving around the nature of God, Christ, and the Holy Spirit, church discipline, church structure, baptism, how to respond in times of persecution, and a plethora of other issues that would need to be resolved if the church was to continue advancing into the future. The first five hundred years of church history is a record of how the church dealt with many of these issues.

In the earlier days of the church, the greatest enemy and persecutor was the Jewish establishment, because they viewed Christianity as another heretical Jewish sect. Many in the Jewish community, primarily the Jewish leaders, resented the success of the apostles' preaching and felt threatened by the large number of people who, by believing the gospel's message, rejected their authority. Initially, the hostility was between Jews who believed Jesus was the Messiah and those who did not. It is important to note that the early Christians did not think they were rejecting their Jewish faith but were living in the days of its fulfillment.

Persecution in the first centuries of the church was not continual but did erupt, with great intensity, from time to time. As already noted, the Jews were the first persecutors of the church, but the Romans took up this role not long after the church's inception. Nero was the first Roman emperor to persecute the church, and it is believed that both Peter and Paul were martyred during his reign—sometime between 64 and 68 AD. The next great persecution took place under Emperor Domitian, who reigned from 81–96 AD. During this persecution, Domitian exiled the apostle John to the island of Patmos where John received and recorded the book of Revelation.[3]

Undoubtedly, apart from the birth, life, death, resurrection of Jesus Christ, and the Day of Pentecost, the most significant event in the first century was the destruction of Jerusalem in 70 AD. Jesus predicted its demise in Luke 21:20–22, "When you see Jerusalem being surrounded by armies, you will know that its desolation is near. Then let those who are in Judea flee to the mountains, let those in the city get out, and let those in the country not enter the city. For this is the time of punishment in fulfillment of all that has been written." The armies surrounding Jerusalem were the Roman legions led by General Titus, who destroyed Jerusalem and the Jewish temple. The destruction of Jerusalem is significant because

---

3. Eusebius, *History of the Church*, 125.

it publicly demonstrated that God's kingdom was no longer centered in the nation of Israel but in the New Testament church.

Second Century

The second century witnessed many significant developments within the Church. Persecution continued under Emperor Trajan and Emperor Marcus Aurelius, resulting in the deaths of several famous leaders, including Ignatius of Antioch (c.35–108), Polycarp (c.69–155), and Justin Martyr (c.100–65). We also see the beginnings of the early apologists who sought to provide a defense for the Christian faith. The "Didache" or "the Teaching of the Twelve Apostles" is a very ancient Christian document that contrasts the way of life and death.[4] It is unknown where or when it was composed. Many scholars date it in the first century, which would make it one of the most ancient Christian documents outside the New Testament that we possess. We also have the *The Epistle of Diognetus*, written by an unknown author in the second century to a man named Diognetus. This is probably the earliest surviving defense of Christianity. The purpose of the letter was to teach Diognetus about the Christian religion. The best-known apologist from this period is Justin Martyr. He wrote two apologies and a dialogue with a Jewish man. The most significant part of his works is the detailed and delightful description of an early second-century worship service.

One of the great theological heresies of the second century was Gnosticism.[5] So-called Christian Gnosticism was a thorn in the church's flesh, yet it was the church's struggle with Gnosticism that forced it to clarify its teaching on several issues. First, the church was compelled to determine which books of the Bible should be included in the canon of Scripture. Second, the church produced the Apostles' Creed as a theological defence against the Gnostic onslaught upon Christian doctrine and continues to be used in thousands of churches around the world to the present day. Third, the church argued for apostolic succession, a compelling argument in the second century but not especially useful today,

4. Thomas O'Loughlin, *Didache*.

5. The term "Gnosticism" comes from the Greek word *gnosis*, which means "knowledge." Gnosticism was a syncretistic religious movement that drew together elements from Judaism, Greek philosophy, Pagan religions, and Christianity and was thus characterized by great diversity.

and as we shall see, was one of the main causes of the separation of the eastern and western branches of Christianity.

The second century also saw the rise of the first great teachers of the church, after the apostles. Irenaeus of Lyons (c.115–202), Clement of Alexandria (c.150–215), Tertullian (c.155–220)—who introduced the word "Trinity" into Christian theology—and Origen of Alexandria (c.184–c.253), all key leaders within the church during this period. Their writings reveal the challenges they faced in formulating complex theological concepts as they sought to understand the nature of God and Christ as revealed in Scripture. Roland Bainton rightly observed, "the history of Christian thought is the record of man's wrestling with the implications of the self-disclosure of God in the man Christ Jesus."[6] This struggle would continue in the centuries to come. While we may object to some of their theological conclusions, we cannot deny the positive contributions they have made to our understanding of Christian theology today.

Third Century

The third century opened with another wave of persecution promulgated by Emperor Septimius Severus who ruled from AD 193–211. In the year 202, Severus issued an edict that required everybody to participate in the cult of worship of the Unconquered Sun. For Christians who had sworn allegiance to Jesus Christ, this was a problem, and it led to the martyrdom of Irenaeus; Origen's father, Leonides; Perpetua, and Felicitas, along with numerous unnamed Christians. In the mid-third century, Emperor Decius, who ruled only two years (249–51), initiated the first empire-wide persecution against the Christians. Up to this time, the persecutions were more local and sporadic. The death of Decius in 251 provided some short-lived hope for suffering Christians. Valerian became the emperor in 253, and initially seemed to be favorable toward Christians, but before long his attitude toward them changed, and he initiated a horrendous persecution against them.[7]

During these periods of persecution, a movement known as Novatianism[8] arose, posing a genuine threat to the unity of the church. Novatianism was a debate about whether Christians who lapsed in times

6. Gonzales, *History of Christian Thought*, 15.

7. Eusebius, *History of the Church*, 298.

8. Novatianism was named after its founder, Novatian (c.200–58).

of persecution should be allowed back into membership. Novatianism's hard-line stance against receiving lapsed Christians back into membership led to a rupture in the church's unity.

Fourth Century

Following a period of relative calm, Emperor Diocletian (284–305)—under whose administration the empire was divided into four sections under four sub-emperors with Diocletian retaining ultimate power—initiated the last, and worst, widespread persecution against the church. In 303, he issued four edicts against the Christians and a fifth one in 304. All church buildings were to be destroyed, Christian books were to be confiscated, all Christians were to be dismissed from the government and army, the clergy were to be imprisoned, and finally, all Christians were required to offer sacrifices to the pagan gods. This last edict was, of course, unacceptable to genuine Christians. Despite widespread persecution in the early part of the century, the fourth century would see Christianity legalized under Emperor Constantine (306–37) and declared the Roman Empire's official religion by Emperor Theodosius (379–95).

One of the great theological struggles of the fourth century concerned the nature of Jesus Christ. Arianism, which teaches that Jesus was a man, but not God, emerged and the church entered into a serious struggle with this contentious heresy. The Council of Nicaea (the first ecumenical council) was called by Emperor Constantine I in 325 AD to address this crucial issue. At this council, the famous Nicene Creed was produced, a creed that defined the parameters of orthodoxy for the Christian church, which continues to present day. The First Council of Constantinople (the second ecumenical council) was called in 381 to address the issue of the nature of the Holy Spirit. The language used in the creeds produced by these two councils continues to impact the language we use today when describing the triune nature of God.

One of the great defenders of the Nicene Creed came to the forefront at this time. Athanasius (296–373), an African bishop, was destined to become the greatest theologian of his generation. He was an ardent defender of the Nicene Creed and the greatest opponent of those who defended the Arian position. His book, *On the Incarnation*, is a wonderful defense of the divine nature of Jesus Christ. Athanasius was also the first to refer to the twenty-seven books of the New Testament as the Canon of Scripture.

Monasticism also emerged at this time and became a great spiritual and intellectual force in the church. Monasticism arose in response to the influx of vast numbers of people, many of whom were not true Christians into the church, after Constantine legalized Christianity. The church had become so influential that the great powers of the world acknowledged her strength and began to court her in the same way that a man might attempt to win the favour of a wealthy and influential woman. Wealth, luxury, pomp, and political influence had infiltrated the church. Church leaders now lived in lavish homes with increasing wealth and influence. Many devout Christians were disgusted with this new development, viewing it as great apostasy. In response to this corruption, a number of these pious Christians retreated to the desert to live out their Christian lives away from the corruption of both the world and the church. This retreat to the desert marked the beginning of the monastic movement. Prominent leaders in early monasticism include Paul of Thebes (c.226/27–c.341), Anthony (c.251–356), Pachomius (c.292–348), Basil the Great (330–79), and Jerome (342–420).

Another great leader of the fourth century was Chrysostom, known as the "golden-mouthed preacher." He was born around 350 and died in 407. He served much of his ministry in the city of Constantinople (modern-day Istanbul). We possess many of his sermons and an excellent work entitled *On the Priesthood*, which provides directions for men who serve in pastoral ministry.

Fifth Century

Augustine, one of the greatest and most influential theologians in the church's history, was born in 354 and died in 430. His theological shadow casts itself over both Roman Catholicism and Protestantism. He influenced Roman Catholic theologians Bernard of Clairvaux and Thomas Aquinas and sixteenth-century Protestant Reformers Martin Luther and John Calvin. His ideas have shaped the life of the church for over fifteen hundred years. His most popular and well-known work is entitled *Confessions*. There were three main controversies in his life: Manichaeism, Donatism, and Pelagianism, which he countered through his various writings.

Two major councils met in the fifth century. The First Council of Ephesus (the third ecumenical council that met in 431) addressed the Nestorian controversy—the belief that there are two separate persons in the incarnate Christ, one divine and one human. The Council of Chalcedon (the fourth ecumenical council that met in 451) dealt with the Eutychian heresy—the belief that there was only one nature in Christ.

During the fifth century, another significant Christian movement known as Celtic Christianity developed under the great Irish missionary, Patrick. Patrick was born around 389 in Roman Britain but was destined to become a missionary to the Irish.

Another significant fifth century leader was Leo the Great (400–61), who lived in a time of considerable change. In the final years of Rome's world dominance, the barbarians (people outside the boundaries of the Roman empire) were overrunning the land, and few men had the strength of character to stand up and lead during this tumultuous time. Leo was an exception. He was a man of great gifts and abilities, and his work prepared the church to take a leading role in the rebuilding of Europe after the fall of the Roman empire. Leo is considered by many to be the first pope of the church. He certainly committed himself to furthering the claim of the Roman bishop's supremacy over the universal church. Despite his push towards centralized control in the church, he was theologically orthodox.

Finally, one of the great monks born in the fifth century was Benedict; who was born in 480 and died in 547. He began his life as a secluded hermit, eventually leaving his solitary life to establish monasteries for communities of both men and women. Benedict's most outstanding achievement was his production of a seventy-three-chapter rule book for monastic living, known as *The Rule of Benedict*. Written around AD 516, it provided a standard for monastic life in the western church. The new rule book corrected some of the excesses of the past and provided sensible and reasonable codes of conduct. Its reasonableness is undoubtedly one of the reasons it became so popular as a basis for monastic life. It seemed to strike the right balance between work, study, prayer, community, and rest.

Conclusion

In addition to the six reasons mentioned earlier for studying church history, understanding church history is also crucial for comprehending the history of the western world. I remember a non-Christian professor in a class on sixteenth-century English history telling his students that he would be talking a great deal about theology. It was not a class in theology, but the historical issues of sixteenth-century England were theological in nature, as they were for Europe generally. From the time of Constantine I, the church and state were bound together like the strands of a tightly woven rope. You cannot understand one without understanding the other.

A knowledge of church history is vital in our understanding of both the western and eastern world. Eastern Orthodoxy, the Coptic Church; the Greek Orthodox Church; the Russian Orthodox Church, and the various other Orthodox communities share the same early history as the Western Church. Although this book will not be covering Eastern Orthodoxy, it is important to note that the first five hundred years of church history is the common heritage of virtually every Christian community on earth. While there are very significant theological differences between these various branches of the church, they share the same foundation.

As an introduction to early church history, this book is not intended to cover any subject exhaustively. Its goal is to provide an overview of the most significant leaders of the church while adding heartwarming stories of ordinary Christians who remained faithful to the Lord in the face of persecution. It will introduce readers to how the church, in its first five centuries, sought to answer the primary theological questions of the day. In writing this book, I hope to whet the appetite of those who have never read early church history and refresh the minds of those who have. For some, I hope the reading of this book will be the beginning of a journey that will lead to a deep and abiding love for the history of God's sovereign working in the church and in the world.

Chapter 1

Alexander the Great and the Romans

IN ORDER TO UNDERSTAND the first-century church, we must have some knowledge of the events that transpired prior to the birth of the New Testament church. Some significant events include the destruction of the northern kingdom of Israel in 722 BC, the fall of the southern kingdom of Judah and its capital Jerusalem, in 586 BC; the Hellenization of the known world under Alexander the Great in the fourth century BC; the establishment of the synagogue, and the rise of Rome. We will explore how some of these events influenced and impacted early Christianity.

Diaspora Judaism

For centuries leading up to the time of Christ, the Jewish people were scattered throughout the known world. In 722 BC, the ten northern tribes of Israel were defeated by the Assyrians and the people were relocated throughout the Assyrian Empire. In 586 BC, the southern kingdom of Judah was destroyed by the Babylonians, along with the temple in Jerusalem, and the Jews were scattered throughout the Babylonian empire. While it is true that Jerusalem and the temple were eventually rebuilt, most Jews did not go back to Israel. A whole generation had passed since they were sent into exile and so there was little reason for them to relocate to a place that had never been their home country. By the time of the Roman Empire, a sizable population of Jews lived in most major cities spread throughout the Mediterranean world. These scattered Jews are called the "Diaspora" or the "Dispersion." The dispersion of the Jews played a significant role in preparing the way for the dispersion of Christianity throughout the world. There are two significant reasons for this:

1

the translation of the Hebrew scriptures into Greek (the Septuagint); and the rise of the Jewish synagogue.

Alexander the Great and the Septuagint

One of the most influential men of the fourth century BC was Alexander III, King of the Macedonians, more commonly known as Alexander the Great. Born in 356 BC, he was educated by the philosopher Aristotle, and was known for his military prowess from a young age.[1] He succeeded his father Philip II of Macedon in 336 BC. Philip II had been an effective king who consolidated Macedon and the surrounding regions forming a united Greek confederation, with the lone exception of Sparta.[2] He planned to attack the mighty Persian empire but was assassinated by Pausanias of Orestis, one of his royal bodyguards, just before beginning his campaign. Following the death of Philip, Alexander was declared king. He spent the next decade fulfilling his father's dream of crushing the once-mighty Persian empire and extending Greek interests throughout the world. Alexander pressed on as far as India, forging a vast Macedonian kingdom that stretched from Greece to India.[3] While leading his army back to Persia following his Indian campaigns, Alexander contracted an unknown disease—possibly malaria or Typhus. He died in Babylon in 323 BC at thirty-three years of age.[4] After his death, his newly formed empire was divided by his generals into four smaller Greek-ruled kingdoms, each still mighty in its own right. Ptolemy took control of Egypt, starting the Ptolemaic empire; Seleucus took control of Syria and Mesopotamia, forming the Seleucid empire; Cassander ruled Macedonia and Greece, creating the kingdom of Macedon, and Lysimachus took Thrace and much of Asia Minor. The Romans would eventually absorb all of these kingdoms into their own empire.

Although Alexander died relatively young, the influence of his life and legacy profoundly impacted the spread of the gospel throughout the early centuries of the Christian church. As Alexander extended his empire, he founded new cities (many named after himself). He established Greek colonies, resulting in the spread of Greek culture, and inaugurating

---

1. Miles Doleac, *Footsteps of Alexander*, 24.
2. Miles Doleac, *Footsteps*, 38.
3. Frank Welsh, *History of the World*, 57–59.
4. Miles Doleac, *Footsteps*, 176.

a new Hellenistic civilization, which lasted from 323–31 BC.[5] The Greek language became the language of the people, forming a linguistic link in this period. The importance of this linguistic shift cannot be exaggerated. Even though the Hellenistic empire technically came to an end in 31 BC, the Romans inherited Greek culture, blending it with their own. The Greek language became the common language of the Roman Empire.[6] It has been rightly said that while "the Romans conquered Greece, the culture of the Greeks conquered the Romans."[7]

One consequence of the spread of Hellenism was that many Jews of the diaspora forgot how to read and speak Hebrew—the language of their forefathers. For this reason, it became necessary for the Hebrew scriptures to be translated into Greek, enabling the large number of Jews to have access to them. This translation was known as the Septuagint. The legend surrounding the production of the Septuagint is that seventy (or seventy-two) scholars translated the Old Testament independently. When they compared their translations, it was found that they were in complete agreement.[8] While this story is most likely fabricated, or at least highly embellished, it provided proof for some that the translation received divine approval. Irenaeus, a second-century Greek bishop, believed the story to be accurate and deemed the Septuagint as superior to all other translations.[9] The Roman numeral LXX is used when referring to the Septuagint.

The influence the Septuagint had on the spread of Christianity cannot be overstated. The world in which Jesus was born was a Greek world. The common language of the people was Greek. To have an Old Testament Greek translation meant not only that Hellenized Jews but the vast majority of non-Jews who lived in the Roman Empire could hear the scriptures preached in their own language. The Septuagint was the Scripture of the early church, and most of the Old Testament quotes found in the New Testament come not from the Hebrew text but from the Septuagint.

5. Miles Doleac, *Footsteps*, 193.

6. Miles Doleac, *Footsteps*, 211.

7. Wylen, *Jews in the time of Jesus*, 36.

8. Richard Kalmin, "Miracle of the Septuagint," 245.

9. Irenaeus, *Against Heresies*, 3.21.2–3.

The Rise of the Synagogue

Another important development in the centuries leading up to the New Testament church was the rise of the Synagogue. As a result of the Jewish dispersion, the temple in Jerusalem was no longer the central place of worship for many Jews. It was probably sometime after the Babylonian Exile that the local synagogue emerged as the focal point of the religious life of the Jewish community.[10] During the Maccabean era (167–37 BC), there was a religious revival that resulted in the emergence of religious communities in which the law of Moses was discussed and interpreted. These religious circles formed the basis for many of the synagogues that were established for the public reading and teaching of the law.[11] While we do not know when the first synagogues appeared, the New Testament tells us they were scattered throughout the Roman Empire in the first century AD. It is estimated that there were between three hundred and ninety-four and four hundred and eighty synagogues in the city of Jerusalem alone during the first century AD.[12] Both Jesus and the original disciples were Jews and regularly worshiped in the synagogue. It was the practice of the apostle Paul when he first visited a new town, to visit the synagogue to preach. While he was in Ephesus, he preached for three months in the synagogue until he was forced to withdraw.[13]

The structure and worship of the synagogue profoundly influenced the early church as it began to organize itself into assemblies. In the ancient synagogue, there appear to have been five components in their gatherings. First, the Shema which was the recitation of various passages from the book of Deuteronomy. Second, the offering of prayer. Third, readings from the Law. Fourth, the reading of the Prophets, and fifth, the sermon.[14] There does not seem to have been a regular ministry performed by one man, but any qualified male was permitted to read the scriptures or give the sermon. This would explain why Paul was able to preach in

10. Schaff, *History of the Christian Church*, 1:456.

11. *Encyclopedia of Ancient Christianity*, 3:670.

12. Schaff, *History of the Christian Church*, 1:457. Alfred Edersheim, *Temple*, says that "tradition fixes the number at from 460–480," 35.

13. Acts 19:8,9. The Greek word translated "assembly" is συναγωγή.

14. Leon Morris, *Saints and the Synagogue*, 42.

the synagogues as he traveled from town to town.[15] Interestingly, James refers to a Christian church as a synagogue in his New Testament letter.[16]

The influence the Jewish synagogue had on the Christian assembly cannot be fully understood. Nevertheless, the five components of early Jewish worship are also part of early Christian worship with a new Christocentric emphasis. The reading of Scripture, prayer, recitation of Scripture, and preaching were central elements in early Christian worship. We see this in Paul's instruction to Timothy when he wrote, "Until I come, devote yourself to the public reading of Scripture, to exhortation, to teaching."[17] He also said, "Preach the word."[18] In addition to readings from the Old Testament, the New Testament church included the apostles' writings. The book of Acts tells us, "And they devoted themselves to the apostles' teaching and the fellowship, to the breaking of bread and the prayers."[19] Peter tells us that Paul's letters were as authoritative as Old Testament Scripture,[20] and Paul expected that his letters would be read in the church and his teaching obeyed.[21]

As already stated, the Jewish synagogue allowed multiple men to participate in the public reading and preaching of the Word. We see this same freedom in the early church. Jesus went to the synagogues, read Scripture, and explained Scripture to the people. The apostles were invited to preach in the synagogues wherever they went. Many Jewish men could participate publicly in a Jewish worship service. Paul indicates that this same freedom was present in the early church. Paul wrote, "What then, brothers? When you come together, each one has a hymn, a lesson, a revelation, a tongue, or an interpretation. Let all things be done for building up."[22]

Although we do not know precisely what took place in the Jewish synagogue of the first century, it is safe to say that the Christians adopted the general pattern of the synagogue and adapted it for Christian worship and the administration of the church.

15. Wilkins Worship, *Theology and the Ministry in the Early Church*, 43.

16. Jas 2:2.

17. 1 Tim 4:13.

18. 2 Tim 4:2.

19. Acts 2:42.

20. 2 Pet 3:16.

21. 1 Tim 4:1–3.

22. 1 Cor 14:26.

Alexander the Great and the Persecution of the Church

Alexander the Great was not only a brilliant and successful military tactician but he also demonstrated political proficiency when assimilating new regions into his expanding empire. Under the Persian occupation, there was little respect given to deities of conquered peoples, and the Persian kings were more likely to destroy foreign gods than to incorporate them into their own religious policy. This hardline attitude certainly did not win the hearts of the local people.[23] Alexander approached the situation differently. Many of the cities he inherited from the Persians were religiously and culturally diverse, and Alexander possessed a deep reverence for the innumerable deities worshipped. It has been said, "to take Alexander's historians at face value, one would have to conclude that the king of Macedon never met a god whom he did not like. He never found an oracle unworthy of consultation. He never encountered a myth that did not merit investigation."[24] Rather than destroying the local temples and statues of the gods, he offered sacrifices to them and honoured them before the people. We see this most vividly demonstrated when he arrived in Egypt in the winter of 332/1 BC. He ordered the reconstruction of both the Karnak and Luxor temple and was willingly crowned as Pharaoh and declared king of Egypt.[25] It is impossible to know if Alexander's actions resulted from a feeling of genuine religious connection to these various gods or simply was an act of political expediency—it could have been both. Whatever the reason, it certainly was a brilliant tactic in his attempt to win the support and loyalty of the people.[26]

As Alexander conquered more Persian territory, he continued his policy of religious syncretism, even adopting the lofty ways of the Persian kings. When he entered Babylon, it was in the manner of a triumphal procession, surrounded by celebratory chants of the people who viewed him as a deliverer. Alexander offered sacrifices to Marduk and ordered the rebuilding of the temple of Marduk. As he moved further east, Alexander took on the role of a Babylonian monarch adopting the Persian belief that the king was a god-King. He even had his own men bow before him in acknowledgment of his royal status. Although the Persians were accustomed to this kind of behavior, the Greeks were not, and before the

---

23. Miles Doleac, *Footsteps of Alexander*, 179, 180.

24. Miles Doleac, *Footsteps*, 190.

25. Miles Doleac, *Footsteps*, 189.

26. Miles Doleac, *Footsteps*, 180–185.

time of Philip II of Macedon's reign, kingship was scorned amongst the Greeks.[27] This was, however, in keeping with Alexander's belief that he was a descendant of the gods and had divine blood coursing through his veins. Having set the pattern for kingship, Alexander's successors carried this idea forward into their reigns, and the concept of kingship become deeply entrenched in the Hellenistic world.[28] Every successor claimed that they were a "god-king" and that their right to rule was rooted in their quasi-divine status.[29]

When the Romans came to power in the Mediterranean world, it was a small leap for the people to transfer divine status to their generals. Although men like Flaminius in 196 BC and Mark Antony, who ruled the Eastern empire from 42–31 BC, were accorded divine status by the Greeks, it was not until the time of the Caesars that the Romans would accept divine status for the emperors. Caesar Augustus, the first emperor of Rome, who ruled from 27 BC to 14 AD, was worshiped as a god-king throughout Egypt and Asia Minor. Large numbers of people worshiped at the many altars and temples built in honour of his divine status, including a large altar in Lyon, Gaul (modern day France). Despite his refusal to be worshipped in Rome or Italy because the Romans would have considered this scandalous, he was declared to be divine following his death by none other than the Roman Senate.[30] Subsequent Caesars, then, had no problem claiming divine status even while they were still alive. It is not surprising that Emperor Nero (54–68) believed that he was a manifestation of the sun god Helios and that Emperor Domitian demanded that he be called "Lord and God." In the first century, these emperors were the most vicious persecutors of the church. This claim of divine status was one reason the Romans persecuted the Christians. When the Roman authorities demanded that a pinch of incense be given in honour of the emperor, the Christians would not participate. Emperor worship was unacceptable in the mind of the Christian because there was only one God-king, and his name is Jesus.

27. Miles Doleac, *Footsteps*, 188–95.

28. Miles Doleac, *Footsteps*, 194.

29. Miles Doleac, *Footsteps*, 207.

30. Miles Doleac, *Footsteps*, 422.

Roman Infrastructure

One reason for the rapid spread of the gospel throughout the Mediterranean world was Roman infrastructure. The Roman Empire was magnificent in so many ways. Its architecture, deeply influenced by the Greeks, was extravagant and unparalleled anywhere in the world. Its temples were enormous, and public buildings were grand in scale. Triumphal arches graced many cities, gargantuan and elaborately decorated Imperial baths were constructed for the people's pleasure. The Circus Maximus in Rome was designed for horse racing and other games to amuse the people. The aqueduct system that supplied water for the major cities was unparalleled, and the sewage system was so advanced that it was not surpassed until modern times. One of the greatest architectural wonders was the Colosseum in Rome, which opened in 80 AD. and is the largest amphitheater ever built, seating up to eighty thousand people. Even today, the Roman ruins continue to spark wonder in those who visit them.

Although the buildings and infrastructure of the Roman Empire were impressive, it was the peace (Pax Romana) that the Romans imposed upon the Mediterranean world and the elaborate Roman road system that helps explain how the gospel blew like the wind throughout the Empire. The gospel was so successful that the apostle Paul could write to the church in Colossae in 52/53 AD,—only twenty years after the resurrection of Jesus Christ— "the gospel is bearing fruit and growing throughout the whole world."[31] No empire had ever come close to developing the spiderweb-like network of roads that connected the city of Rome to the far reaches of the empire. Initially, Roman reoads were constructed for the swift moment of troops, but it was not long before they were used for civilian travel as well.[32] Paul and his companions traveled on these roads from city to city, preaching the gospel and establishing churches. While the Roman emperors who constructed these roads had the glory of Rome and the growth of the Roman empire in mind, the early Christians traveled these roads for the glory of God and the spread of His kingdom.

The Roman army also played a significant role in the spreading of the gospel. Some Roman soldiers became Christians and continued to serve in the Roman army. They were stationed throughout the empire and carried the gospel with them to faraway lands. Many believe Christianity

31. Col 1:6.

32. Nigel Rogers, *Roman Empire*, 160.

was first introduced to Britain by faithful Roman Christian soldiers who shared the message of Jesus Christ wherever they went.[33]

Roman Religion

The ancient Roman world was polytheistic, and their gods and goddesses were associated with every aspect of life. War, hunting, love, marriage, family, weather, rivers, forest glades, agriculture, blacksmithing, and virtually every other facet of life was related to a god or a goddess. A god ruled every domain. Some gods ruled the sky, others ruled the sea, and others ruled the underworld. There was no part of the visible or invisible world that was not governed by a deity.

Religion was an essential part of Roman life and its roots sunk deep into the soil of Greek religion. When Rome defeated the Greeks, much of Greek religion was assimilated into their own, resulting in a Graeco-Roman religion. The main Greek gods and goddesses are known as the Olympians because it was believed that they lived on Mount Olympus in Greece. The names of the prominent Olympians were Zeus, the god of the sky; Demeter, the goddess of nature; Apollo, the god of light; Aphrodite, goddess of love; Hera, the goddess of the family; Athena, goddess of wisdom; Artemis, goddess of hunting; Hephaestus, the god of fire; Poseidon, the god of the sea; Dionysus, the god of wine; Ares, the god of war; and Hermes, the messenger of the gods. The Romans renamed these gods and welcomed them into their belief system under different names. Zeus became Jupiter; Demeter became Ceres; Apollo kept his name; Aphrodite became Venus; Hera became Juno; Athena became Minerva; Artemis became Diana; Hephaestus became Vulcan; Poseidon became Neptune; Dionysus became Bacchus; Ares became Mars, and Hermes became Mercury. As Rome grew in influence and power, other gods made their way into the Roman Pantheon: Sarapis, a Graeco-Egyptian deity from Egypt, Mithras, a Zoroastrian deity, and Cybele of Phrygia, to name a few. The cults associated with these newer deities promised a mystical experience to their adherents which sharply contrasted with the ritualistic but spiritually unfulfilling official religion of the empire.[34]

Roman religion was highly ritualistic. The gods needed to be appeased, and there was a ritual to be performed in association with every

33. Cairns, *Christianity Through the Centuries*, 39.

34. Nigel Rogers, *Roman Empire*, 415.

activity, whether it be the maintenance of public infrastructure, diplomatic relationships, or any number of everyday endeavors.[35] The Romans were distrustful of personal spiritual experiences, which they deemed unnecessary. The proper performance of rituals was necessary to discern the will of the gods or to placate their anger. The external form of religion was of greater concern than what was going on in the heart.[36] If you held a public office in Rome, you spent a lot of your time participating in ceremonial rituals.

This emphasis on ceremony was embedded in the Roman mind from the beginning. From the time of Romulus, who founded Rome in 713 BC, it was understood that these rituals were to be perfectly performed if they were to be acceptable to the gods. Every spoken word, every movement needed to be done according to a prescribed manner, or the ceremony would have to be repeated until it was flawless.[37] There was an established calendar of sacred and secular days, colleges for training priests, and various cults.[38] On the days dedicated to the gods, businesses shut down so that the entire city could participate in the games and festivities. The celebrations were offered to the gods as an expression of thanksgiving for a great victory or to appease the deity's wrath.[39] Many Roman deities lived in temples, which often included a statue of the god. The temple was not a place to gather for worship, like a church building, but the house of the god. The worshipers would meet outside but would rarely enter the inner precincts of the temple. On religious holidays the statue of the deity would be taken from the temple and carried throughout the city.[40]

Although deemed necessary for the maintenance of the empire, this pragmatic religion of the Romans did not meet the deep spiritual needs of the people. The influx of mystery religions filled the empty religious experience offered by Roman religion. The mystery religions became popular because they emphasized individual spiritual experience and promised secret knowledge and immortality to the individual.[41] They

35. Anthony Everitt, *Rise of Rome*, 62.

36. Anthony Everitt, *Rise of Rome*, 168.

37. Anthony Everitt, *Rise of Rome*, 26.

38. Anthony Everitt, *Rise of Rome*, 60.

39. Anthony Everitt, *Rise of Rome*, 298.

40. Nigel Rogers, *Roman Empire*, 416.

41. R.H. Barrow, *Romans*, 142.

became so popular that the Roman Senate sought to inhibit their growth out of fear that people would neglect their public duties to the empire.[42] Some of these foreign cults were officially recognized but had to pass three tests before they received official sanction: First, would they be a threat to the dominance of the Roman cults? Second, were they politically dangerous? Third, were they morally objectionable?[43]

The Romans believed that Christianity was nothing more than a mystery cult. The problem was that Christianity failed to meet the criteria for official recognition. Several issues faced the early Christians as they inevitably came into conflict with the religion of the Roman Empire. First, there was the issue of food sacrificed to idols. Like most other ancient religions, sacrificing animals was of primary importance in Roman worship. Animals were regularly sacrificed to the gods to procure their blessing or turn away their wrath. A portion of the slaughtered animal was offered as a burnt sacrifice, and the worshipers ate the rest. Other offerings might include flours or cakes.[44] It was the sharing of the sacrifice with the worshipers that presented the greatest problem for the Christian. When you ate the meat sacrificed to an idol, it was believed that you were communing with the god to whom the sacrifice was offered. It was such a serious issue that the apostle Paul addressed it in his letter to the Corinthian church.[45]

Second, there was the issue of Emperor worship. From the time of Augustus' reign (63 BC–14 AD), emperor worship was added to unite the Empire. As already noted, in the eastern empire, there was a long history of attributing divine qualities and titles to rulers. Alexander's successors were endowed with many lofty titles that blurred the lines between God and man. For the eastern portion of the empire, worshipping the emperor was entirely acceptable. This was also true in Egypt that had a long history of attributing divine attributes to the Pharaoh. While the Romans did revere their great heroes of days gone by, the idea of ascribing deity to a man was abhorrent to them. Nonetheless, in Augustus' time, a cult of "Rome and Augustus" was established so that people could express their loyalty to Rome. As Roman emperors took on greater divine status, they claimed more divine titles. This cult became especially problematic for

42. Nigel Rogers, *Roman Empire*, 424.

43. R.H. Barrow, *Romans*, 144.

44. Nigel Rogers, *Roman Empire*, 416.

45. 1 Cor 8:1–13.

Christians who refused to worship the emperor or acknowledge him as Lord and God. This refusal resulted in harsh persecution.[46]

Third, there was the issue of idols. The Roman Empire was filled with a great number of idols. The book of Acts says, "Now while Paul was waiting for them at Athens, his spirit was provoked within him as he saw that the city was full of idols."[47] This was true of the entire Roman world. In the ancient world, votive statuettes were mass-produced and sold to people as they visited the various temples. Workshops were set up near popular temples where artisans would sell figurines made of bronze, silver, or a less expensive material like terracotta. The selling of statues was a very lucrative trade, and those who profited from it did not take kindly to the Christians, whose message of the gospel threatened their livelihood. An example of this is found in the book of Acts which says, "About that time there arose no little disturbance concerning the Way. For a man named Demetrius, a silversmith, who made silver shrines of Artemis, brought no little business to the craftsmen. These he gathered together, with the workmen in similar trades, and said, "Men, you know that from this business we have our wealth. And you see and hear that not only in Ephesus but in almost all of Asia this Paul has persuaded and turned away a great many people, saying that gods made with hands are not gods.'"[48] Demetrius was more concerned with the loss of sales and profit than he was with honouring Artemis.

Christianity was a new religion without temples, statues, and animal sacrifices. It was the religion of the invisible God who did not live in temples made by men. Polycarp was a Christian pastor condemned to death in the second century. During his trial, the people in attendance cried out, "He is the teacher of Asia, the father of the Christians, the destroyer of our gods." Christians were a threat to the gods of Rome, and therefore Roman security, and it was only a matter of time before there arose conflict between them.

Discussion Questions

1. In ancient Rome, the road system enabled the quick dissemination of the gospel. What aspects of our culture today contribute to the

46. Barrow, *Romans*, 144, 145.
47. Acts 17:16.
48. Acts 19:23–26.

spreading of the gospel? Discuss how they can be utilized for the preaching of the gospel?

2. Are Christians ever justified in disobeying the government? In what areas should Christians submit to the government and in what areas should they not submit?

3. In what ways does religion meet people's needs? How does true Christianity differ from other religions?

Chapter 2

Jews and Gentiles

ALTHOUGH THE JEWS WERE a small nation of people originally centered in Palestine, they were destined to have a profound effect on the Roman world. The kingdom of Israel was established around 1050 BC when Saul was anointed the first king. After the death of Saul, David became king, and then David's son, Solomon, after him. Around 930 BC, at the beginning of the reign of king Rehoboam, son of Solomon, and the fourth king of Israel, the kingdom of Israel split into two nations. Ten of the twelve tribes of Israel broke away, forming the northern kingdom of Israel, and two tribes formed the southern kingdom of Judah. As mentioned in chapter one, the Assyrians destroyed the northern kingdom of Israel in 721/722 BC, and the Jews were scattered throughout the Assyrian empire. The Babylonians destroyed the southern kingdom of Judah in 586/587 BC, and the Jews were scattered throughout the Babylonian kingdom. These events marked the beginning of the Jewish diaspora.

With the fall of the southern kingdom in 586, Palestine was incorporated into the Persian empire and then later the Macedonian empire under Alexander the Great. Under Persian and Macedonian rule, the Jews were free to practice their faith openly. The Seleucids, one of the four Macedonian kingdoms to emerge after the death of Alexander, were more intentional in forcing Hellenism on the Jews. Many Jews embraced Hellenistic culture. They learned the Greek language, studied Greek philosophy, participated in public life, and there was little to differentiate them from the native Greeks around them.

Antiochus IV Epiphanes was the ruler of the Seleucid empire from 175–164 BC. He was impatient with the Jews and wanted to eradicate the Jewish faith and religion completely. During his reign, he imposed Greek culture on the Jews who resisted Hellenization. Among other practices, he outlawed circumcision, Sabbath observance, and the reading of the Torah. His most shocking act of oppression against the Jews was the erection of an altar to Zeus in the Jewish temple in Jerusalem, and the offering of pigs as sacrifices to pagan gods. The scriptures refer to the desecration of the temple as "the abomination that causes desolation."[1] This kind of blasphemy against the Jewish faith was certain to cause a reaction from the Jews.

The resistance came when Mattathias and his five sons, John, Simon, Judas (also know as Maccabeus), Eleazar, and Jonathan of the priestly Hasmonean family, led a Jewish rebellion against the Seleucid empire, lasting from 167–63 BC. This rebellion is known as the Maccabean revolt. Mattathias died in 166 and appointed his son Judas as commander of the Jewish forces. Contrary to all expectations, the Jews defeated Antiochus in 165, regaining their religious freedom and national independence. The temple was cleansed and rededicated in 164, and this event is still observed as the festival of Hanukkah. Josephus described the dedication of the temple as follows:

> He and the rest of his men purified the temple, which had become desolate, with weeds growing inside the sanctuary. Rebuilding the altar and restoring the sacred implements, they rekindled the lampstand and burned incense there, three years to the day since Antiochus defiled the temple. Judas and his men celebrated a great feast which lasted for eight days, and which we continue to observe as the festival of Lights.[2]

After the war was over, the Jews began to rebuild their nation. Judah's brother, Simon, was appointed high priest and ruler of the Jews in about 140 BC. This marked the beginning of the Hasmonean Dynasty that, despite many internal divisions, lasted for about a hundred years. In 37 BC, Caesar Augustus installed Herod the Great (37 BC–4 AD) as king of Judea, marking the end of the Hasmonean and the beginning of the Herodian dynasty. During Herod's reign, Judea became a vassal of the Roman Empire, but shortly after the death of Herod, it was brought under direct Roman administration in 6 AD and was made a province of the empire. Judea was governed by a Roman prefect who was granted authority to execute criminals. Roman officials were now involved in virtually

1. Dan 9:27; 11:31; 12:11.
2. *Josephus, Complete Works* (Ant. 12.265).

every aspect of peoples' lives. The people also paid taxes directly to Rome. There was great unrest throughout the Jewish community because of Roman rule. Jewish independence was a recent memory, and Roman domination was difficult for the Jewish people to accept. Bitterness simmered for decades until it resulted in an open revolt against Rome in 66 AD, leading to the destruction of Jerusalem in 70 AD.

The Christian church was born into this tumultuous Roman and Jewish world. The church began in Jerusalem on the day of Pentecost in c.30 AD when the first disciples received the gift of the Holy Spirit, and from the very beginning, the church experienced conflict with both the Jews and the Romans.

First Century Jewish Communities

In the first century AD, there were four significant Jewish groups: the Pharisees, the Sadducees, the Zealots, and the Essenes.

The Pharisees

The term Pharisee means "separated ones." The Pharisees were members of one of three major parties in Judaism dating from the last centuries BC to the destruction of the temple in 70 AD. Josephus (37–c.100 AD), a Romano-Jewish historian, mentions their existence in the second century BC,[3] and yet it is difficult to determine the extent of their influence at that time. While we do not know precisely when the Pharisees began, they may have emerged out of the Hasidim at the time of the Maccabean revolt.[4] After the Babylonian exile, in 586 BC, the Law replaced the temple as the fundamental aspect of Jewish worship. Desiring to re-establish the historic Jewish faith, the Pharisees made the Torah[5]—the first five books of Genesis—central in the Jewish community. As teachers of the "Law," they publicly read the "Torah" and expounded it to the people.

Because they believed it was essential to follow the Torah, they debated the meaning of the law and sought to apply it to virtually every area of life. As a result, a large body of commentary, called the Mishnah, was developed to reinforce and supplement the text of the Torah. The

---

3. *Josephus, Complete Works* (Ant. 13.171).

4. Everett Ferguson, *Backgrounds of Early Christianity*, 636.

5. The Torah is also called the Pentateuch.

Pharisees produced this body of extra-biblical writings to help the people interpret the law of God. Unfortunately, it led to a legalistic approach to the Jewish faith, where works became central for salvation, and faith was of lesser importance. This legalism is the focus of Jesus' criticism of the Pharisees throughout the New Testament.[6] While he acknowledged that the Pharisees were righteous men, at least outwardly, and possessed the authority to expound Moses and the prophets to the people, he condemned them for their self-righteousness and failure to grasp the central place of repentance.[7] This is illustrated in Jesus' interaction with Nicodemus, who did not even understand the basic need to receive a new heart if a person were to enter God's kingdom.[8] Jesus had more disputes with the Pharisees than with any other Jewish group.

After the destruction of Jerusalem in 70 AD, the Pharisees appear to have taken the lead in giving the Jewish people a new center of religious life apart from the temple. The Pharisaic scholars at Jamnia and Usha, after the Bar Kokhba revolt against Rome (132–36 AD), were recognized by Rome as the governing body of the Jewish people; so the Pharisees again became a party with political power and religious influence. The Judaism that survived was primarily Pharisaic Judaism.[9]

The Sadducees

The Sadducees were present during the Hasmonean dynasty and were active in the first century AD. Their name seems to be a derivation of Zadok, the high priest in Israel.[10] They came mainly from the wealthy and priestly class[11] and held the majority of seats on the Sanhedrin—Jewish elders appointed as adjudicators. They collaborated with the Romans as much as possible because their position of power depended on Rome's goodwill.[12] The temple was at the heart of their religious system and was the seat of their political power in Israel. Anyone who appeared to attack the temple would be considered a significant threat to their authority. On

6. Matt 15:12–14; 16:5–12; 23:1–36.

7. Luke 11:43.

8. John 3:10.

9. Ferguson, *Backgrounds of Early Christianity*, 631.

10. 2 Sam 8:17.

11. Acts 4:1; 5:17.

12. John 11:45–56.

one occasion, Jesus said to the Jews, "Destroy this temple, and in three days I will raise it up,"[13] which in the minds of the Sadducees were undoubtedly the most menacing words Jesus ever spoke. It is not surprising with this kind of blunt speech that the chief priests and elders wanted Jesus dead.[14] The false witnesses at Jesus' trial identified these words as the reason why Jesus should be condemned.[15]

Theologically speaking, the Sadducees were extremely liberal. They denied the resurrection of the dead, the immortality of the soul, and the world to come, as well as the presence of angels and demons.[16] The problem with the Sadducees was their lack of biblical understanding.[17] They were essentially unbelievers who enveloped themselves in religion for the sake of wielding power and authority in the community.[18] John the Baptist condemned both the Sadducees and the Pharisees as hypocrites.[19] With the destruction of the temple in 70 AD and the collapse of their program and way of life, they ceased to be an influence in Jewish religious life.[20]

The Zealots

Despite Roman efforts to create unity in Palestine through Hellenization, some groups would not accept Roman rule under any conditions. The Zealots were one such radical group. They were a Jewish faction whose origin can be traced back to the Maccabean revolt in the second century BC. Josephus also identifies them as the Jewish rebel fighters in the war for independence from Rome (66–73 AD).[21] They were active during the reign of Herod the Great (37–4 BC), aggressively resisting his idolatrous practices.

The Zealots opposed Jews who conformed to Roman ways, often breaking out in open rebellion. They regularly resorted to violence and

13. John 2:19.

14. Matt 26:2–4.

15. Matt 26:61.

16. Luke 20:27; Acts 23:6–8.

17. Mark 12:24.

18. Josephus, *Complete Works*, 18.1.

19. Matt 3:7–11.

20. Ferguson, *Backgrounds of Early Christianity*, 636.

21. Josephus, *Jewish War* 4.147.

assassination against the Romans. Judas of Galilee, a revolutionary leader of the Zealots, rebelled against Rome in response to the taxation census of Cyrenius in 6 AD.[22] He argued that God was the only master of Israel, and that Rome had no legitimate authority over the Jews. The revolt was suppressed, and Judas was killed. He is mentioned in Acts 5:37. The Zealots were also active in the uprising against the Romans that resulted in the temple's destruction in Jerusalem in 70 AD. The Zealots took their final stand against the Romans, under the leadership of Eleazer ben Yair, at Masada, their mountain top fortress near the Dead Sea in Israel. After a long siege, the Romans captured the fortress on April 16, 73 AD, but not before all the inhabitants, except two women, committed suicide.[23] Simon, who Jesus called to become one of the twelve apostles, may have been a member of the Zealot party.[24] Theologically they agreed with Pharisees but were unwilling to live in submission to a foreign power.[25]

The Essenes

The Essenes were more mysterious than the other three main Jewish groups, functioning at the fringe of Jewish society. Like the Pharisees and the Sadducees, they were active during the Hasmonean Dynasty. They were a separatist group that never moved outside of Palestine and had about four thousand members at the time of Christ. They appear to have originated in the second century BC but disappear in the second century AD. Their lifestyle was highly disciplined, and they required a three-year training program before allowing anyone to become part of their community. The Essenes were likely the ones who copied and collected the famous Dead Sea scrolls of the Qumran community.[26] Like the Pharisees, the Essenes believed in life after death, but because they used a different purification ritual for their sacrifices, they were forbidden access to the temple.[27]

22. Josephus, *Complete Works*, 18.1.

23. Josephus, *Jewish War* 7.389.

24. Matt 10:4.

25. Josephus, *Complete Works*, 18.1.

26. Cross and Livingstone, *Dictionary of the Christian Church*, 562.

27. Josephus, *Complete Works*, 18.1.

The Jewishness of the Early Church

The early church began in Jerusalem and was a Jewish church at its inception. It grew out of Judaism, and the Christians did not believe they were abandoning their Jewish faith but were experiencing the Messianic fulfillment of that faith. It has been rightly said that "Christianity regarded itself as a continuation and development of Judaism, and initially flourished in regions with which Judaism was traditionally associated, supremely Palestine."[28] The first Christians kept the Sabbath, continued to attend the temple worship, and celebrated the resurrection of Christ on the first day of the week. The one hundred and twenty who gathered in an upstairs room in Jerusalem waiting for the outpouring of the Holy Spirit were all Jews. The twelve apostles, including Matthias, who replaced Judas, were all Jews. The first converts to Christianity were predominantly Jewish. Peter described the three thousand converts on the day of Pentecost as "men of Israel."[29] So initially, the church was composed mainly of ethnic Jews, with Jewish customs and the belief that they were experiencing the fulfillment of Old Testament prophecy.

Friction between Jewish and Gentile Converts

The Jewishness of the early church inevitably led to tension between Jewish and Gentile converts. Initially, this tension revealed itself within the Jewish community. The book of Acts records the schism developing between the Hebraic Jews and the Hellenistic Jews over the distribution of food to the widows.[30] Seven men were chosen to address this problem, and it is noteworthy that the names of all seven men were Greek. This may have been intentional to help offset the tendency of Jewish favoritism.

This friction is also seen in the conversion of Cornelius and his family. In the book of Acts, Peter goes to the home of a Gentile centurion named Cornelius and preaches the gospel to him and his family. They believed the message of salvation in Christ, received the gift of the Holy Spirit, spoke in other languages, and were baptized. When Peter returned to Jerusalem, the circumcision party criticized him for entering the home of an uncircumcised man and eating with him. However, upon hearing

28. McGrath, *Historical Theology*, 18.

29. Acts 2:22.

30. Acts 6:1–7.

Peter's report of what had happened, they rejoiced because they realized that the Gentiles had been granted the gift of repentance.[31] This rejoicing, however, did not put an end to the struggle between Jewish and Gentile converts.

The ongoing friction between Jewish and Gentile converts led to the gathering of the church's first general council. Acts chapter fifteen says that the council met in Jerusalem to address the question of circumcision. Some men were teaching that Gentile converts must be circumcised if they were to be saved; so Paul, Barnabas, and some others were appointed to go to Jerusalem to meet with the other apostles and the church's elders to address this issue. After much debate, they concluded that circumcision was not necessary for salvation. The Gentile converts were instructed to do four things—do not eat meat sacrificed to idols, abstain from sexual immorality, do not eat meat from strangled animals, and avoid eating blood.[32] The first twelve chapters of the book of Acts focuses primarily on Peter's ministry, mainly to the Jews. Chapter thirteen to the end of the book focuses on Paul and his ministry to the Gentile world. As larger numbers of Gentiles entered the church, the Jewish cultural character of the church diminished until it was essentially non-existent.

The Ministry of the Apostle Paul

Saul is introduced in the book of Acts as a zealous, young, pharisaic Jew, who supported the stoning of Stephen, a deacon and preacher in the early church. After Stephen was killed, Saul committed himself to a program of persecution, attempting to wipe out the church of Jesus Christ before it could get firmly established. Despite his violent and murderous beginning, Saul was destined to become a preacher of the same message he sought to eradicate.

Saul was converted to Christianity around 36 AD, while traveling to Damascus to arrest the Christians there. As he was approaching the city, a bright light appeared and blinded him. Jesus spoke to him from the light, and Saul, who was to become Paul, was a transformed man. In a moment, he went from Saul the persecutor to Paul the preacher. Three days after Jesus appeared to him, his sight was restored, he was baptized,

31. Acts 11:1–18.
32. Acts 15:20.

and he immediately began to preach Jesus as the Son of God.[33] Great opposition arose against him among the Jews, so Paul was forced to leave Damascus and go to Jerusalem, where the Christians were hesitant to accept him. They remembered him as Saul, who had been, "breathing out murderous threats" against the Christians.[34] Barnabas spoke up for him and Paul then joined the believers in Jerusalem and began to preach throughout the city. Once again, there was significant opposition, so the Christians sent Paul to the city of Tarsus.

After spending several years in Tarsus, Barnabas went to find Paul and bring him back to Antioch to help in the teaching ministry of the church. They spent a year in the city teaching and encouraging the people of God. Barnabas and Paul then went to Jerusalem to bring a financial gift from the church in Antioch to relieve the physical suffering of the people living in Judea. While in Antioch, the Holy Spirit told the church to "Set apart for me Barnabas and Saul for the work to which I have called them."[35] This marked the beginning of the first of Paul's three missionary journeys.[36]

Paul and Barnabas left Antioch and first went to Seleucia, where they boarded a ship and sailed to Cyprus. Upon arriving, they preached the gospel in the synagogues scattered throughout the island. Shortly after that, they sailed to Paphos and Perga in Pamphylia. From Perga, they traveled to Antioch, in Pisidia, and went to the synagogue to preach the gospel. Many of the Jews rejected their message, so they began preaching the gospel to the Gentiles, who were more receptive. When the Gentiles heard that the gospel was not only for the Jew, but also for the Gentile, "they began rejoicing and glorifying the word of the Lord, and as many as were appointed to eternal life believed."[37] The local Jews stirred up opposition against Paul and Barnabas, so they left the city and went to Iconium.

---

33. Luke says in Acts 9:23 "when many days had passed . . ." Many commentators believe the "many days" refers to a three-year period in which Paul journeyed into Arabia to preach. Galatians 1:16, 17 says, [God] "was pleased to reveal his Son to me, in order that I might preach him among the Gentiles, I did not immediately consult with anyone; nor did I go up to Jerusalem to those who were apostles before me, but I went away into Arabia, and returned again to Damascus."

34. Acts 9:1.

35. Acts 13:2

36. Paul's first missionary journey is recorded in Acts 13 and 14 (46–48 AD).

37. Acts 13:48.

When they arrived in Iconium, they went to the Synagogue and preached the gospel with great success. Many Jews and Gentiles believed the message, but once again, the unbelieving Jews stirred up opposition, so they left the city and went to Lystra to preach. The unbelieving Jews in Antioch and Iconium went to Lystra and turned the people against Paul. They stoned him, dragged him out of the city, and left him for dead, but Paul got up, and he and Barnabas went to Derbe. After preaching the gospel in Derbe, they retraced their steps, teaching in the cities they had previously visited. They eventually arrived back in Antioch, where the Holy Spirit first told the church to send them out. This marked the end of Paul's first missionary journey. Many scholars believe that Paul wrote his letter to the Galatian church (c.49 AD) while on his first missionary journey.

After preaching and teaching in Antioch, Paul and Barnabas traveled to the council in Jerusalem to participate in the debate about the role of circumcision and the Mosaic law in Christianity. After the council concluded, they went back to Antioch, shared the council's conclusions with the Christians, and remained there preaching and teaching the Word of God. Paul told Barnabas that they should go back to the churches they previously visited to see how the Christians were doing. Barnabas agreed, but they had a heated dispute over taking John, also called Mark, with them on the journey. Paul did not think it wise to bring him because he had abandoned them on a previous trip, but Barnabas insisted. They could not agree, so they went their separate ways. Barnabas and Mark went to Cyprus

Paul left on his second missionary journey and took a Christian brother named Silas with him.[38] They began their journey by preaching in the churches scattered throughout Syria and Cilicia. They went to Derbe and then Lystra, where Paul recruited Timothy as a fellow worker in the gospel. They preached in many churches and informed the Christians about the Jerusalem council's decision. Paul's ministry was very fruitful, and the churches grew in number every day. They traveled through the region of Phrygia and Galatia, passed through Mysia, and then to Troas. While in Troas, Paul had a dream in which a man said, "Come over to Macedonia and help us."[39] In response to the dream, Paul went to Samothrace, Neapolis, and finally to Philippi, an important city in Macedonia.

---

38. Paul's second missionary journey is recorded in Acts 16–18. (49–52 AD)

39. Acts 16:9

While in Philippi, Lydia, a wealthy lady, was converted, and she and her household were baptized and became followers of Christ. Shortly after that, Paul and Silas were thrown into prison after casting a demon out of a young girl. While in prison, there was an earthquake that destroyed the doors of the prison. Paul and Silas did not escape but used the opportunity to preach the gospel to the jailor and his entire family, who became followers of Jesus Christ.

After leaving Philippi, they traveled through Amphipolis and Apollonia, eventually arriving in Thessalonica. Paul, following his usual practice, went to the synagogue and preached the gospel to the Jews. Some Jews believed, but others did not. The unbelieving Jews began to stir up the crowds against them. In response, the Christian brothers of the city sent Paul and Silas away under cover of darkness. After leaving the city, they went to Berea and preached the gospel in the local synagogue. When the unbelieving Jews in Thessalonica heard that they were in Berea, they went to the city and stirred up the people against them. Silas and Timothy stayed in Berea, but Paul boarded a ship and sailed for Athens. While in Athens, Paul preached the gospel on the Areopagus, a prominent rock outcropping, and as in most places, he had a mixed response. Some people mocked him for his teaching on the resurrection of the dead, but others believed the message and became followers of Jesus.

After preaching the gospel in Athens, Paul went to Corinth, where he preached in the synagogue every Sabbath. He met a couple named Aquila and Priscilla, who, like Paul, were tentmakers, so he stayed with them. Once again, Paul received opposition from the unbelievers, but this time he did not flee. God assured Paul in a dream that he had many followers in the city, so Paul stayed for a year and a half, teaching whoever would listen to him. After further opposition, he sailed to Syria, along with Priscilla and Aquila. They arrived in Ephesus, where Paul, as was his custom, went to the synagogue and reasoned with the Jews. He left Ephesus shortly after and went to Caesarea and on to Antioch. This marked the end of Paul's second missionary journey. During his second missionary journey, Paul wrote 1 and 2 Thessalonians (c.50, 51 AD).

After spending time with the believers in Antioch, Paul set out on his third missionary journey.[40] He first went and preached the gospel in the churches throughout Galatia and Phrygia to strengthen the believers. He then went to Ephesus, where he encountered some disciples who had

---

40. Paul's third missionary journey is recorded in Acts 18:23–21:14 (53–57 AD).

never heard of the Holy Spirit. Paul explained the baptism of the Spirit to them; they believed his message and were baptized in the name of the Lord Jesus Christ. He then went to the synagogue and spent three months reasoning with the Jews until they became antagonistic to his teaching. He left the synagogue and continued to teach every day for two years in the hall of Tyrannus. Paul performed many miracles, and large numbers of people put their faith in Jesus Christ. Acts 19:20 sums up Paul's ministry well, "so the word of the Lord continued to increase and prevail mightily." In response to the success of the gospel, a riot broke out in Ephesus, and Paul was forced to leave the city. He traveled throughout Macedonia, strengthening the churches, eventually ended up in Greece, where he stayed for three months until he fled in response to a plot to kill him. Paul probably wrote the letter to the Romans during these three months.

Paul traveled through Macedonia to Troas and stayed there for seven days. On one occasion, on the Lord's Day, Paul gathered with God's people, broke bread, and preached a very long sermon that lasted until midnight. While Paul was preaching, a young man named Eutychus was sitting in an upper-story window and fell asleep during the message. He fell out of the window and was presumed dead. However, Paul healed the young man and then continued to speak with God's people until morning.

Paul departed from Troas and went back to Ephesus, where he met with the elders and encouraged them in their work as shepherds of the church of Christ. After a brief stay, he sailed to Cos, Rhodes, and then on to Patara. He boarded another ship and returned to Tyre, where he stayed for seven days with the disciples. He left Tyre and stayed for one day with Christians in Ptolemais. He sailed for Caesarea and remained in the home of Philip, the evangelist, for some time. Agabus, the prophet, warned Paul not to go to Jerusalem because he would be arrested, but Paul was determined and ignored the warning. He made his way to Jerusalem and immediately informed James and the elders of all God had done amongst the Gentiles. This marked the end of his third missionary journey. Paul wrote 1 and 2 Corinthians in Ephesus during his third missionary journey (53–55 AD).

Shortly after Paul arrived in Jerusalem, he was falsely accused, beaten by an angry mob, and arrested, just as Agabus had predicted. The Roman tribune bound Paul but allowed him to stand before the Jewish chief priests and the council to discover the nature of the accusations made against him. This meeting did not proceed well. A verbal altercation broke out between the Sadducees and the Pharisees, who made up the council. The tribune, concerned for Paul's safety, had him removed and placed in the barracks. A plot against Paul's life was discovered, and to protect Paul, the tribune had him sent to Caesarea to stand before Felix, the governor. Paul would spend two years in Caesarea. At the end of the two years, Felix was succeeded by Festus. Festus intended to have Paul sent to Jerusalem to stand trial, but Paul, being a Roman citizen, appealed to Caesar and was sent to Rome to stand before the emperor. On the way to Rome, Paul was shipwrecked, bitten by a poisonous snake on the island of Malta with no ill effect, and then healed all the sick people on the island. After leaving, they sailed to Rome, arriving in the city in 60 AD. Paul was permitted to live alone, with one soldier guarding him. He lived there for two years, and he saw a constant flow of people to whom he proclaimed the message of salvation. The book of Acts ends with the words, "He lived there two whole years at his own expense, and welcomed all who came to him, proclaiming the kingdom of God and teaching about the Lord Jesus Christ with all boldness and without hindrance."[41]

There is some evidence that Paul was released from prison in 62 AD and preached the gospel in the western empire, but was arrested again and executed, in Rome by the Emperor Nero, sometime between 64 and 68 AD.[42] 1 and 2 Timothy were written sometime between 64 and 68. The letter to Titus is dated between 62 and 64. He also wrote the letters to the Ephesians, Philippians, Colossians, and Philemon, known as the prison epistles, while in Rome.

It is fitting that the book of Acts does not conclude with Paul's death but with the continuation of his ministry in Rome. The story does not end with Paul. The preaching of the gospel continued after the death of the apostles and will continue until the second coming of Jesus Christ.

The Death of the Apostles

The death of James, (the brother of John), and Judas Iscariot,[43] are the only two apostle deaths recorded in the Bible. Although the New Testament

41. Acts 28:30, 31.

42. See Paul under the heading, "The Death of the Apostles."

43. Matt 27:3–10.

does not provide any information on the apostles' deaths, extra-biblical sources tell us where many of them preached and how they died. Although some of these sources have been embellished and need to be read with caution, they provide some interesting details on the lives and deaths of the apostles.

Peter

According to Eusebius (260–340 AD), Peter preached the gospel in Pontus, Galatia, Cappadocia, Bithynia, Italy, and throughout Asia.[44] Ancient testimonies on the death of Peter tell us that he was crucified upside down in Rome sometime between 64 and 68 AD, during the persecution under the emperor Nero. Jesus' prophecy recorded in John 21:18,19 foreshadows these events where it says, "…when you are old, you will stretch out your hands, and another will dress you and carry you where you do not want to go." (This he said to show by what kind of death he was to glorify God)."

Eusebius, quoting Clement (c.35–99 AD), informs us that Peter watched his wife taken away to be executed. He wrote, "They say, accordingly, that when the blessed Peter saw his wife led out to die, he rejoiced because of her summons and her return home, and called to her very encouragingly and comfortingly, addressing her by name, and saying, 'Oh thou, remember the Lord.' Such was the marriage of the blessed, and their perfect disposition toward those dearest to them."[45] Eusebius also said that Peter was crucified upside down at his own request.[46]

Clement of Rome, in his letter to the Corinthians, wrote concerning the death of Peter, "through envy and jealousy, the greatest and most righteous pillars [of the church] have been persecuted and put to death. Let us set before our eyes the illustrious apostles. Peter, through unrighteous envy, endured not one or two, but numerous labours; and when he had at length suffered martyrdom, departed to the place of glory due to him."[47] Hippolytus (c.170–235 AD) said that Nero crucified Peter with

44. Eusebius, CH, 3.1.

45. Eusebius, *Church History, Life of Constantine the Great, and Oration in Praise of Constantine*, book 3.30.

46. Eusebius, CH, 3.1.

47. Clement, *First Epistle of Clement to the Corinthians*, Chapter 5.

his head turned downward.[48] Tertullian indicated that Peter endured a death like that of the Lord.[49]

Andrew

The apostle Andrew preached to the Scythians and Thracians[50] and throughout the cities of Achaia. According to tradition, he established many churches throughout that region. On one occasion, the proconsul, Ægeates, while in the city of Patras, arrested Andrew and put him on trial. Upon cross-examination, he threatened Andrew with torture and crucifixion, but Andrew would not deny the Lord Jesus. Filled with rage at Andrew's stubborn refusal to deny Christ and offer incense to the Roman gods, he had him severely tortured. Once again, he was brought before Ægeates, who threatened to crucify him. Andrew's response was as follows:

> I am a slave of the cross of Christ, and I ought rather to pray to attain to the trophy of the cross than to be afraid; but for you is laid up eternal torment, which, however, you may escape after you have tested my endurance, if you will believe in my Christ. For I am afflicted about your destruction, and I am not disturbed about my own suffering. For my suffering takes up a space of one day, or two at most; but your torment for endless ages shall never come to a close. Wherefore hence-forward cease from adding to your miseries, and lighting up everlasting fire for yourself.[51]

Once again filled with rage, he ordered that Andrew be fastened to the cross. One tradition says that he was bound with ropes rather than pierced with nails to prolong his agony. While on the cross, Andrew preached to the large crowd of disciples that stood before him, exhorting them and encouraging them with thoughts of eternal life. After several days of suffering, he died.[52] Hippolytus said that Andrew was crucified and suspended on an olive tree.[53]

48. Hippolytus, *Hippolytus on the Twelve Apostles*, 255.

49. Tertullian, *On Prescription Against Heretics*, chapter 36.

50. Hippolytus, *On the Twelve Apostles*, 255.

51. Old English words updated by author.

52. *Acts of Andrew and Matthias*, 517–25.

53. Hippolytus, *Ante-Nicene Fathers*, 5:255.

James, the son of Zebedee, the brother of John

We know that James, the brother of John, was martyred because it is recorded in Scripture. Acts 12:1–3 tells us that he was killed by King Herod with the sword.

John

Most accounts indicate that John died around 98 AD during the reign of Emperor Trajan. Jerome (c.347–419/420 AD) also affirmed that John was sent to the island of Patmos, where he received and recorded the Revelation. After the death of Domitian, he returned to Ephesus and died sixty-eight years after the death of Jesus Christ, which places his death at the end of the first century.[54] Hippolytus said that John died during Trajan's reign and is buried in the city of Ephesus, but the location is unknown.[55] Tertullian noted that John was "plunged unhurt, into boiling oil" and was then banished to the island of Patmos.[56] Eusebius affirmed what Tertullian said,

> After fifteen years of Domitian's rule Nerva succeeded to the throne. By a vote of the Roman senate Domitian's honours were removed, and those unjustly banished returned to their homes and had their property restored to them. This is noted by the chroniclers of the period. At that time too (96 AD) the apostle John, after his exile on the island, resumed residence at Ephesus, as early Christian tradition records.[57] Eusebius also confirmed that he was buried in Ephesus.[58]

Philip

According to Hippolytus, Philip preached in Phrygia.[59] *The Acts of Philip* is a non-canonical book probably written in the mid-fourth century. Although this is not a reliable record of Philip's death, the recorded story of Philip's martyrdom says that during the reign of Emperor Trajan, Philip

---

54. Jerome, *Lives of Illustrious Men*, 364.

55. Hippolytus, *On the Twelve Apostles*, 3.

56. Tertullian, *On Prescription Against Heretics*, ch.36.

57. Eusebius, *History of the Church*, 3.20.

58. Eusebius, *History of the Church*, 3.31.

59. Hippolytus, *On the Twelve Apostles*, 5.

and Bartholomew were preaching in the city of Ophioryma (Hierapolis). Large numbers of people listened to their preaching, and many believed in the Lord Jesus. One of the many who believed was a woman named Nicanora, the wife of the proconsul. She was sick in bed, but through faith in Christ, she was healed and immediately went to Philip, Bartholomew, and Philip's sister Mariamne who was with them. When Nicanora's husband heard about his wife's conversion to Christianity, he was furious. He arrested Philip, Bartholomew, and Mariamne, had them beaten, dragged through the streets, and held captive in a pagan temple until he could decide how to execute them. They were then taken from the temple, stripped of their clothing, and exposed for all to see. Then "he ordered Philip to be hanged, and his ankles to be pierced, and to bring also iron hooks, and his heels also to be driven through, and to be hanged head downwards, opposite the temple on a certain tree; and stretch out Bartholomew opposite Philip, having nailed his hands on the wall of the gate of the temple." While Philip was hanging upside down, he spoke to the people, and many more believed in the message of Christ. Some of the disciples sought to remove the iron hooks from his feet and set him free, but Philip would not allow them, choosing instead to die as a martyr for the Lord. Both Bartholomew and Mariamne were set free, but Philip died in the presence of the people.[60] Hippolytus also said that Philip was crucified with his head downward.[61] According to Eusebius, he was buried in Hierapolis, along with his four daughters, who were prophetesses.[62]

Nathanael/Bartholomew

Many scholars believe that Nathanael and Bartholomew refer to the same person. Early church records suggest that he preached the Word of God in India. It appears that he was highly successful in his ministry and that many idol worshipers abandoned their pagan worship and believed in Christ. One tradition says that he was beaten with rods, then scourged, and finally beheaded.[63] Another tradition says he was tied in a sack and

---

60. *Acts of Philip,* Ante-Nicene Fathers, 8:497–503.

61. Hippolytus, *On the Twelve Apostles,* 5.

62. Eusebius, *Church History,* 3.31.

63. *Martyrdom of the Apostle Bartholomew,* Ante-Nicene Fathers, 8:557.

cast into the sea. Still, another says he was crucified upside down and was buried in the town of Allanum.[64]

Matthew/Levi

According to Hippolytus, Matthew, also known as Levi, died in Parthia, in the town of Hierees.[65] The earliest traditions say that he was burned at the stake. Others say he was crucified.

Thomas

The apostle Thomas preached to the Parthians, the Medes, the Persians, the Hyrcanians, the Bactrians, and the Margians. *The Acts of Thomas*, an apocryphal text from the early third century, says that Thomas preached the gospel in India. Many question the reliability of the text, and it indeed does contain many embellishments, however the Christian church has been present in India from ancient times and claims Thomas as its founder. According to Hippolytus, while in the city of Calamen, India, Thomas was speared to death and was buried in the same town.[66]

James, Son of Alphaeus

James was martyred sometime in 62 AD. Some believe he was martyred later in the century because of a reference to the siege of Jerusalem, which began in 67 AD. Eusebius tells us that the siege took place shortly after James' death. He also said that James was thrown from the walls of the temple and beaten with a club.[67] Heggesippus, born at the end of the first century AD, said that after James was thrown from the temple, he was stoned and then killed when he was struck in the head with a fuller's club.[68] Hippolytus confirmed that he was stoned to death and buried next

64. Hippolytus, *On the Twelve Apostles*, 6.

65. Hippolytus, *On the Twelve Apostles*, 7.

66. Hippolytus, *On the Twelve Apostles*, 8.

67. Eusebius, CH 2.1

68. Eusebius, CH 2.23.

to the temple.[69] Many paintings and stained-glass depictions of James have him holding a club in his hand.

Simon, the Zealot

According to Hippolytus, Simon became the bishop of Jerusalem after the death of James. He died at one hundred and twenty years of age and was buried there.[70] One tradition says he was crucified in Samaria during a revolt and another that he was killed with an axe in Suanir, Persia.

Thaddaeus, Judas, Son of James (not Iscariot)

Judas preached the gospel to the people of Edessa and throughout Mesopotamia. He may have died at Berytus, the ancient city of modern-day Beirut in Lebanon, and was buried there.[71]

Judas—the Traitor

Judas, the traitor, filled with inconsolable grief over his betrayal of Jesus, hung himself.[72]

Matthias

Matthias was chosen to take the place of Judas, the traitor.[73] According to Hippolytus, he preached in Jerusalem and died there.[74]

Paul

Paul was possibly beheaded during the Neronian persecution.[75] Early writers tell us that Paul was allowed to defend himself before Emperor

69. Hippolytus, *On the Twelve Apostles*, 9.

70. Hippolytus, *On the Twelve Apostles*, 11.

71. Hippolytus, *On the Twelve Apostles*, 10.

72. Matt 27:3–5.

73. Acts 1:23.

74. Hippolytus, *On the Twelve Apostles*, 12.

75. Hippolytus, *On the Twelve Apostles*, 13.

Nero in Rome, and the Emperor set him free, thus allowing Paul to preach the gospel in the western part of the empire. Paul says,

> At my first defense no one came to stand by me, but all deserted me. May it not be charged against them! But the Lord stood by me and strengthened me, so that through me the message might be fully proclaimed and all the Gentiles might hear it. So I was rescued from the lion's mouth.[76]

Jerome said that the "first defense" refers to his defense before Nero when he was taken to Rome for the first time (62 AD). "The lion" refers to Nero, who set him free, a rescue Paul attributes to the Lord. It appears that Paul was arrested a second time when he returned to Rome. Jerome indicated he was beheaded in the fourteenth year of Nero (68 AD), on the same day that Peter was crucified.[77]

Conclusion

Though we cannot be sure of all the details, it appears that most of the apostles died as martyrs of the faith. Even John, who probably died a natural death, suffered much in his service to Jesus Christ. It is not surprising that the apostles suffered and died for the faith because Jesus predicted that his followers would be hated and would suffer. Jesus said, "Blessed are you when others revile you and persecute you and utter all kinds of evil against you falsely on my account. Rejoice and be glad, for your reward is great in heaven, for so they persecuted the prophets who were before you."[78] He also said, "Therefore I send you prophets and wise men and scribes, some of whom you will kill and crucify, and some you will flog in your synagogues and persecute from town to town."[79] Many other biblical passages warn Christians of the suffering that comes to those who serve Jesus Christ. The courage and faithfulness of the apostles in their suffering should encourage us to endure suffering willingly in our service for Jesus Christ.

76. 2 Tim 4:16–17.

77. Jerome, NPNF, 3:363.

78. Matt 5:11, 12.

79. Matt 23:34.

Discussion Questions

1. In the first-century church, the conflict between Jewish and Gentile converts was severe.
   What are some of the divisions that divide the church today, and how do we seek to resolve them?

2. Is there a place for church councils today to help resolve division in the church?

Chapter 3

Persecution and the Fall of Jerusalem

THE EARLY CHRISTIANS DID not believe they were rejecting their Jewish faith. They believed Christianity was a fulfillment of biblical Judaism. Initially, the Romans themselves considered the rise of Christianity to be a struggle within the Jewish community and did not deal with Christians as a separate entity. Acts 18:2 says, "After this Paul left Athens and went to Corinth. And he found a Jew named Aquila, a native of Pontus, recently come from Italy with his wife Priscilla, because Claudius had commanded all the Jews to leave Rome." Emperor Claudius (10 BC–54 AD) ruled from 41–54 AD. Suetonius, a Roman historian, referring to this expulsion, wrote, "Because the Jews at Rome caused continuous disturbances at the instigation of Chrestus, he expelled them from the city."[1] Many historians believe that "Chrestus" refers to Christ, and the disturbance in Rome refers to Jewish opposition to the preaching of the gospel. Over time, as more Gentile converts entered the church, the Romans dealt with the Jews and Christians as two distinct groups. Two significant periods of persecution occurred in the first century during the reigns of Emperor Nero and Emperor Domitian.

Emperor Nero (r. 54–68 AD)

Nero was born on December 15, 37 AD, in Antium. His father's name was Domitius, and his mother was Agrippina. His father died when he was three years of age, and Emperor Gaius took the family estate and banished his mother. As a result, Nero was raised by his aunt, Domitia

1. Suetonius, *Twelve Caesars*, 25.

Lepida, in relative poverty until Emperor Claudius succeeded Gaius and restored Nero's inheritance to him and recalled his mother from banishment.[2] Agrippina became the third wife of Claudius and exercised great influence over his actions. She convinced him to adopt her son Nero. At forty-one years of age, Claudius died on October 13, 54 AD, while eating mushrooms. Many people believed Agrippina poisoned him.[3] Suetonius says that Nero was directly involved in his murder.[4] Nero, who was only sixteen years of age at the time, was immediately declared Emperor. During the funeral of Claudius, Nero described his mother as "The best of mothers," and they were often seen riding through the streets together.[5] There were also whispers suggesting an incestuous relationship. It appeared that she would wield significant influence during her son Nero's reign.

At the beginning of his reign, Nero showed great potential and appeared to possess a humble heart. He lowered taxes, gave out gifts of money and grain, and refused to allow great honours to be given to him until he was older. He also wrote and recited his poems, and the people appear to have been delighted with his stage performances, although this may have been feigned delight. He provided games for the people, such as chariot racing, gladiatorial battles, sea battles, and a variety of stage plays. He also gave out many expensive gifts throughout the games. All of this won the hearts of the people.[6]

Although he started well, public opinion quickly turned against him when he murdered his mother Agrippina; his wife Octavia; his second wife Poppaea, who he kicked to death while she was pregnant;[7] his aunt Domitia who raised him, and possibly other contenders for the throne.[8] He also murdered many others in his own family and numerous noblemen who were not of his family but were considered a threat to his power.[9] As time went on, he began to murder anyone who slighted him in any way whatsoever.[10]

2. Suetonius, *Twelve Caesars*, 244.

3. Tacitus, *Agricola and the Germania*, 36, 37.

4. Suetonius, *Twelve Caesars*, 262.

5. Suetonius, *Twelve Caesars*, 246.

6. Suetonius, *Twelve Caesars*, 246, 247.

7. Suetonius, *Twelve Caesars*, 266.

8. Tacitus, *Agricola and the Germania*, 38.

9. Suetonius, *Twelve Caesars*, 266.

10. Suetonius, *Twelve Caesars*, 267.

As the years progressed, Nero became a pleasure-seeking, debauched, delusional man whose mind was filled with dreams of grandeur. He would often roam the streets at night looking for trouble and was even known to stab innocent men in the alleyways, break into shops to rob them and then auction the stolen goods off for personal profit.[11] Suetonius tells us of a game that Nero invented where he dressed up in the skins of wild animals and then attacked the private parts of men and women who were tied to stakes.[12] On one occasion, he even participated in a wedding ceremony with a man named Pythagoras. Dressing in women's bridal clothing, he shared the wedding bed with him in public for witnesses to see.[13] He often appeared in public dressed like a singer and charioteer and participated in various singing, acting, and racing events, usually receiving the trophy for first place. On one occasion, he didn't even finish the chariot race, but the judges still awarded him the prize.[14] He also fancied himself a poet, which brought great dismay to those who were true poets. He was also reckless and exorbitant in his expenditures, resulting in bankruptcy.[15] It wasn't long before it was whispered that he had gone mad.

An example of Nero's delusions of grandeur is seen in the construction of his personal pleasure palace known as "the golden house." Nero expropriated approximately two hundred acres of the best land in Rome to build his new palace, and the final product was extravagant and magnificent to behold. Suetonius provided an excellent summary description of its resplendent glory:

> A house whose size and elegance these details should be sufficient to relate: Its courtyard was so large that a one hundred and twenty-foot colossal statue of the emperor himself stood there; it was so spacious that it had a mile long triple portico; also there was a pool of water like a sea, that was surrounded by buildings which gave it the appearance of cities; and besides that, various rural tracts of land with vineyards, cornfields, pastures, and forests, teeming with every kind of animal both wild and domesticated. In other parts of the house, everything was covered in gold and adorned with jewels and mother-of-pearl;

11. Suetonius, *Twelve Caesars*, 258.

12. Suetonius, *Twelve Caesars*, 259.

13. Tacitus, *Annals of Rome*, 362.

14. Suetonius, *Twelve Caesars*, 256.

15. Suetonius, *Twelve Caesars*, 262.

dining rooms with fretted ceilings whose ivory panels could be turned so that flowers or perfumes from pipes were sprinkled down from above; the main hall of the dining rooms was round, and it would turn constantly day and night like the Heavens; there were baths, flowing with seawater and with the sulfur springs of the Albula.[16]

When it was completed, Nero inaugurated the house, and he showed his satisfaction by remarking that "finally he could begin to live in a house worthy of a human being."[17] Adding to this extravagance, the valley was turned into an artificial lake for the personal pleasure of the emperor and those close to him. The entire center of the city of Rome was now taken up with this opulent display of imperial glory.[18]

If one were to approach Nero's palace, he would be confronted immediately by the colossal statue of Nero that stood in the vestibule atrium, and was made by the Greek sculptor Zenodorus, a famous bronze caster. The statue was almost one hundred and twenty feet tall (one hundred and nineteen and a half feet according to Pliny). It was made of bronze and was dedicated to the sun-god Helios, which was meant to invest Nero with the sun's attributes. The statue was nude, with the left foot behind the right standing on the toes. The front foot bore the weight of the statue. The right hand was held slightly forward, leaning on a support, with the left arm bent and lifted with a globe in the hand. There was also a crown on the head with seven spikes representing the rays of the sun. It is believed the inspiration for the statue came from the Colossus of Rhodes. The statues are the same height, and both are meant to convey the idea of imperial power and authority.[19] Indeed, the globe in the left hand was meant to represent the imperial right of the emperor of Rome to rule the world.

Nero began to present himself more in relation to the sun god, believing that he was the one who would usher in a new golden age for the empire. Not only was his statue made from bronze, but there was gold leaf on the frescoes and stuccoes, gold and gems covered much of the palace, jewels and precious stones were abundant, all meant to reflect that his palace was to be the royal palace of the sun. The palace was built using a stone called *phengites*, which emitted a natural glow that gave the

16. Tranquillus, Suetonius, *Lives of the Twelve Caesars*, "Nero," 261.

17. Suetonius, *Lives of the Caesars*, 261.

18. Sciortino, DOMVS AVREA, 10.

19. Sciortino, DOMVS AVREA, 11.

impression that light did not flow into the palace but flowed out of it. Along with this light illusion, one can only imagine the sparkling glare reflecting off the statue of Nero when the sun struck the bronze surface. Along with the statue, the entire palace would have given the impression that the sun-god Helios truly dwelt there.[20]

Nero is probably one of the best-known emperors, not so much for his architectural achievements (of which there are many), or even his lascivious behaviour, but his acts of cruelty, especially against the Christians. This man, believing himself to be the sun god and the rightful ruler of the entire world, was the source of many great cruelties perpetrated against the Christians. Tertullian, a second and third-century theologian, said this about Nero:

> Study your records: there you will find that Nero was the first to persecute this teaching when, after subjugating the entire East, in Rome especially he treated everyone with savagery. That such a man was author of our chastisement fills us with pride. For anyone who knows him can understand that anything not supremely good would never have been condemned by Nero.[21]

Eusebius described him as "the monster of depravity."[22] Not only did Christians believe Nero to be a cruel man, but so did many Romans. Tacitus, a first and early-second-century Roman Senator and historian, possessed no love for the Christians and yet did not deny their unjust treatment at the hands of Nero. He wrote:

> But neither human resources, nor imperial munificence [generosity], nor appeasement of the gods, eliminated sinister suspicions that the fire had been instigated. To suppress this rumour, Nero fabricated scapegoats—and punished with every refinement the notoriously depraved Christians (as they were popularly called). Their originator, Christ, had been executed during Tiberius' reign by the governor of Judaea, Pontius Pilatus. But despite this temporary setback the deadly superstition had broken out afresh, not only in Judaea (where the mischief had started) but even in Rome. All degraded and shameful practices collect and flourish in the capital."[23]

<hr>

20. Suetonius, "Nero," 39.

21. Eusebius, *Ecclesiastical History*, 104.

22. Eusebius, CH, 2.25.

23. Tacitus, *Annals of Imperial Rome*, 365.

This quote refers to the great fire that broke out in Rome on June 18, 64 AD. The fire burned for an entire week, and even after it stopped, there were flair-ups for several days afterward. There are many theories about how the fire began, but many believed that Nero started the fire, and as Tacitus implies, he blamed the Christians to cover it up. Nero was in Antium, not in Rome when it began, possibly to deflect any accusations that might be leveled against him. While it is true that he did not personally set the fire, there is evidence that he had others do the work for him. Suetonius states Nero's guilt as a fact, "…he brazenly set fire to the city, and though a number of former consuls caught his attendants trespassing on their property with tar and blazing torches, they dared not interfere."[24] He went on to say that while the city was burning, Nero watched the conflagration from the tower in the Gardens of Maecenas, enraptured by what he called "the beauty of the flames," then put on his tragedian's costume and sang *The Fall of Troy* from beginning to end."[25] Tacitus wrote, "Rome burned while Nero fiddled."[26] Many believed that he ordered the fire to be set to make way for him to rebuild the city of Rome according to his vision for the city. Tacitus further described the cruelties of Nero against the Christians:

> First, Nero had self-acknowledged Christians arrested. Then, on their information, large numbers of others were condemned—not so much for incendiarism as for their anti-social tendencies (or because the human race detested them). Their deaths were made farcical. Dressed in wild animals' skins, they were torn to pieces by dogs, or crucified, or made into torches to be ignited after dark as substitutes for daylight. Nero provided his Gardens for the spectacle, and exhibited displays in the Circus, at which he mingled with the crowd—or stood in a chariot, dressed as a charioteer. Despite their guilt as Christians, and the ruthless punishment it deserved, the victims were pitied. For it was felt that they were being sacrificed to one man's brutality rather than to the national interest.[27]

It was during the persecutions of Nero that Paul was beheaded, and Peter was crucified upside down.[28]

24. Suetonius, *Twelve Caesars*, 268.

25. Tranquillus, Suetonius, *Lives of the Twelve Caesars*, Nero, 38.

26. Tacitus, *Agricola and the Germania*, 38.

27. Tacitus, *Annals of Rome*, 365–66.

28. Eusebius, CH 2.25.

In 68 AD, Nero was overthrown by a rebellion and then committed suicide by stabbing himself in the throat when the Senate proclaimed him a public enemy.[29] He was only thirty-two years of age. It is said that leading up to his suicide he was constantly repeating, "What an artist the world is losing in me!"[30] After his death, the Christians were left alone and appear to have been ignored by the next several emperors. This would change in the year 81 AD when Domitian became emperor of the Roman Empire. But, before looking at the reign of Domitian, there is a first-century event of eschatological importance that must be covered—the fall of Jerusalem in 70 AD.

The Fall of Jerusalem (70 AD)

The destruction of Jerusalem in 70 AD was an exceptional event in the history of God's dealings with the nation of Israel. Since the calling of Abraham, the people of Israel were at the center of God's plan, and the entire Old Testament focuses on God's dealings with that nation. Jerusalem was the capital of Israel and was called the city of David and the city of God. The temple, the center of Israelite worship, was located in that illustrious city. Despite the uniqueness of Israel and Jerusalem in God's plan, a dramatic shift took place when Jesus came into the world two thousand years ago. The church, which included both believing Jews and Gentiles, came to the forefront in God's plan. In the Old Testament, people approached God with animal sacrifices and worshipped at the temple in Jerusalem, but in the New Testament era, people approached God through Jesus Christ, who offered the final sacrifice for our sins. A graphic demonstration of this new shift was seen when the temple curtain that separated the Holy Place from the Holy of Holies was torn from top to bottom when Jesus died on the cross. This event signified that the way into God's presence was now open for all who would seek Him through believing in Jesus Christ. Jerusalem and the temple were no longer central in God's plan, and God would destroy them. This is not just hearsay but was predicted in the New Testament. In the gospel of Matthew, Jesus tells the disciples that all the stones of the temple would be thrown down, and then he goes on to describe the coming destruction

---

29. Tacitus, *Agricola and the Germania*, 38.
30. Tacitus, *Agricola and the Germania*, 38.

of the city of Jerusalem.[31] The gospels of Mark[32] and Luke[33] record the same event. Luke provided even greater detail when he wrote, "But when you see Jerusalem surrounded by armies, then know that its desolation has come near."[34] This refers to the Roman armies that surrounded Jerusalem and destroyed it forty years after Jesus made this prediction. Josephus, a first-century Jewish historian, provided eyewitness testimony of the event.

The Romans took over Palestine in 63 BC, about sixty years before the birth of Jesus Christ. The Jewish people were unhappy with Roman rule, and many looked forward to the day when they could throw off the Roman yoke and become an independent nation again. The first great attempt took place between 66 and 73 AD and is known as the Great Revolt or the first Jewish-Roman war. When the war began, Emperor Nero appointed General Vespasian to suppress the rebellion, and Vespasian's son Titus was sent to support him in the effort. When they entered Judea, they did not immediately set out for Jerusalem but attacked the smaller fortified strongholds of the rebels. Once they crushed these surrounding regions, the rebel leaders fled to Jerusalem along with thousands of refugees.

Jerusalem was a divided city. Many of the younger people wanted to continue the fight against the Romans, while others desired peace and mourned over the future of Jerusalem. This division led to a bloody battle within the city's walls, between the Zealots, who sought to take control of the city, and the Jews who opposed them. Eventually, the Zealots took the city, slaughtering thousands of people in the process, especially those who came from noble and high-placed families. Upon hearing of the turmoil and division in the city, the Romans urged Vespasian to attack, but he refused. He believed that God was on their side and was allowing their enemy to destroy one another, giving the Romans a victory without putting their own soldiers in harm's way.[35] The situation in Jerusalem continued to deteriorate rapidly. There was a steady stream of people deserting the city attempting to get away from the Zealots, but many of them were caught and killed before they could escape.

31. Matt 24:1, 2.

32. Mark 13:1–23.

33. Luke 21:5–24.

34. Luke 21:20

35. Josephus, *Wars of the Jews*, 4.6.2.

Vespasian was now compelled to attack Jerusalem, but he was informed that Emperor Nero had died during his preparations for battle. Vespasian sent his son Titus to get their orders from Galba, the new emperor. While enroute, Galba was assassinated after having reigned for only seven months and seven days. Otho was then proclaimed emperor but committed suicide after only three months and two days in office. The German legions then chose Vitellius to be emperor, and he went to Rome with his army. Vespasian and his men were unhappy with this choice. After much dialogue, the soldiers declared Vespasian as emperor. While he initially refused, when they threatened to kill him if he did not accept the emperorship, he submitted to their will. After an eight-month struggle, Vitellius was murdered and Vespasian was now fully recognized as Emperor. Vespasian traveled to Rome and sent his son Titus to destroy the city of Jerusalem.[36]

While Titus traveled to Jerusalem with his army, the city was plagued with civil strife as several factions within the city sought to gain control. Upon arriving at Jerusalem, Titus put the city under siege and began to press the attack. The Roman threat served to unite the Jewish factions in the city against them, and the Romans were forced to fight long and hard against the desperate and courageous Jewish forces.[37]

As the siege continued, famine began to spread throughout the city. Josephus described the desperate condition of the people:

> Famine now raged in the city, and the rebels took all the food they could find in a house-to-house search, while the poor starved to death by the thousands. People gave all their wealth for a little measure of wheat, and hid to eat it hastily and in secret so it would not be taken from them. Wives would snatch the food from their husbands, children from fathers, and mothers from the very mouths of infants. Many of the rich were put to death by Simon and John [Zealot leaders], while the sufferings of the people were so fearful that they can hardly be told, and no other city ever endured such miseries. Not since the world began was there ever a generation more prolific in crime than this bastard scum of the nation who destroyed the city.[38]

Further to this, he wrote:

36. Josephus, *Wars of the Jews*, 4.585.

37. Josephus, *Wars of the Jews*, 5.21.

38. Josephus, *Wars of the Jews*, 5.424, 347.

> All hope of escape and all food supplies were now cut off from the Jews, and famine devoured thousands upon thousands. The alleys were choked with bodies, the survivors not having enough strength to bury the dead and even falling into graves with them. No mourning was heard in Jerusalem, for famine stifled all emotions, and an awful silence shrouded the city. The rebels at first ordered the bodies buried at public expense, finding the stench unbearable, but then flung them into the ravines when they became too numerous.[39]

The atrocities within the city continued. Within eleven weeks, there were 115,880 corpses carried out of the city, and it was reported that 600,000 more bodies from the lower class were thrown out. People were so desperate for food that they began to eat cow dung,[40] shoes, leather, belts, hay, and in one case, a mother killed, cooked, and ate her child.[41] Those who were captured by the Romans while escaping were crucified outside the walls of the city. Josephus wrote, "out of rage and hatred, the soldiers nailed their prisoners in different postures, and so great was their number that space could not be found for the crosses."[42] These and many more atrocities were experienced in Jerusalem at this time.

After a great struggle, the Romans took the city, and against the wishes of Titus, who wanted to save the temple, it was plundered of its treasures and burned to the ground by his unruly and enraged soldiers. They looted the city, slaughtering men, women, and children without consideration of age or status.[43] After Jerusalem was taken, Josephus described the ongoing slaughter that took place, "Pouring into the streets [of the upper city], they massacred everyone they found, burning the houses with all who had taken shelter in them. So great was the slaughter that in many places the flames were put out by streams of blood."[44]

Jerusalem fell to the Romans on September 26, 70 AD. When Titus entered the city for the first time and saw the strength of its defenses, he said, "Surely God was with us in the war, who brought the Jews down from these strongholds, for what could hand or engine do against these

---

39. Josephus, *Wars of the Jews*, W V, 491.

40. Josephus, *Wars of the Jews*, W V, 541.

41. Josephus, *Wars of the Jews*, W VI, 193.

42. Josephus, *Wars of the Jews*, W V, 424.

43. Josephus, *Wars of the Jews*, W VI, 271.

44. Josephus, *Wars of the Jews*, W VI, 403.

towers?"[45] There were 1,100,000 Jews who died during the war, and 97,000 were taken as prisoners. These are staggering numbers, even for today. Jesus was right when he said, concerning the fall of Jerusalem, "For then there will be great tribulation, such as has not been from the beginning of the world until now, no, and never will be."[46]

Someone might ask the question, "What happened to the Christians in Jerusalem?" There were a substantial number of Christians who lived in and around Jerusalem since the day of Pentecost. Where did they go? The simple answer to the question is that they left before the Zealots took over the city. This is confirmed by Eusebius who wrote:

> Meanwhile, before the war began, members of the Jerusalem church were ordered by an oracle given by revelation to those worthy of it to leave the city and settle in a city of Perea called Pella. Here they migrated from Jerusalem, as if, once holy men had deserted the royal capital of the Jews and the whole land of Judea, the judgment of God might finally fall on them for their crimes against Christ and his apostles, utterly blotting out all that wicked generation.[47]

It is not difficult to believe that God would warn his people[48] before the coming judgment on the city and lead them to a safe place during this time of tribulation for the city of Jerusalem. The destruction of the temple put an end to the sacrificial system. The whole concept of temple worship ended, along with the power and influence of the Sadducees.

Emperor Domitian (81–96 AD)

Domitian became Emperor in 81 AD, after the death of his brother Titus, who had served as Emperor from 79-81. From the beginning of his reign, he had some peculiar habits. It is said that he would spend many hours alone catching flies and then piercing them with a sharp pen.[49] It seems like an odd obsession considering that from a young age Domitian did not enjoy the idea of bloodshed. He even passed an edict outlawing the sacrifice of cattle. In his earlier years, he was kind to his friends,

45. Josephus, *Wars of the Jews*, W VI, 403.

46. Matt 24:21.

47. Eusebius, CH. 3.5.

48. Matt 24:15–21.

49. Suetonius, *Twelve Caesars*, 345.

self-controlled, generous and it appeared he would be a good ruler.[50] Not unlike previous emperors, he provided grand entertainment for the people. There were chariot races, gladiator battles, wild-beast hunts, foot racing, music competitions, and much more. He even had an artificial lake dug next to the Tiber River for full-scale naval battles.[51] He was a conservative leader who wanted to maintain, restore, and promote Roman traditions. He made many social and judicial changes meant to improve public manners and to strengthen the integrity of the judiciary.[52]

Although Domitian started well, it was not long before his hidden cruelty began to come to the surface. He was described as "a man of considerable ability, but of cruel and difficult temperament."[53] Suetonius believed that "fear of assassination made him cruel."[54] His brutal behaviour was seen in his willingness to have a man executed for the smallest of offenses. One man who said something rude about the emperor was thrown into the ring with wild dogs and torn to pieces.[55] He also executed many senators. As time went on, his cruelty reached new heights. He would torture prisoners by having their testicles scalded, or their hands cut off.[56] His extravagant spending on public games and his aggressive building program led to financial problems. To solve these problems, he began to seize people's property for any and every reason. Even a minor insult to the emperor could lead to the loss of your estate.[57]

Domitian was also given to self-aggrandizement. He rebuilt many important buildings that were destroyed by fire, but would only allow his name to be inscribed on the building.[58] He also started referring to himself as "Lord God." The introduction in his written letters began with the words, "Our Lord God instructs you to do this." This became a standard title in both verbal and written discourse. He also ensured that all his statues in the city of Rome were fashioned from gold and silver. In

50. Suetonius, *Twelve Caesars*, 350.

51. Suetonius, *Twelve Caesars*, 345, 346.

52. Suetonius, *Twelve Caesars*, 348.

53. Tacitus, *Agricola and The Germania*, 40.

54. Suetonius, *Twelve Caesars*, 345.

55. Suetonius, *Twelve Caesars*, 351.

56. Suetonius, *Twelve Caesars*, 352.

57. Suetonius, *Twelve Caesars*, 353.

58. Suetonius, *Twelve Caesars*, 347.

addition to this, he erected many porticos and arches to the glory of his own name.[59]

It is not surprising that during his emperorship, he persecuted the Christian church. Eusebius described the persecution as follows:

> Many were the victims of Domitian's appalling cruelty. At Rome, great numbers of men distinguished by birth and attainments were executed without a fair trial, and countless other eminent men were for no reason at all banished from the country and their property confiscated. Finally, he showed himself the successor of Nero in enmity and hostility to God. He was, in fact, the second to organize persecution against us, though his father Vespasian had had no mischievous designs against us.[60]

Tertullian said this about Domitian, "A similar attempt [to destroy the Christians] had once been made by Domitian, who almost equaled Nero in cruelty; but—I suppose because he had some common sense—he very soon stopped, even recalling those he had banished."[61] During this persecution, the apostle John was exiled to the island of Patmos, where he received the Revelation of Jesus Christ.

Eusebius also tells us that Domitian ordered that all those of David's line should be executed.[62] This is a reference to the Jewish people. It was only twenty years since the destruction of Jerusalem and about twenty years since the Roman siege took place against Masada. The last thing Domitian wanted to deal with was another Jewish uprising. The Jews were considered a rebellious and seditious group, and Domitian believed there should be strict laws to keep them in line.

Although persecution under Domitian was intense, it did not last long. Domitian, who had lost support because of his tyranny, was murdered by a knife-wielding assassin in his palace on September 18, 96 AD. He was forty-four years of age and reigned for fourteen years. The Roman Senate ordered that his name be erased from every inscription so that future generations would forget him.[63] After his death, the Christians enjoyed a time of peace.

59. Suetonius, *Twelve Caesars*, 354.

60. Eusebius CH 3.17.

61. Eusebius CH 3.20.

62. Eusebius CH 3.19.

63. Suetonius, *Twelve Caesars*, 360.

Discussion Questions

1. How should the church respond to a pagan government that oppresses Christianity?

2. Discuss the significance of the destruction of Jerusalem.

Chapter 4

Persecution in the Second Century

Persecution continued into the second century, but it was concentrated during the reigns of Emperor Trajan, who ruled from 98 to 117, and Marcus Aurelius, who reigned from 161 to 180. Throughout this century, many unnamed Christians were martyred for their faith, whose stories have been lost in time, but the testimonies of two men, Ignatius and Polycarp, both executed during the reign of Emperor Trajan, have been preserved for our encouragement and edification.

Emperor Trajan (r. 98–117)

Emperor Trajan was born in 53 AD in Italica, close to the city of Seville in modern-day Spain. His father served as a senator during the reign of Emperor Nero and as a consul under Emperor Vespasian. He was a commander during the First Jewish-Roman War (66–70) and served as governor of Syria from 73–77. Trajan served with his father in Syria. He became a successful military commander, was appointed consul in 91, and then became governor of Germania in 97.[1] When he was appointed emperor in 98, he had already been well-groomed for the position.

Trajan was a successful military strategist, and during his reign, he defeated the Dacians (modern day Romania) and incorporated their vast territory into the empire, establishing new sources of wealth for Rome. With this new wealth, Trajan set out to rejuvenate Italy, which had been in a state of decline for many years. New projects included low-interest loans to revitalize the Italian farm communities; funds for the education of poor and disadvantaged children; new roads; new ports to enable

1. Carlos Gomez, ed. *Encyclopedia of the Ancient Roman Empire*, 209, 210.

easier access to Rome and to facilitate trade; aqueducts to provide fresh water for the cities; temples to honour the gods, and bridges for the faster movement of troops and people in general. He also constructed a massive basilica in Rome which became the administrative center for the city and provided the blueprint for future basilicas built as Christian churches. He provided money to support the free distribution of grain and gave lavish gifts to the people. He also financed gladiatorial contests, races, and various games for the entertainment of the masses. Needless to say, he was popular with both the people and the Senate.[2]

Even though he was a generous and effective ruler, he was also a persecutor of the Christian church. Eusebius informs us that there were sporadic outbursts of persecution during his reign in various cities. In one of these outbursts, Symeon, the bishop of the church in Jerusalem, was martyred at the age of one hundred and twenty after being tortured for many days. Ignatius of Antioch was also killed during his reign in 107, when he was fed to the lions in the Roman Colosseum. We do not know the exact number of Christians martyred during his reign, but the numbers were large enough to alarm Pliny the Younger, governor of Bithynia, who wrote a letter to Emperor Trajan asking him for advice on dealing with those who were accused of being Christians.[3]

Pliny the Younger

Pliny was born in either late 61 or early 62 AD. Although little is known about his early life, we know that he rose to positions of great influence in the Roman empire, eventually serving as governor of Bithynia on the northern shore of modern-day Turkey. While governor of Bithynia, he wrote to Trajan around 112, inquiring about how he should treat those accused of being Christians.[4] It is evident when reading the letter that although the Christians were persecuted, and the persecution was widespread and violent, there was no legal process in place to provide direction when the accused were brought before the judge. Pliny expressed his lack of experience when dealing with Christians and his need for guidance. He wrote:

2. Gomez, ed. *Encyclopedia of the Ancient Roman Empire*, 214–18.

3. Eusebius, *Church History*, 3.32.

4. Pliny, *Letters of Younger Pliny*, 10.96.

> I have never been present at an examination of Christians. Con-
> sequently, I do not know the nature of the extent of the punish-
> ments usually meted out to them, nor the grounds for starting
> an investigation and how far it should be pressed. Nor am I at
> all sure whether any distinction should be made between them
> on the grounds of age, or if young people and adults should be
> treated alike; whether a pardon ought to be granted to anyone
> retracting his beliefs, or if he has once professed Christianity, he
> shall gain nothing by renouncing it; whether it is the mere name
> of Christian which is punishable, even if innocent of crime, or
> rather the crimes associated with the name.[5]

Pliny then outlined the approach he had taken up to that point. When an accused person was brought before him, he would ask him three times if he was a Christian. If he persisted in claiming to be a Christian, Pliny would have him led away and executed. Although he admitted his failure to understand the reason for their punishment, he indicated that their stubborn and obstinate attitude was enough to merit the punishment meted out to them. If the accused denied he was a Christian and was willing to offer incense to the gods, Pliny would release him:

> Amongst these I considered that I should dismiss any who de-
> nied that they were or ever had been Christians when they had
> repeated after me a formula of invocation to the gods and had
> made offerings of wine and incense to your statue (which I had
> ordered to be brought into court for this purpose along with the
> images of the gods), and furthermore had reviled the name of
> Christ: none of which things, I understand, any genuine Chris-
> tian can be induced to do.[6]

Pliny even had two women who were called "deaconesses" by the church tortured in an attempt to gather more information on Christian gatherings and concluded that it was no more than "a degenerate sort of cult carried to extravagant lengths." Pliny offered hope that many people caught up in Christianity might be reclaimed to the traditional gods of the empire with the proper guidance.

Emperor Trajan provided a threefold response to Pliny's letter. First, he wrote that Christians should not be hunted down, but if they were brought before him and the charge of being a Christian was accurate, they should be punished. Second, if anyone denied being a Christian and

5. Pliny, *Letters of Younger Pliny*, 10.96.
6. Pliny, *Letters of Younger Pliny*, 10.96.

proved it by offering sacrifices and prayers to the gods, they should be set free. Third, anonymous pamphlets should be rejected and never be used as a basis to accuse someone.[7] Trajan's policy became the policy of the empire into the third century. While this policy was very pragmatic and had the interests of the empire in mind, Tertullian (a late second, early third-century theologian) was not impressed. He wrote in the early third century concerning this edict:

> What a necessarily confusing sentence! It refuses to seek them out, as if they were innocent, and orders that they be punished as if they were guilty. It pardons, and yet is cruel. It ignores, and yet punishes. Why do you circumvent your own censure? If you condemn, why do you not inquire? And, if you do not inquire, why do you not also absolve?[8]

Although the edict did quell persecution in some places, it did not entirely prevent recurrent attacks against Christians throughout the Roman provinces, nor did it protect Christians against false accusations or prevent the authorities from punishing Christians for their faith. It would not be until the reign of Emperor Constantine in the fourth century that the Christian faith would be legalized, allowing Christians to practice their religion openly.

Ignatius of Antioch (c.35–108)

Ignatius of Antioch, also known as Ignatius Theophoros (God-bearer), was an influential church leader in the first century and early part of the second century AD. Other than a few allusions to his life recorded in his letters, we know little about him. He was born between 30–35 AD, was an early bishop in Antioch,[9] was arrested and condemned during the reign of the emperor Trajan, was sent to Rome, and was fed to wild animals in the Roman Coliseum sometime between 107 and 117. He was a friend of Polycarp and a disciple of the apostle John.[10] He may also have known Mary, the mother of Jesus.[11]

---

7. Pliny, *Letters of Younger Pliny*, 10.97.

8. Tertullian, *Apology* 1.2.

9. Eusebius, CH, 3.21.

10. Eusebius, CH, 3.36.

11. Ignatius, *Epistle of Ignatius to the Virgin Mary*, 126, 1:123.

While enroute to Rome to be executed, Ignatius wrote letters to seven different churches covering various topics. His letters addressed issues such as martyrdom, the role of bishops, elders, and deacons in the church, the centrality of the death and resurrection of Christ, as well as other theological subjects. One desire that stands out when one reads the letters of Ignatius is his yearning to be martyred for Christ. He admonishes the Christians in Rome not to intercede with the government on his behalf but allow him the privilege of being martyred for Jesus. He wrote:

> I write to all the churches, and I bid all men know, that of my own free will I die for God, unless ye should hinder me. I exhort you, be ye not an unseasonable kindness to me. Let me be given to the wild beasts, for through them I can attain unto God. I am God's wheat, and I am ground by the teeth of wild beasts that I may be found pure bread [of Christ]. Rather entice the wild beasts, that they may become my sepulcher and may leave no part of my body behind, so that I may not, when I am fallen asleep, be burdensome to anyone. Then shall I be truly a disciple of Jesus Christ, when the world shall not so much as see my body.[12]

As Ignatius traveled to Rome, he looked forward, with great delight, to the moment when he would be killed for his faith and enter into the presence of the Lord Jesus Christ. He believed that martyrdom was the ultimate expression of discipleship and faithfulness to the Lord. As he anticipated his martyrdom, he wrote, "now I am beginning to be a disciple."[13] In his letter to the Ephesians, he indicated that through his death, he would "have the power to be a disciple."[14] Even the ill-treatment by the soldiers who accompanied him was helping him to "become more completely a disciple."[15] Ignatius desired to get to Jesus, and he believed that his suffering would enable him to do this. He wrote, "come fire and cross and grapplings with wild beasts, [cuttings and manglings,] wrenching of bones, hacking of limbs, crushings of my whole body, come cruel tortures of the devil to assail me. Only be it mine to attain unto Jesus Christ."[16] The desire for worldly things had faded away, and his longing to be like Jesus in his suffering and to be with Jesus took hold of his heart.

12. Ignatius, *To the Romans*, 4.

13. Ignatius, *To the Romans*, 5.

14. Ignatius, *To the Ephesians*, 1.

15. Ignatius, *To the Romans*, 5.

16. Ignatius, *To the Romans*, 5.

Ignatius was granted his desire to be fed to wild animals in the Roman Colosseum. After his arrest, he was brought before Emperor Trajan, who questioned him before condemning him to death. Trajan had already stated that anyone unwilling to sacrifice to idols would be put to death. The following is the record of the questioning that took place at his trial.

> Trajan - "Who are you, wicked wretch, who sets himself to transgress our commands, and persuades others to do the same, so that they should miserably perish?"
>
> Ignatius - "No one ought to call Theophorus (lit. "one who carries God") wicked; for all evil spirits have departed from the servants of God. But if, because I am an enemy to these (spirits), you call me wicked in respect to them, I quite agree with you; for inasmuch as I have Christ the King of heaven [within me], I destroy all the devices of these [evil spirits]."
>
> Trajan - "And who is Theophorus?"
>
> Ignatius - "He who has Christ within his breast."
>
> Trajan - "Do we not then seem to you to have the gods in our mind, whose assistance we enjoy in fighting against our enemies.?"
>
> Ignatius - "You are in error when you call the demons of the nations gods. For there is but one God, who made heaven, and earth, and the sea, and all that are in them; and one Jesus Christ, the only-begotten Son of God, whose kingdom may I enjoy."
>
> Trajan said, "Do you mean He who was crucified under Pontius Pilate?"
>
> Ignatius - "I mean He who crucified my sin, with him who was the inventor of it, and who has condemned (and cast down) all deceit and malice of the devil under the feet of those who carry Him in their heart."
>
> Trajan - "Do you then carry with you He that was crucified?"
>
> Ignatius - Truly so; for it is written, 'I dwell in them, and walk in them."
>
> Trajan then pronounced sentence against Ignatius,
>
> "We command that Ignatius, who affirms that he carries about within him, He that was crucified, be bound by soldiers, and carried to the great (city) Rome, there to be devoured by the beasts, for the gratification of the people."

When Ignatius heard this he cried out with joy, "I thank you, O Lord, that you have vouchsafed to honour me with a perfect love towards you, and have made me to be bound with iron chains, like the Apostle Paul."

Having spoken thus, he then, with delight, clasped the chains about him; and when he had first prayed for the church, and commended it with tears to the Lord, he was hurried away by the savage cruelty of the soldiers, like a distinguished ram, the leader of a goodly flock, that he might be carried to Rome, there to furnish food to the bloodthirsty beasts."[17]

The Teachings of Ignatius

Though they do not provide a systematic theology, Ignatius' letters reveal some of his beliefs that influenced the church's development of theology and church practice.

Church Leadership

Ignatius placed a heavy emphasis on the role of leadership in the church. He promoted a tripartite system that included a bishop, elders, and deacons. He had a very high view of the bishop, in particular, teaching that the bishop stood in the place of Christ. In the same way that Jesus Christ submitted to his Father, the congregation should submit to the bishop and not resist him in any way.[18] He said that "we ought to regard the bishop as the Lord Himself,"[19] and that the people should not do anything without the consent of the bishop.[20] In another place, he compares the bishop to the Father in heaven and that all should be in submission to him.[21] Love feasts, baptisms, weddings, or any other activity in the church should not be done without his approval.[22] The elders were under the bishop but also carried considerable authority in the church. He wrote, "Therefore as the Lord did nothing without the Father, [being united with Him], either by Himself or by the Apostles, so neither do ye anything without the bishop and the presbyters."[23] He described the relationship between the bishop and the elders as strings to a harp. When they sound together in harmony,

---

17. *Martyrdom of Ignatius*, 129–30.

18. Ignatius, *To the Ephesians*, 5.

19. Ignatius, *To the Ephesians*, 6.

20. Ignatius, *To the Trallians*, 2.

21. Ignatius, *To the Trallians*, 3.

22. Ignatius, *To the Smyrneans*, 8.

23. Ignatius, *To the Magnesians*, 7.

they make wonderous music to God.[24] Likewise, the deacons were to be honoured for the task they performed. Ignatius wrote, "I advise you, be ye zealous to do all things in godly concord, the bishops presiding after the likeness of God and the presbyters after the likeness of the council of the Apostles, with the deacons also who are most dear to me, having been entrusted with the diaconate of Jesus Christ."[25] Ignatius went as far as to say that without the bishops, elders, and deacons, the church did not exist.[26] While a bishop ruling over several churches within a geographical region was not a practice in the early second century, the idea of a monarchical bishop in each church with the elders, deacons, and congregation in subjection to him was becoming well established. Ignatius did not teach that the bishop of Rome was superior to other bishops. This would be a later development.

While it appears that the tripartite system of leadership was already established in the church in the early second century, it is crucial to recognize that first century; extra-biblical writings only refer to two positions of leadership. *The Didache,* also known as *The Teaching of the Twelve Apostles,* is believed by many scholars to have been written in the first century, making it the oldest Christian document we have outside the New Testament. Concerning the election of leaders in the church, it says, "elect for yourselves bishops and deacons."[27] There is no distinction made between bishops and elders in this document. The same is true in the letter of Clement of Rome, who wrote late in the first century:

> From land to land, accordingly, and from city to city they preached, and from their earliest converts appointed men whom they had tested by the Spirit to act as bishops and deacons for the future believers. And this was no innovation, for, a long time before the Scripture about bishops and deacons; for somewhere it says, "I will establish their overseers in observance of the law and their ministers in fidelity."[28]

The New Testament as well only mentions two positions of leadership in the church—elders and deacons.[29] It appears that the distinction

24. Ignatius, *To the Ephesians,* 4.

25. Ignatius, *To the Magnesians,* 6.

26. Ignatius, *To the Trallians,* 2.

27. *Didache,* 15.

28. Clement of Rome, *Epistle to the Corinthians,* 42.4,5.

29. 1 Tim 3:1–13; Titus 1:5–9.

between bishops, elders, and deacons was not fully established in the Christian church until the early decades of the second century.

The Lord's Supper

Ignatius was the first to teach that the bishop or someone authorized by the bishop must preside at the Lord's Supper to make it valid. He wrote, "Let no one do anything touching the church, apart from the bishop. Let that celebration of the Eucharist be considered valid which is held under the bishop or anyone to whom he has committed it."[30] He also emphasized that The Lord's Supper (Eucharist) is the flesh and blood of Christ against the docetist's denial of the incarnation. He wrote, "The Eucharist is the flesh of the Lord Jesus Christ."[31] Ignatius was also the first one to identify the Eucharist as a sacrificial altar. He said, "Take care, then, to partake of one Eucharist; for, one is the Flesh of Our Lord Jesus Christ, and one the cup to unite us with His Blood, and one altar."[32] When writing to the Magnesians he wrote, "Come together, all of you, as to one temple and one altar."[33] Ignatius' main concerns seem to be preserving the humanity of Jesus Christ and unity in the church. It is not clear whether or not he believed that the bread and the wine were the actual flesh and blood of Jesus Christ, although his statements certainly imply that he did. While he could not anticipate the full implications of his teaching, his statements on the Lord's Supper would contribute to the development of the doctrine of transubstantiation celebrated in the Roman Catholic Church up to the present time.

The Humanity and Deity of Jesus Christ

Multiple times in Ignatius' letters he explicitly states that Jesus Christ is God. In the introduction of his letter to the Ephesians, he wrote, "by the will of the Father and of Jesus Christ our God."[34] He also referred to "Jesus Christ our God" in his letter to the Romans.[35] While warning the

30. Ignatius, *To the Smyrnaeans*, 8.1

31. Ignatius, *To the Smyrnaeans*, 7.1.

32. Ignatius, *To the Philadelphians*, 4.

33. Ignatius, *To the Magnesians*, 7.2.

34. Ignatius, *To the Ephesians*, introduction.

35. Ignatius, *To the Romans*, 13.

church about heretical teachers, he wrote, "There is one only physician, of flesh and of spirit, generate and ingenerate, God in man, true Life in death, Son of Mary and Son of God, first passible and then impassible, Jesus Christ our Lord."[36] Further to this, "For our God, Jesus the Christ, was conceived in the womb by Mary according to a dispensation, of the seed of David but also of the Holy Ghost." Later he wrote, "God appeared in the likeness of man."[37] These quotes reveal how concerned Ignatius was that the Christians in Ephesus understand that Jesus is both God and man. In the first century world, the influence of Docetism and Gnosticism on Christian theology led many professing Christians to deny or at least struggle with the humanity of Jesus Christ. Gnosticism taught that all matter is evil and that God would never pollute himself by taking on human flesh. Wanting nothing to do with this anti-Christian view, Ignatius emphasized the true deity and the true humanity of the Saviour. One of his strongest statements on the humanity of Christ is in his letter to the Romans, where he wrote:

> Jesus Christ, who was of the race of David, who was the Son of Mary, who was truly born and ate and drank, was truly persecuted under Pontius Pilate, was truly crucified and died in the sight of those in heaven and those on earth and those under the earth; who moreover was truly raised from the dead, His Father having raised Him, who in the like fashion will so raise us also who believe on Him."[38]

This quote is similar to the statement on Jesus Christ in the Apostle's Creed. It indicates that the creed was already developing in the second century but would not appear in its more complete form until the fourth and fifth centuries.

Marcus Aurelius

Marcus Aurelius became emperor by the nomination of the Roman Senate in 161 and ruled until 180. Unlike many of the emperors who preceded him, he was an enlightened leader with a philosophical mind and was inclined to live a contemplative life. He held to the teachings of Stoic philosophy and sought to live according to its tenets. As Emperor,

36. Ignatius, *To the Ephesians*, 7.

37. Ignatius, *To the Ephesians*, 20.

38. Ignatius, *To the Romans*, 9.

Aurelius faced many challenges, including an invasion by a revitalized, expansionist Parthian Empire from the east in 161 AD. Under his leadership, the Romans roundly defeated the Parthians. There was, however, little time to enjoy this glorious victory because the Germanic tribes were raiding in the north on the Danube frontier. A plague ravaged the land in 166–167 AD and diminished the Roman forces in the north. This emboldened the Germans to invade the Empire.[39] Leading the Roman legions in defending the northern border, Aurelius was able to impose peace upon the region by allowing some Germans to settle within the empire's borders.[40] He hoped they would provide a source of recruits for a depleted Roman army.[41]

While on campaign, the emperor kept a record of his thoughts in a book entitled *Meditations*. It is not a book in the traditional sense but a journal in which Marcus wrote down those thoughts he considered worthy of preserving. Some have called it one of the world's greatest books, while others view it as a collection of pointless thoughts of a pretentious thinker.[42] However one might view his writings, he was a very generous and conscientious ruler. He cared for the people and sought to pass legislation that would help the neediest in society, such as widows, orphans, and slaves.[43]

Although Marcus Aurelius was a good and levelheaded leader, he was also a superstitious man. He offered sacrifices before he embarked on any important activity and often sought the advice of Seers. The early part of his reign had many problems, including invasions, floods, plagues, natural disasters, and foreign invasions. Many believed the Christians were to blame because they refused to honour the traditional gods, and for this reason, sporadic persecution broke out against them. Marcus' view of the Christians is seen in the one mention of them in his *Meditations*. He considered them obstinate and unreasonable in their willingness to die.[44] Marcus followed the policy of Trajan when dealing with Christians,

39. Nigel Rogers, *Roman Empire*, 35.

40. R.H. Barrow, *Romans*, 156.

41. Nigel Rogers, *Roman Empire*, 126.

42. R.H. Barrow, *Romans*, 156.

43. Gomez, ed. *Encyclopedia of the Ancient Roman Empire*, 250.

44. Meditations 11.3.

ordering that Christians should be tortured to death if they did not deny Christ but released if they did.[45]

Several accusations were made against the Christians in the first and second century to justify the violence perpetrated against them. First, they were accused of participating in Thyestean feasts.[46] In Greek mythology, there is a story of a violent dispute between Thyestes and his brother Atreus over who had the right to rule as king of Mycenae. With the help of Zeus, Atreus became king and invited his brother to attend a banquet that they might be reconciled. Thyestes attended the banquet but was unaware that the main dish consisted of his own sons who were cut up and stewed. Thyestes willingly ate and, at the end of the meal, asked that his sons be brought in. The heads, hands, and feet of his sons were carried into the banquet hall, and it was revealed to him that he had just feasted on his son's flesh.[47] Because the Christians were said to eat the body and drink the blood of Christ, many concluded that the flesh of sacrificed children was eaten during their gatherings.

Second, they were accused of Oedipean incest.[48] Greek Mythology tells the story of a man named Oedipus who, after destroying a terrible monster that was preying on the people of Thebes, was declared king. He married the widowed Queen, not realizing she was his birth mother, and they had four children together.[49] The Christians were accused of Oedipean incest because even husbands and wives referred to one another as brothers and sisters. They were charged with committing incestuous sexual acts with one another when they met together to celebrate what they called the "love feast."

As these rumors spread throughout the community, the people turned on the Christians. Even family members who tolerated the faith of their relatives joined with those who persecuted them.[50] Eusebius described the suffering they endured:

> When the tyrant's tortures had been overcome by Christ through the perseverance of the blessed saints, the Devil thought up other devices: imprisonment in filth and darkness, stretching feet

45. Eusebius, 5.1.

46. Eusebius, 5.1.

47. Jenny March, *Penguin Book of Classical Myths*, 434.

48. Eusebius, 5.1.

49. Jenny Marsh, *Classical Myths*, 476.

50. Eusebius, 5.1.

in stocks to the fifth hole, and other atrocities that angry jailers, full of the Devil, inflict on prisoners. Thus, many of them were strangled in prison, while others were tortured so cruelly that it seemed impossible for them to survive, yet they did so, deprived of human help but strengthened by the Lord to encourage the rest. But the young, recently arrested and unaccustomed to torture, could not endure confinement and died in prison.[51]

Some Christians were forced to run a gauntlet of whips, others were mauled to death by wild animals, and many were fastened to hot iron chairs that roasted their flesh.[52] In some cases, just the name Christian was enough to condemn you to death. On several occasions, Christians were asked the simple question, "Are you a Christian?" If they answered, "yes," they were taken away and punished.[53]

Following the death of Marcus Aurelius, there was a period of peace for the Christians until the time of Emperor Septimius Severus.

Polycarp (c.65–155)

We have little information about the early life of Polycarp. We know that he was a friend of Ignatius, who visited Polycarp while being transported to Rome to be executed. Ignatius wrote a letter to Polycarp in 115 AD, encouraging him to be a faithful shepherd of the flock of God. Both of these men knew the apostle John and may have been discipled by him. Polycarp was the bishop of Smyrna and rose to become a significant leader in the second century. His prominence in the Christian church was attested to during his trial when he was referred to as "the teacher of Asia, the father of the Christians, the destroyer of our gods." He was possibly the bishop of Smyrna when the apostle John received the Revelation while on the island of Patmos. Because of this, some scholars identify him with the Angel of Smyrna mentioned in Revelation 2:8.[54]

Irenaeus, a disciple of Polycarp, gave a brief description of his memory of the man:

51. Eusebius, 5.1.

52. Eusebius, 5.1.

53. Eusebius 5.1.

54. *Martyrdom of Saint Polycarp*, 6:87. The entire dialogue is quoted from this section.

> I can describe the place where blessed Polycarp sat and talked,
> his goings out and comings in, the character of his life, his
> personal appearance, his addresses to crowded congregations.
> I remember how he spoke of his communication with John
> and with others who had seen the Lord; how he repeated their
> words from memory; and how the things that he had heard
> them say about the Lord, His miracles and His teaching, things
> that he had heard direct from the eye-witnesses of the Word of
> Life, were proclaimed by Polycarp in complete harmony with
> Scripture.[55]

Although we know little about Polycarp, there is a beautiful record of his trial and martyrdom in a letter written by the church of God in Smyrna to the church of Philomelium. The letter was written shortly after the execution of Polycarp around 155 AD and was intended to receive wide distribution.

When Polycarp first heard that the authorities were searching for him, he refused to leave town, but his friends persuaded him to go into hiding. He withdrew to a farm not far from the town and spent his time in prayer and meditation. While he was praying, he saw a vision of his pillow on fire and concluded that it was God's will that he be burned alive. As the authorities were determined to find him, he went to another farm, but a household member betrayed him to the authorities. He refused to run, accepting that it was God's will to be arrested. The police chief questioned him and encouraged him to offer incense to the emperor and declare Caesar as Lord. Polycarp refused and was taken to the stadium to be examined by the Proconsul. As he entered the stadium, he heard a voice say, "Be strong, Polycarp, and act manfully." The following is the record of Polycarp's trial and execution:[56]

> Proconsul - "Respect your age," and all the rest they were ac-
> customed to say; "Swear by the Fortune of Caesar; change your
> mind; say, "Away with the atheists!"
>
> Polycarp - But Polycarp looked with a stern mien at the
> whole rabble of lawless heathen in the arena; he then groaned
> and looking up to heaven, said, with a wave of his hand at them:
> "Away with the atheists!"
>
> Proconsul - "Take the oath and I will set you free; revile
> Christ,"

55. ANF, "Fragments from the Lost Writings of Irenaeus, "1:2.
56. *Martyrdom of Saint Polycarp*, 8–16.

Polycarp - "For six and eighty years I have been serving Him, and He has done no wrong to me; how, then, dare I blaspheme my King who has saved me."

Proconsul - "Swear by the Fortune of Caesar."

Polycarp - "If you flatter yourself that I shall swear by the Fortune of Caesar, as you suggest, and if you pretend not to know me, let me frankly tell you: I am a Christian! If you wish to learn the teaching of Christianity, fix a day and let me explain."

Proconsul - "Talk to the crowd."

Polycarp - "You, I indeed consider entitled to an explanation; for we have been trained to render honor, in so far as it does not harm us, to magistrates and authorities appointed by God; but as to that crowd, I do not think it proper to make an appeal to them."

Proconsul - "Well, I have wild beasts, and shall have you thrown before them if you do not change your mind."

Polycarp - "Call for them, to change from better to worse is impossible'; but it is noble to change from what is evil to what is good."

Proconsul - "If you make little of the beasts, I shall have you consumed by fire unless you change your mind."

Polycarp - "The fire which you threaten, is one that burns for a little while, and after a short time goes out. You evidently do not know the fire of the judgment to come and the eternal punishment, which awaits the wicked. But why do you delay" Go ahead; do what you want."

"As he said this and more besides, he was animated with courage and joy, and his countenance was suffused with beauty. As a result, he did not collapse from fright at what was being said to him; the proconsul, on the other hand, was astounded, and sent his herald to announce three times in the centre of the arena; Polycarp has confessed to being a Christian."

The crowd cried out, "This is the teacher of Asia, the father of the Christians, the destroyer of our gods! He teaches many not to sacrifice and not to worship!" They demanded that a lion be let loose on him, but the proconsul could not do this because the hunting sports were closed, and presumably, the animals were already back in their cages. The crowd then demanded that he should be burned alive. Wanting to participate in his death, many in the crowd rushed forward and prepared the wood for the fire. When they finished, Polycarp was placed on the woodpile, where he immediately prayed to God. After he prayed, they set the fire. The record of Polycarp's death says that the fire miraculously did not consume him but formed a wall around him, making him "like a loaf in the oven." Since they could not burn him with fire, it was ordered that an executioner stab him with a dagger. It was reported that after stabbing him, a dove flew from the wound, and there was so much blood that it extinguished the fire. Most scholars agree that the dove and the blood section is a later addition to the text.[57] After Polycarp died, they burned his body to prevent the Christians from taking it. However, the Christians did gather up his bones and bury them so that they could meet each year at his grave to celebrate the anniversary of his martyrdom.

We have a letter written in 110 by Polycarp to the Philippian church.[58] In his letter, he was not as concerned with the leadership structure as Ignatius was but focused instead on relationships in the church. He urged the people to live a holy life, instructed wives to be faithful to their husbands, and train their children in the things of God. Widows should devote themselves to prayer; deacons are to live upright lives and fulfill their duties as servants of the Lord. Elders were to be busy visiting the sick, caring for the widow, the orphan, and the poor, and being devoted to a life of personal holiness. All Christians should become imitators of Jesus Christ who took our sin upon himself when he died on the cross even though he did nothing wrong. Christians should be willing to endure suffering for his sake patiently.

Polycarp also taught that salvation is of grace. He wrote, "You are assured that you have been saved by a gratuitous gift, not by our actions—no, but by the will of God through Jesus Christ."[59] Along with Ignatius, Polycarp condemned those who denied that Jesus Christ had come in the flesh and identified them as "Antichrist" and "the first-born of Satan."[60]

While we do not know the exact number of Christians who were tortured and killed for the faith in the second century, there was a considerable number who refused to deny Jesus Christ in the face of persecution. The faithfulness of men like Ignatius and Polycarp, and the multitude of nameless Christians who died for Jesus, should encourage us to remain faithful to our Saviour in the face of persecution in our day.

57. "The Letter of the Smyrnaeans," *On the Martyrdom of S. Polycarp*, 88.

58. Polycarp, *Epistles to the Philippians*.

59. Polycarp, "The Second Epistle," 1.

60. Polycarp, "The Second Epistle," 7.

Discussion Questions

1. Was Ignatius right to seek out martyrdom? Why or why not?

2. Is martyrdom the ultimate expression of discipleship?

3. Does the New Testament support the tripartite system of leadership promoted by Ignatius?

4. What can Christians learn today from the example of Polycarp?

Chapter 5

The First Apologists

BECAUSE THE EARLY FOLLOWERS of Jesus were predominately Jewish, the theology of the Christian church was communicated using Jewish terms and concepts. However, through the ministry of the apostle Paul and other early preachers, the gospel spread to the far corners of the Roman Empire, bringing many Gentiles into the church. With the influx of Gentiles, the language of Christian theology began to incorporate many Greek words and concepts.

The growing church caught the notice of Roman officials who began viewing its growth as a threat to the political stability of the Empire. Rumours of Christians committing acts of murder, cannibalism, and incest began circulating in the general population. And while Roman officials did not generally make decisions based upon rumours, it did influence their judgment.[1] In response to the false accusations made against the Christians, the first apologists made their appearance in the second century to provide a defense of the Christian faith.

Many intellectuals viewed Christianity with great disdain and were not shy in speaking out against it. Celsus, a second-century Greek philosopher, wrote:

> In some private homes we find people who work with wool and rags, and cobblers, that is, the least cultured and most ignorant kind. Before the head of the household, they dare not utter a word. But as soon as they can take the children aside or some women who are as ignorant as they are, they speak wonders...If you really wish to know the truth, leave your teachers and your

1. Justin Martyr, *First and Second Apologies*, 1.

father, and go with the women and the children to the women's quarters, or to the cobbler's shop, or to the tannery, and there you will learn the perfect life. It is thus that these Christians find those who will believe them.[2]

He also wrote in another place,

Let no uncultured person draw near, none wise and none sensible, for all that kind of thing we count evil; but if any man is ignorant, if any man is wanting in sense and culture, if anybody is a fool, let him come boldly (to become a Christian)…We see them in their own houses, wool dresses, cobblers, the worst, the vulgarest, the most uneducated persons…they are like a swarm of bats or ants creeping out of their nest, or frogs holding a symposium around a swamp, or worms convening in mud.[3]

This kind of thinking was pervasive throughout the upper classes in Roman society. When combined with the general belief that Christians participated in cannibalism and incestuous sexual relationships, it painted an ugly picture of Christianity. Therefore, it was necessary to provide a refutation of these accusations, which is where the apologists come in.

An apology is an oral or written defense of the Christian faith, and an apologist is the one who provides that defense. There were several apologies written in the first and second centuries of the Christian church. We will look at three: The Didache; The Epistle of Diognetus; and the apologies of Justin Martyr.

The Didache or The Teaching of the Twelve Apostles

The manuscript of the Didache, dated around 1056 AD, was discovered in 1873 at Constantinople (Istanbul). It is not known where or when it was composed. Many scholars date it in the first century, which would make it the oldest Christian document, outside the New Testament, that we possess; while others date it in the third century AD. The Didache claims to be the teachings of the twelve apostles given for the instruction of unbelievers who wanted to become Christians.[4] While it may be an accurate representation of the apostles' teaching, it was not written by the apostles themselves.

2. Origen, *Against Celsus* 3.55.

3. Origen, *Against Celsus*, 3.59.

4. *Introduction to the Didache*, Ancient Christian Writers, 3.

It begins by contrasting two diametrically opposed ways of life. "Two Ways there are, one of Life and one of Death, and there is a great difference between the Two Ways." In describing the way of life, the writer begins with the two greatest commandments: "love the God who made you; secondly, your neighbor as yourself." It goes on to list a series of commands from the teaching of Jesus and the Ten Commandments. "Do not murder; do not commit adultery; do not practice pederasty [sex between a man and a boy]; do not fornicate; do not steal; do not deal in magic, do not practice sorcery; do not kill a fetus by abortion, or commit infanticide," etc. The followers of Jesus Christ were called to repent of these activities and no longer participate in them. After urging the believer to turn away from sin, the writer urges the new believer to "be gentle, and long-suffering, and merciful, and guileless, and quiet, and good." He warns against pride and instructs the believer to be willing to associate with the lowly; to make proper judgments; to provide for the needy; to treat one's servants well, and confess one's sins to God.

The way of death is described as a life of sin: "murders, adulteries, lustful desires, fornications, thefts, idolatries, magical arts, sorceries, robberies, false testimonies, hypocrisy, duplicity, fraud, pride, malice" and the like. Those who follow the Way of Life put sin to death and cultivate a holy lifestyle, while those who follow the Way of Death know nothing of repentance but give free rein to their sinful desires.

After explaining the difference between the Way of Life and the Way of Death, it provides instruction on the correct procedures for baptism. The new believer is to be baptized in the name of the Father, the Son, and the Holy Spirit. The water used in baptism should be cold running water, but warm water was acceptable if cold water was not available. If running water was not available, it was appropriate to pour water on the head three times in the name of the triune God. The candidate for baptism should be fasting for a day or two before his baptism. The Didache assumes Christians fast and instructs them to do so on Wednesdays and Fridays because the hypocrites fast on Mondays and Tuesdays. The Christian should also pray the Lord's Prayer three times a day.

The church met on Sunday for worship, and when they gathered, they ate together, confessed their sins to one another, reconciled with those with whom they were separated, and celebrated the Lord's Supper. The celebration of the Lord's Supper was to be accompanied by prescribed prayers. When praying for the cup, it should be prayed,

> We give Thee thanks, Our Father, for the Holy Vine of David
> Thy servant, which Thou has made known to us through Jesus,
> Thy Servant. To Thee be the glory for evermore.[5]

The prayer for the bread is as follows,

> We give Thee thanks, Our Father, for the life and knowledge
> which Thou has made known to us through Jesus, Thy Servant.
> To Thee be the glory for evermore. As this broken bread was
> scattered over the hills and then, when gathered from the ends
> of the earth into Thy Kingdom. For Thine is the glory and the
> power through Jesus Christ for evermore."[6]

There were also prescribed prayers to be offered at the end of the celebration. The Lord's Supper in the first century included a full meal. It says, "after you have taken your fill of food, give thanks as follows."[7] It then records a lengthy prayer. Only those who were baptized were permitted to participate in the Lord's Supper.

The Didache also provides instructions on how to determine whether a visiting preacher is a false teacher. If he proves to be a true teacher of the word and settles in the area, the people should financially support him in his labour, but he should be rejected as a false prophet if he asks for money. The same is true for new people who join the church. If they have a trade, they should work for their living and not expect the church to provide for them. The congregation was responsible for electing their own bishops and deacons.

The letter ends with an appeal to live in anticipation of the Lord's coming. Many false teachers seek to lead God's people astray, and they must be diligent and watchful until Jesus comes to take them home.

The Epistle to Diognetus

An unknown author wrote this letter in the second century to a man named Diognetus. It may be the earliest surviving defense of Christianity. The letter is addressed to the "most excellent Diognetus," and its purpose is to teach him concerning the religion of the Christians. The writer

5. *Didache*, 9.

6. *Didache*, 9.

7. *Didache*, 10.

responds to three questions: Who is the God of the Christians? What is the source of Christian love? Why is Christianity such a young religion?

He answers the first question— "Who is the God of the Christians?—by highlighting how ridiculous idol worship is. He argued that the idols were made of the same perishable substance as pots and pans and that they do not possess the ability to speak, see, feel, move, think or reason, and are also subject to decay. He wrote,

> This is stone, like the pavement under the feet; that one, metal, no better than the utensils forged for our use; this one, wood, and perhaps rotten wood by now; that one, silver, which needs a watchman to keep it from being stolen; another, iron, subject to corrosion by rust; still another, earthenware, no better to look at than anything fashioned for the most ignoble service. Is it not so? Are they not all of perishable material? Have they not been forged by iron and fire? On this one, a stonecutter has plied his craft, on that, a coppersmith, on a third, a silversmith, and on a fourth, a potter. Is it not so? … are they not all deaf and blind and lifeless and senseless and motionless?…these things you call gods; these you serve; these you worship; and in the end you become like them![8]

Because Christians rejected these so-called gods, they were hated by those who did worship them.

After highlighting the foolishness of pagan idol worship, the writer then went on to distance the Christians from the worship of the Jews. While acknowledging that the Jews also reject the Greek gods and claim to honour the one true God, he says they are mistaken in their worship of God. Their sacrifices are unnecessary because God does not need anything. Their food laws, Sabbath regulations, circumcision, feast days, and new moon celebrations are of no value and display a lack of understanding of true religion. The weakness in his argument is his failure to acknowledge that God did require these things in the Old Testament but find their fulfillment in Christ. It is not that the religious practices of the Jews were "ridiculous," they were just no longer necessary because of the death, burial, and resurrection of Jesus Christ.

He answered the second question—"What is the source of Christian love?—by emphasizing the holy Word[9] [Son of God] that has entered the

8. *Epistle to Diognetus*, 2, 3.

9. The author does not mention the name of Christ in the letter, preferring to refer to him simply as "Word."

soul of the Christian. Although Christians live in this world, they are not of this world. They love one another and all men because their religion is of divine origin. In terms of appearance, Christians are not distinguished by their country, clothing, culture, or any other worldly distinctions. They speak the same language as their non-Christian neighbours. They do not have cities of their own or eat special food. They marry, have children, care for others, and while doing so live in a state of rejection by both the Jews and the Greeks. The world hates Christians, not because of the way they look, the language they speak, or the types of homes they live in, but because Christians do not participate in the world's sinful pleasures. They do not kill their infants through infanticide, nor do they live an adulterous lifestyle. They love all people. The holy life of the Christians is a rebuke to the sinful life of non-Christians, and they detest them because of it.

He answered the third question—"Why is Christianity such a young religion?"—by stressing that Christian truth is not of human origin but was revealed by God according to his divine purpose. God demonstrated his kindness and love for mankind when he sent his Son to become a man and to establish the truth among men. Up until that time, God demonstrated his patience for humanity by tolerating their sin. He did not love our sin but tolerated it because he was preparing for the day when his Son would bring the reign of righteousness into the world. God gave his own Son as a ransom for our sin. The innocent Son of God took the sins of the wicked upon himself when he died. The innocent died in the place of the wicked. He goes on to explain that the invisible God sent "the designer and Architect of the universe in person."[10] He did not send an angel or some other lesser being, but God himself, took on human flesh. He wrote, "His mission was an act of gracious clemency, as when a king sends his son who is himself a king! He sent Him as God. He sent Him <as Man> to men.[11] He sent his Son into the world, not to condemn the world, but to persuade people to come to God and be saved. One of the most beautiful passages in the letter highlights the wonder of the sacrifice of Jesus Christ:

> O the surpassing kindness and love of God for man! No, He
> did not hate us, or discard us, or remember our wrongs; He ex-
> ercised forbearance and long-suffering! In mercy, of His own

10. *Epistle to Diognetus*, 7.
11. *Epistle to Diognetus*, 7.

accord, He lifted the burden of our sins! Of His own accord He gave up His own Son as a ransom for us—the Saint for sinners, the Guiltless for the guilty, the Innocent for the wicked, the Incorruptible for the corruptible, the Immortal for the mortal! Indeed, what else could have covered our sins but His holiness? In whom could we, the lawless and impious, be sanctified but in the Son of God alone? O sweetest exchange! O unfathomable accomplishment! O unexpected blessings—the sinfulness of many is buried in One who is holy, the holiness of One sanctifies the many who are sinners![12]

Justin Martyr (c.100–165)

Justin Martyr was born in Flavia Neapolis in Syria-Palestine, modern-day Nablus, sometime in the early second century AD. As a young man, he attached himself to several different philosophers in his pursuit of knowledge, and after discovering all there was to learn from one man, he would move on to the next. He spent a considerable amount of time studying and delighting in Plato's writings which introduced him to invisible realities. One day, while meditating in a field, an old man approached him and presented Christ to him as the only means by which a man can know true wisdom.[13] After the man left, Justin said, "Straightway a flame was kindled in my soul; and a love of the prophets and of those men who are friends of Christ, possessed me; and while revolving his words in my mind, I found this philosophy alone to be safe and profitable."[14] From this point on (c.135), he embraced the Christian faith.

Even before becoming a Christian, Justin was impressed with the Christian's fearlessness in the face of persecution and death. He wrote, "For I myself too, when I was delighting in the teachings of Plato, and heard the Christians slandered, and saw them fearless of death, and of all other things which are counted fearful, saw that it was impossible that they could be living in wickedness and pleasure."[15] He reasoned that if a person were addicted to the pleasures of this world, he would do all that was necessary to preserve this earthly life.

12. *Epistle to Diognetus*, 9.

13. Justin Martyr, *Dialogue with Trypho*, 3.

14. Justin Martyr, *Dialogue with Trypho*, 8.

15. Justin Martyr *The Second Apology*, 12.

His early immersion in pagan thinking made him uniquely qualified to defend the Christian faith to the second-century world. It appears that Justin was so successful at pointing out the inconsistencies in the thought and lifestyle of the philosophers that they sought to have him put to death. Crescens, a pagan philosopher who wrote against Christianity, was especially offended by Justin and worked hard to have him killed. Eusebius wrote:

> Crescens, who made his den in the great city, surpassed all in pederasty and love of money. He advised others to despise death but feared it so much himself that he conspired to inflict it on Justin as a great evil since Justin convicted the Philosophers of gluttony and hypocrisy simply by proclaiming the truth.[16]

Crescen's plan to have Justin executed was realized sometime between 160 and 167 when Justin was condemned to death.

Justin was the first great apologist of the Christian faith, and he produced many written works in defense of Christianity. Only three of these works have been preserved: *The First Apology*, *The Second Apology*, and, *Dialogue with Trypho, a Jewish rabbi.*

The First Apology

The *First Apology* was written sometime between 151 and 155 AD and consists of sixty-eight chapters. It was addressed to Emperor Antoninus Pius, his son Verissimus, Lucius the philosopher, the Senate, and the Roman people. Chapter 2 begins with an appeal for justice and calls on Roman leaders to investigate the Christian faith more thoroughly before passing judgment on them. Chapters 3–14 provide a refutation of slanders leveled against Christianity, such as the charges of atheism, immorality, and disloyalty to Rome. In chapters 14–20, he demonstrated the moral superiority of Christianity, contrasting it with the irrationality of paganism in chapters 21–22. In chapters 23–29, he argued that the teaching of Christ and the apostles are older than all other writers. Jesus is the only begotten son of God, and demons are the authors of the ancient myths and the instigators of persecution against the Christians. Chapters 30–53 focus on the coming of Christ as the fulfillment of Old Testament prophecy. In chapters 54–60, Justin argued that Christ was partially revealed through the fables and myths of Greeks and that God

16. Eusebius, CH, 4.16.

revealed Jesus, the Word of God, in part through the Greek philosophers who were influenced by the teaching of Moses. Chapters 61–67 provide the only description we have of a Christian worship service in the second century.

Christian Worship in the Second Century

Justin began this section by describing what takes place when a person is made new through faith in Jesus Christ. Those who believe the gospel and desire to live according to the precepts of the Christian faith were instructed to fast and pray for the forgiveness of sins in preparation for their baptism. Justin described baptism as a new birth and was the first one to refer to it as "a washing of illumination." Illumination refers to the power of God that is dispersed throughout the entire being of the person being baptized, giving him the divine power necessary to live a holy life.[17] There is an ongoing debate as to whether or not Justin believed in baptismal regeneration. It is important to note that Justin taught repentance and belief in the gospel were necessary before baptism was administered.[18] When new believers arrived at the place of baptism, they were baptized in the name of the Father, the Son, and the Holy Spirit. The baptism took place away from the church, and after the baptism, the newly baptized went to the church where the congregation was meeting. When they arrived, prayers were offered for the congregation and for those who were baptized. After the prayers, they greeted one another with a holy kiss. Immediately following this expression of affection, the "ruler" [Pastor] of the assembly led in the celebration of the Lord's Supper. The bread and cup of wine mixed with water were brought to the "ruler," who then offered thanksgiving to God. After he finished praying, the people said, "Amen." The deacons then came forward to distribute the bread and wine to those present and take some to those absent from the meeting. Only those who believed the gospel and were baptized were permitted to participate in the Lord's supper. Justin described the bread and the wine in the following manner,

> For we do not receive these things as common bread nor common drink; but in like manner as Jesus Christ our Savior having been incarnate by God's logos took both flesh and blood for our

17. Justin Martyr, *First and Second Apologies*, 174, n377.
18. Justin Martyr, *First Apology*, 61.

salvation, so also we have been taught that the food eucharistized through the word of prayer that is from Him, from which our blood and flesh are nourished by transformation, is the flesh and blood of that Jesus who became incarnate.[19]

This is a confusing statement, seen in the fact that Calvinists, Lutherans, and Roman Catholics each quote this passage to support their interpretation of the Lord's Supper.

Justin provided a detailed description of what took place when the Christians gathered together. On Sunday, all who live in either the city or the country assembled in one place. The writings of the apostles and the prophets were read to the gathered assembly. After the reading, "the Ruler" verbally instructed and exhorted the people. After the exhortation, they stood for prayer, and then the bread and wine mixed with water were brought for the celebration of the Lord's Supper. The rich gave offerings to "the ruler," who was responsible for distributing them to the poor, orphans, widows, prisoners, and traveling visitors. There are two reasons they met on Sunday: first, because God created the universe on Sunday, and second because Jesus Christ rose from the dead on Sunday.

Second Apology

The *Second Apology* was written around 160 AD and consists of fifteen chapters. It is written to the Roman Senate and addressed the outrageous execution of a man named Ptolemaeus who led a woman to leave her life of sin and follow Jesus Christ. The woman's husband was furious over his wife's conversion and directed his rage at the teacher, who led her to embrace Christianity. He had Ptolemaeus arrested and ultimately condemned to death.

Justin also responded to the question, "why do Christians not kill themselves and go directly to God?" First, they have been left in the world to imitate God. Second, they are to instruct others in the things of God, and third, if they killed themselves, they would be acting in opposition to the command of God, "you shall not murder." Yet, while it is true that Christians will not commit suicide, this does not mean that they fear death. Justin argued that their willingness to die for the faith was evidence that they did not feast on human flesh and give themselves over

19. Justin Martyr, *First Apology*, 66.

to pleasure-oriented lifestyles. If they did, they would not be willing to leave this world but would do all they could to hold on to it.

He also answered the question, "why are those who serve God often oppressed and persecuted by wicked people?" He said that people who have sought to live holy lives have been hated by those under the influence of demonic powers. Satan is the ultimate source of persecution, and it is the demons who have blinded the eyes of unbelievers and convinced them to believe the lies told about Christians.

He concluded by expressing a desire that his little booklet be published so that people could have a correct understanding of what Christians believe.

Dialogue with Trypho

Justin's *Dialogue with Trypho* was written around 160 and is the most ancient defense of the Christian faith written to the Jews. It is the longest of his three surviving works and provides an account of a conversation he had with a Jewish man named Trypho about the Christian faith. At this time, Justin continued to wear the Philosopher's robe. Trypho the Jew, approached Justin and wanted to speak with him on philosophical subjects, especially those that pertain to God. Justin's primary purpose in the Dialogue was to convince Trypho that Jesus is the Messiah. He spent a considerable amount of time demonstrating that the Old Testament pointed forward to the coming of Christ and that Jesus is the fulfillment of the Old Testament law. All the Jewish rites such as fasting, circumcision, sacrifices, observing holy days, eating only clean animals, and others pointed to the need for a new heart in Christ.

He also emphasized that Jesus, as the logos, was divine. He wrote, "Christ is called both God and Lord of hosts."[20] Justin makes a clear distinction between the Father and the Son, arguing that it was the Son who appeared in the theophanies of the Bible. He spoke to Moses in the burning bush and both Moses and Aaron in the pillar of cloud. He was one of the three that appeared to Abraham before the destruction of Sodom and Gomorrah, and he is the Angel of the LORD who appeared to Jacob and spoke to him in his dreams. He also says that Jesus is to be worshiped "as God and as Christ."[21]

20. *Dialogue with Trypho*, 36.
21. *Dialogue with Trypho*, 63.

Justin highlighted the prophecies pointing to the death of Christ and the centrality of the cross in the Christian faith. He believed that the tree of life in the garden of Eden, the rod of Moses that parted the Red Sea, the branch that sweetened the bitter waters of Marah, the branches used by Jacob to produce streaks and spots on the sheep of Laban, along with many other examples of wood and rods, all pointed forward to the cross of Jesus Christ. Justin took samples from the Psalms and the Prophets to demonstrate that the death of Jesus was predicted throughout the Old Testament. He showed from Old Testament prophecy that the Messiah would be killed and hung from a tree in the shape of a cross and that he would take the curse of sin upon himself on behalf of the entire human race. He also demonstrated that the resurrection and the first and the second coming of Christ are foretold in the Old Testament as well.

The Death of Justin Martyr

Justin Martyr was executed during the reign of Marcus Aurelius sometime between 162 and 167 AD.[22] It should be noted that "Martyr" is not Justin's surname but was given to him as an honorific title because he died for the faith. The following is an account of his trial and death.

> Rusticus the prefect, had Justin brought before his judgment seat.
>
> Rusticus: "Obey the gods at once, and submit to the kings." (emperors)
>
> Justin: "To obey the commandments of our Saviour Jesus Christ is worthy neither of blame nor of condemnation."
>
> Rusticus: "What kind of doctrines do you profess?"
>
> Justin: "I have endeavoured to learn all doctrines; but I have acquiesced at last in the true doctrines, those namely of the Christians, even though they do not please those who hold false opinions."
>
> Rusticus: "Are those the doctrines that please you, you utterly wretched man?"
>
> Justin: "Yes, since I adhere to them with right dogma."(orthodoxy)
>
> Rusticus: "What is the dogma?"
>
> Justin: "That according to which we worship the God of the Christians, whom we reckon to be one from the beginning, the maker and fashioner of the whole creation, visible and invisible;

22. Justin Martyr, *First and Second Apologies*, 3.

and the Lord Jesus Christ, the Son of God, who had also been preached beforehand by the prophets as about to be present with the race of men, the herald of salvation and teacher of good disciples. And I, being a man, think that what I can say is insignificant in comparison with His boundless divinity, acknowledging a certain prophetic power, since it was prophesied concerning Him of whom now I say that He is the Son of God. For I know that of old the prophets foretold His appearance among men."

Rusticus: "Where do you assemble?"

Justin: "Where each one chooses and can: for do you fancy that we all meet in the very same place? Not so; because the God of the Christians is not circumscribed by place; but being invisible, fills heaven and earth, and everywhere is worshipped and glorified by the faithful."

Rusticus: "Tell me where you assemble, or into what place do you collect your followers?"

Justin: "I live above one Martinus, at the Timiotinian Bath; and during the whole time (and I am now living in Rome for the second time) I am unaware of any other meeting than his. And if any one wished to come to me, I communicated to him the doctrines of truth."

Rusticus: "Are you not, then, a Christian?

Justin: "Yes I am a Christian."

Rusticus: "Hearken, you who are called learned and think that you know true doctrines; if you are scourged and beheaded, do you believe you will ascend into heaven?"

Justin: "I hope that, if I endure these things, I shall have His gifts." another reading says, "I shall have what he teaches us to expect." For I know that, to all who have thus lived, there abides the divine favour until the completion of the whole world."

Rusticus: "Do you suppose, then, that you will ascend into heaven to receive some recompense?"

Justin: "I do not suppose it, but I know and am fully persuaded of it."

Rusticus: "Let us then, now come to the matter in hand, and which presses. Having come together offer sacrifice with one accord to the gods."

Justin: "No right-thinking person falls away from piety to impiety."

Rusticus: "Unless you obey, you shall be mercilessly punished.

Justin: "Through prayer we can be saved on account of our Lord Jesus Christ, even when we have been punished, because this shall become to us salvation and confidence at the more fearful and universal judgment-seat of our Lord and Saviour."

Rusticus: "Let those who have refused to sacrifice to the gods and to yield to the command of the emperor be scourged, and led away to suffer the punishment of decapitation, according to the laws."

Rusticus the prefect pronounced sentence, saying, "Let those who have refused to sacrifice to the gods and to yield to the command of the emperor be scourged, and led away to suffer the punishment of decapitation, according to the laws. The holy martyrs having glorified God, and having gone forth to the accustomed place, were beheaded, and perfected their testimony in the confession of the Saviour. And some of the faithful having secretly removed their bodies, laid them in a suitable place."[23]

Justin's Philosophy

Understanding the proper relationship between pagan philosophy and Christianity was a pressing question during the early centuries of the church. Some Christian leaders, like Tertullian, believed there was no relationship between the two. Tertullian thought that philosophy was the source of heresy and represented the wisdom of the world, not the wisdom of God. He famously wrote, "What indeed has Athens to do with Jerusalem? What concord is there between the Academy and the church? What between heretics and Christians?"[24] Tertullian taught Christians to reject philosophy and to seek God through the scriptures alone.

On the other hand, Justin, who was deeply influenced by Greek philosophy, considered that all truth is God's truth no matter where it is discovered. He held a much higher view of the philosophers, believing that God had revealed some truth to them. Justin argued that Jesus, who he referred to as "the logos," was present in the lives of people from all nations of the world and that those who were indwelt by the logos were Christians. He mentioned Socrates and Heraclitus as examples of those who had partial knowledge of the logos and were persecuted by those who lived without it. Justin believed that the teachings of Plato were similar to the teachings of Christ because Plato taught according to the knowledge that was revealed to him by the divine logos. Although the philosophers only possessed partial knowledge, it was true knowledge

23. *Martyrdom of the Holy Martyrs*, Ante-Nicene Fathers, 1:1-5.

24. *Prescription against Heretics* 1.7.

nonetheless. This is why Justin could write, "whatever things were rightly said among all people are the property of us Christians.[25]

This same logos was sent into the world by the Father, was born of a virgin, partook in our suffering, died on the cross, rose again from the dead, and ascended into heaven. While Justin argued that the logos was present in the lives of those who lived before the coming of Christ, it was through Jesus Christ that the complete revelation of God's truth is seen.

Though some might praise Justin's attempt to reconcile pagan philosophy with Christianity, it is difficult to reconcile his belief that Greek philosophers possessed the logos with the teaching of Scripture. The apostle Paul wrote, "Where is the one who is wise? Where is the scribe? Where is the debater of this age? Has not God made foolish the wisdom of the world? For since, in the wisdom of God, the world did not know God through wisdom, it pleased God through the folly of what we preach to save those who believe."[26] While one might acknowledge that the pagan philosophers taught true things, this does not mean that they were Christians. In his attempt to reconcile his philosophical presuppositions with Christian theology, Justin was in danger of altering the gospel and unwittingly providing support for believing that people can be saved outside of Christianity.

Despite his weaknesses as a theologian, Justin was a zealous defender of the Christian faith and was willing to lay down his own life in its defense. He was the first educated theologian and Christian thinker after the apostles to use his considerable intellectual gifts for the defense and spread of Christianity. We should admire men like Justin Martyr and pray that God would give us the same passionate devotion in our service to Jesus Christ.

Discussion Questions

1. What is an apology for the Christian faith?

2. In his First Apology, what reasons does Justin give for Christians meeting on Sunday for worship instead of the Sabbath?

25. Justin Martyr, *Second Apology*, 13.
26. 1 Cor.1:20–21.

3. How is twenty-first-century worship in evangelical churches similar to worship as described in the writings of these early church leaders? How is it different?

4. Should twenty-first-century Evangelicals, like these early Christians, require baptism before partaking of the Lord's Supper? Why or why not?

5. Do you agree with Tertullian's rejection of all philosophy and seeking God's truth in the scriptures alone, or is Justin Martyr correct in believing there to be elements of God's truth in the teachings of the philosophers?

Chapter 6

Gnosticism and the Church's Response

Gnosticism

THE TERM "GNOSTICISM" COMES from the Greek word "gnosis," which means "knowledge." Gnosticism was a syncretistic religious movement that drew together elements from Judaism, Greek philosophy, Pagan religions, and Christianity and was thus characterized by great diversity.[1] It has been described as "a crazy quilt of recondite teachings that thrived in the syncretistic climate of the Roman Empire."[2] According to many early church fathers, Gnosticism was a Christian heresy,[3] but it may find its origin in the pre-Christian era.[4] The Gnostics believed they possessed mystical knowledge, which is known only by those with proper understanding. Having this knowledge was the key to salvation.[5]

Gnosticism began sometime early in the first century AD and reached the height of its influence in the second century.[6] Irenaeus, who wrote an extensive work entitled, *Against the Heresies*, identified Simon Magus[7] as the originator of Gnosticism. He referred to him as one "from whom all sorts of heresies derive their origin."[8] While this cannot be proven, it would not be surprising if that were the case. Simon Magus

1. Kelly, *Early Christian Doctrines*, 26.

2. Eusebius, *Church History*, 147.

3. *Encyclopedia of Ancient Christianity*, Ramelli, "Gnosticism," 140.

4. Ramelli, *Gnosticism*, 142.

5. Kelly, *Early Christian Doctrines*, 26.

6. *Encyclopedia of Ancient Christianity*, Ramelli, "Gnosticism," 140.

7. Acts 8:9–12.

8. Irenaeus, *Against Heresies* 1:23.2

was a man with a great following; he was addicted to power and was a false teacher, all of which provide the necessary ingredients for the rise of a heretical religious movement.

Despite the diversity within Gnosticism, it is possible to identify the core beliefs of the movement in general terms. Gnosticism promoted a dualistic world view that taught the spiritual and the material world were incompatible. It made a distinction between the creator god and the supreme, unknowable Divine god. The Supreme Divine god manifested itself by creating a series of spiritual beings called aeons. One of these aeons, often associated with the God of the Old Testament, took it upon himself to create the material world.[9] This was considered a reckless and rebellious act. One Gnostic text represents the God of the Bible as foolish, blind, ignorant, arrogant, the source of envy, and the father of death.[10] By its very nature, this material world was inferior to the spiritual world and was antagonistic to it.

Nevertheless, because a spiritual being created the world, spiritual sparks were implanted in some people. These people are called "spiritual" while those who did not have this divine spark are called "fleshly."[11] If the "spiritual" people are to be freed from their imprisonment in a fleshly body, a messenger is needed to bring the secret knowledge required for their liberation. Professing Christians who embraced Gnosticism claimed that Jesus was that messenger. He came into the world to remind us of our spiritual origin and provide the knowledge key necessary to unlock the door of salvation. Without this knowledge, a man stumbles around like a confused and disoriented drunk, but when he receives it, he becomes sober, and his mind is awakened to the true nature of life and redemption.[12]

Christian Gnosticism, so-called, led to the rejection of many orthodox Christian teachings. It denied the biblical teaching on creation and relegated the God of the Bible to a lesser, rebellious spiritual being. It rejected the incarnation, arguing that Jesus only seemed to be human because a spiritual being would never willingly clothe himself with a fleshly body. This led to the denial of the virgin birth, the humanity of Christ, his real physical sufferings, and his death on the cross for our sin.

---

9. *Dictionary of the Christian Church*, 684.

10. Jones, *Gnostic Empire Strikes back*, 22.

11. *Dictionary of the Christian Church*, Gnosticism, 684.

12. Kelly, *Early Christian Doctrines*, 27.

Concerning his death, one writer noted, "only the Gnostic knows that the real Christ actually sat on the branch of a tree, watching and laughing."[13] Of course, the bodily resurrection of Jesus Christ was rejected because salvation for the gnostic was deliverance from the physical body.

The apostle John addressed an earlier form of Gnosticism in his letters and gospel. In chapter one of his first letter, he wrote, "That which was from the beginning, which we have heard, which we have seen with our eyes, which we looked upon and have touched with our hands, concerning the word of life—the life was made manifest, and we have seen it, and testify to it and proclaim to you the eternal life, which was with the Father and was made manifest to us."[14] He also wrote, "By this you know the Spirit of God, every spirit that confesses that Jesus Christ has come in the flesh is from God, and every spirit that does not confess Jesus is not from God."[15] At the beginning of his gospel, he refers to Jesus as the Word who was not only with God, but was God, and emphasizes that "the Word became flesh and dwelt among us."[16] John is very careful to protect the full humanity of Jesus Christ and says that those who deny that Jesus is God come in the flesh are not of God.

In light of their dualistic worldview, the Gnostics took two approaches to life. Some embraced asceticism, seeking to suppress all earthly desires. In contrast, others gave themselves over to sensual pleasure, arguing that how a man used his body is irrelevant since the spirit cannot be destroyed. Irenaeus illustrated the reasoning behind the second response when he wrote, "Gold when deposited in mud does not lose its beauty, but preserves its own nature, since mud can in no way injure gold. In the same way they themselves, so they indeed claim, neither suffer harm nor lose their spiritual substance regardless of what material practices they may be engaged in."[17]

Marcion

One highly influential promoter of Gnostic ideas in the second century was a man named Marcion. His influence as a heretic theologian was so

13. Jones, *Gnostic Empire Strikes Back*, 25.

14. 1 John 1:1, 2.

15. 1 John 3:2, 3.

16. John 1:1, 14.

17. Irenaeus, *Against Heresies*, 1.6.2.

great that German theologian Adolf von Harnack referred to him as "the most significant figure between Paul and Augustine."[18] Marcion's father was a bishop of Sinope in Pontus, on the southern coast of the Black Sea, and being the son of a bishop, Marcion was taught the doctrines of Christianity. Around 140 AD, Marcion was removed from the church by his father, possibly on the charge of immorality or perhaps because of his heretical opinions. Subsequently, Marcion left Sinope and moved to Rome. For a time, he was a trader and became quite wealthy, buying and selling weapons. He also joined the Christian congregation in Rome, making a sizable financial contribution to the church. In 144, he was removed from the church for heresy, and his donation was returned. From this point on he began to propagate Gnostic ideas, establishing numerous congregations throughout the Roman Empire. Justin Martyr, commenting on the growth of the Marcion church, wrote, "by the aid of demons [he] has caused many of every race of men and women to speak blasphemies and to deny that God is the Maker of this Universe, and to profess that another, who is greater than He, has done greater works." Irenaeus reports that when Polycarp met Marcian in Rome, Marcion asked, "Recognize us?" and Polycarp responded, "I do recognize you as the first-born of Satan."[19] Probably the most scathing description of Marcion is given by Tertullian who described him in this way,

> Nothing, however, in Pontus is so barbarous and sad as the fact that Marcion was born there, fouler than any Scythian, more roving than the waggon-life of the Sarmatian, more inhuman than the Massagete, more audacious than an Amazon, darker than the cloud (of Pontus) colder than its winter, more brittle than its ice, more deceitful than the Ister, more craggy than Caucasus. Nay more, the true Prometheus, Almighty God, is mangled by Marcion's blasphemies. Marcion is more savage than even the beasts of that barbarous region. For what beaver was ever a greater emasculator than he who has abolished the nuptial bond? What Pontic mouse ever had such gnawing powers as he who has gnawed the Gospels to pieces? Verily, O Euxine, thou hast produced a monster more credible to philosophers than to Christians. For the cynic Diogenes used to go about, lantern in hand, at mid-day to find a man; whereas Marcion has quenched the light of his faith, and so lost the God whom he had found.[20]

18. Encyclopedia of Ancient Christianity, 2:676.

19. Irenaeus, *Against Heresies*, 3.3.4.

20. Tertullian, *Against Marcion*, 1.1.

His influence and teaching became a genuine threat to the orthodox church.[21]

Marcion demonstrated both an anti-historical and an anti-semitic bias.[22] He believed Christianity had no relationship with the past but came to us directly from heaven.[23] In his teaching, he emphasized the love of God, but there was no place in his theological system for the law of God. His disdain for the law of God led him to reject the Old Testament in its entirety. He identified the Old Testament God with the lesser rebellious god of the Gnostics and not the God and father of the Lord Jesus Christ. He also rejected the gospels, although he accepted a highly edited version of the gospel of Luke. Only ten of Paul's letters, except for the pastoral epistles, were admitted into his canon of Scripture.[24] Marcion was the first one to create a canon of New Testament writings.

Marcion believed that the Father of Jesus Christ was a loving God who would never punish anyone and that God would accept everyone in the end. He denied the humanity of Christ, arguing that Christ only seemed human. He also denied that the New Testament God would ever raise anyone physically from the dead. Because Marcion and his followers believed that the material world was evil, they sought to suppress all earthly desires. They used only water at the Lord's Table and forbade sexual relations, even in marriage, because it would result in physical pleasure. They also discouraged procreation because the having of children only promoted the material world of the creator.[25]

Ironically, the teaching of Marcion had a positive impact on the church. It forced the church to clarify its position on the Canon of Scripture and to produce an authoritative doctrinal statement for testing a Christian's orthodoxy.[26]

21. *Encyclopedia of Ancient Christianity*, 2:676.

22. Schaff, *History of the Christian Church*, 2:483.

23. Schaff, *History of the Christian Church*, 2:485.

24. *The Dictionary of the Christian Church*, 1034.

25. *Encyclopedia of Ancient Christianity*, Marcion, 676.

26. Kelly, *Early Christian Doctrines*, 58.

The Response of the Church

The church responded to Marcionism and the broader gnostic heresy in three ways: Canon, Creed, and Apostolic succession.[27]

Canon

The word canon means "measuring stick." The books of the Bible are called the canon of Scripture because they measure out and set the boundaries for Christian belief and practice. Although many of the twenty-seven books of the New Testament were already accepted as authoritative by the church from the beginning, there was no fully recognized canon of Scripture in the second century AD. In response to Marcion's diminished Bible, the church began to compile a list of writings that were accepted officially as representing God's authoritative word to the church. This was not done formally, but gradually a consensus developed over time.[28]

Although Marcion rejected the Old Testament in its entirety, the orthodox church accepted all thirty-nine books. The manner in which the New Testament freely quotes the Old Testament demonstrates that there was no debate over the authority of the Old Testament scriptures. From its inception, the church possessed a canon of Scripture and preached the Old Testament as the divinely inspired Word of God.[29]

The New Testament was a different story, and it took time for some of the twenty-seven books to be entirely accepted into the canon of Scripture. The wider church community immediately accepted the Synoptic gospels (Matthew, Mark, and Luke). The gospel of John, written later than the Synoptics, was accepted by the early Fathers and was included with the other three.[30] Justin Martyr mentioned the gospels around 150 AD, referring to them as "the memoirs of the apostles."[31] The Acts of the Apostles was accepted along with Paul's letters, 1 John and 1 Peter. Although some challenged the acceptance of the book of Revelation, Eusebius, writing in the fourth century, included it in the recognized

27. Justo L. Gonzalez, *Story of Christianity*, 62.

28. Kelly, *Early Christian Doctrines*, 59.

29. Warfield, *Revelation and Inspiration*, 451.

30. Eusebius, *Church History*, 3.24.

31. Justin Martyr, *First Apology*, 67.

books.[32] Irenaeus, who wrote in the mid-second century, quoted most of the twenty-seven books included in the New Testament and accepted them as authoritative.[33] The disputed books were Hebrews, James, Jude, 2 Peter, and 2 and 3 John. It was not until 367 AD, in Athanasius's Easter letter, that the twenty-seven books of the New Testament are referred to as the canon of scripture by the eastern church.[34] The western church later approved the canon in the African Councils of Hippo in 393 and Carthage in 397. The criteria for approving a book as part of the canon was complicated. The main guidelines were that a book had to have been written by or approved by an apostle; its content had to be orthodox, and it had to have been in prominent use by the church.

Some find it disturbing that it took more than three hundred years to settle the debate as to which books should be accepted into the New Testament canon. However, the vast majority of the New Testament was never debated, and those few books in question represented a tiny portion of the New Testament. Even if the smaller books like Jude, 2 Peter, 2 and 3 John had been rejected, no Christian doctrine would be affected. These smaller books add richness to the New Testament and are rightly accepted as authoritative, but they introduce no new teaching to the New Testament. Because ninety-five percent of the New Testament was accepted in the first century, immediately after it was written, the debate over whether or not to include these few smaller books in the canon never put the gospel of Jesus Christ at risk.

It is also essential to understand that not every church had the entire New Testament, and they certainly did not have the original letters but copies of those letters. Some churches may have received copies of the gospels, the book of Acts, Paul's letters, John's first letter, and Peter's first letter while not having a copy of Jude, 2 Peter, or 2 and 3 John. They would have relied upon this incomplete canon for many years, and even copied it for other churches, and were thus skeptical of these smaller books when they were presented to them as Scripture. The gradual circulation of some New Testament letters is not an argument against their canonicity. As the twenty-seven books of the New Testament became more widely known,

32. Eusebius, *Church History*, 3.25.

33. *Dictionary of the Christian Church*, Irenaeus, 847.

34. Athanasius, Letter 39.5.

there was minimal dissent and the books we recognize today are the same ones identified in the early church.[35]

Creed

A creed is a confession of faith containing truths essential for salvation. It may also include a more extensive summary of Christian doctrine and is designed to be used for the public edification of the Christian church. The earliest creeds were used for teaching young believers and as a confession of faith spoken at one's baptism. Most of the creeds were written in response to erroneous teaching and provided a safeguard for Christian truth.[36]

One of the greatest and most influential creeds of the Christian church is called *The Apostles' Creed*. Despite its name, the creed was not written by the apostles but does contain an accurate, if not limited, summary of their teaching. It is a universal creed in that it is accepted by the vast majority of Christian denominations, including Evangelicals, Roman Catholics, Eastern Orthodox, and every denomination in between.[37] It has been described as, "the best popular summary of the Christian faith ever made within so brief a space."[38]

The Apostles' Creed is the most ancient of the creeds. It grew out of Peter's confession of faith, "You are the Christ, the Son of the living God,"[39] and the baptismal formula, "Go therefore and make disciples of all nations, baptizing them in the name of the Father and of the Son and of the Holy Spirit."[40] In the earlier centuries of the church, the Creed was not written down but was communicated orally and memorized by new believers. The final form of the creed was not complete until at least the sixth century, but it was not until the eighth century that it became the dominant form in the Latin church.[41]

The creed is structured around the persons of the Trinity, with the greatest emphasis placed upon Jesus Christ, the Son of God.

---

35. B. B Warfield, *Formation of the Canon of the New Testament*, 454.

36. Schaff, *Creeds of Christendom*, 1:4.

37. Schaff, *Creeds of Christendom*, 1:14.

38. Schaff, *Creeds of Christendom*, 1:15.

39. Matt 16:16.

40. Matt 28:19.

41. Schaff, *Creeds of Christendom*, 1:19.

Apostles' Creed

1. I believe in God, the Father almighty, creator of the heavens and earth.

2. and in Jesus Christ, his only Son, our Lord;

3. who was conceived by the Holy Spirit and born of the Virgin Mary;

4. suffered under Pontius Pilate, was crucified, dead and buried; [he descended to hell;]

5. on the third day he was raised from the dead;

6. he ascended into the heavens, and sits at the right hand of God the Father almighty;

7. from where he will come to judge the living and the dead.

8. I believe in the Holy Spirit;

9. in the holy catholic church; [the communion of saints]

10. the forgiveness of sins;

11. the resurrection of the flesh

12. and eternal life.[42]

When one examines the creed, it becomes evident that each line was a response to the false teaching of Marcion and the Gnostics. The first section focuses on the Father. The reference to the Father Almighty as the creator of the heavens and earth identifies him as the one true God who rules and reigns over all things. Rather than being a lessor rebellious god, he is the almighty God. It is implicitly stated that the material world is not evil but is God's good creation.[43]

The second and largest section of the creed focuses on Jesus, and in particular, his humanity. It emphasizes his birth, his suffering during the time of Pontius Pilate, his crucifixion, his death, and his resurrection from the grave. Jesus did not just appear as the Gnostics claimed but was born of flesh and blood. He lived, died, and rose again in the flesh. The creed also says that Jesus will judge the living and the dead, a concept Marcion denied.[44]

---

42. McGrath, ed., *Christian Theology Reader*, 8.

43. Gonzalez, *Story of Christianity*, 64.

44. Gonzalez, *Story of Christianity*, 64.

The third section includes a reference to the Holy Spirit, the third person of the Trinity and emphasizes the fact that there is one universal church. Marcion started a rival church, and the creed denies that it has the right to exist outside of the already established church. The emphasis on the resurrection of the flesh highlights that salvation is not deliverance from the physical body. On the final day, the soul will be reunited with the resurrected body.[45]

Apostolic Succession

The Christian Gnostics claimed that they had access to a secret message revealed through a secret apostolic tradition.[46] They taught that Jesus was the one who brought this message and that only the Gnostics had access to it.

Irenaeus, a second-century teacher, argued that if Jesus came with a message for the world, he would have entrusted it to his apostles, and the apostles would then entrust it to other men. If there were secret teaching, it would come through those whom the apostles themselves taught. The orthodox church argued that the bishops of their churches were in a clear line that reached back to the apostles, and they denied that any secret message existed. Marcion and the Gnostics could not demonstrate the same kind of succession.

It should be noted that this was a powerful and persuasive argument in the second century, but it has lost its force over time. Second-century pastors and churches could demonstrate a direct link to the apostolic era because they were only a generation or two away from the church's inception. As time progressed, new doctrines and practices were introduced into the church that were not of apostolic origin. Still, the apostolic succession argument continued to be used to give authority to these new doctrines. Apostolic succession is used to support the belief that only bishops who could show a direct link to the apostles were qualified to perform ordinations. Even the papal office today claims its authority by tracing itself back to Peter, who Roman Catholics believe to be the first pope.

45. Gonzalez, *Story of Christianity*, 64.
46. Kelly, *Early Christian Doctrines*, 36.

Discussion Questions

1. How should the church handle false teachers today?

2. Study the following passages and think about how they relate to the New Testament Canon. (1 Pet 1:12; 1 Cor.2:13; 1 Thess 4:2; 2 Thess 2:15; 3:14; 5:27; 1 Cor 14:37; Col 4:16; Rev 1:3; 2 Pet 3:16; 1 Tim 5:18; Deut 25:4; Luke 10:7)

3. What are the limitations of the Apostles' Creed as a statement of faith?

4. Is apostolic succession a good argument, and should it be used today?

Chapter 7

Three Great Second and Third Century Teachers

THE SECOND AND THIRD centuries witnessed significant theological developments as theologians provided detailed explanations of biblical teaching about God and his creation. While these theological developments were not without problems, much of the theology was retained and refined in succeeding generations, permanently influencing Christian beliefs and practices. This chapter will look at three of the most important second and third-century teachers: Irenaeus, Tertullian, and Origen.

Irenaeus of Lyons (c.115–c.202 AD)

We know little about the early life of Irenaeus, but there are a few things that can be said with relative confidence. He was probably born in Smyrna, in the Roman province of Asia sometime between 115 and 140 AD, and while still a youth, he sat under the teaching of Polycarp, who he referred to as the "old man" in his writings. He studied in Rome and then went to Gaul, where he became a leader in the church at Lyons. Around 177 AD, he was sent to Rome, with letters, seeking a more tolerant stance towards the Montanus sect. While he was traveling, severe persecution broke out in Lyons, which resulted in the death of Pothinus, the bishop of Lyons. Upon his return in 178, Irenaeus was ordained as the new bishop of Lyons, where he served the Lord faithfully until his death.[1] The time

---

1. *Dictionary of the Christian Church*, Irenaeus, 846–47.

and manner of his death are unknown, but later tradition says that he died in 202 during the persecution of Septimius Severus.[2]

The Teaching of Irenaeus

Irenaeus is recognized as the most orthodox of the ante-Nicene fathers and the first Christian teacher to quote extensively from the entire New Testament. He appears to have been deeply influenced by Justin Martyr and relied heavily upon his writings. His arguments often follow the same line of thought as Justin's, and in some cases, he used his exact wording. It may be, however, that Justin and Irenaeus were using common source material.[3] There are also parallels between Clement of Alexandria and Irenaeus, indicating a common source of information shared among these early writers.[4]

Irenaeus was an excellent and caring pastor and also a prodigious writer. He was concerned with Christian orthodoxy and protecting his flock from the influence of false teaching that was rife in the second century. In particular, he was alarmed about the teaching of Gnosticism and its threat to Christianity and felt compelled to take up his pen against it. Irenaeus was not a systematic theologian, and much of his theology was developed in reaction to the false teaching of his day.[5] His primary and most important work is entitled *Against the Heresies*,[6] which is a refutation of Gnostic thought and an argument supporting the truth of Christianity. He also wrote an essay against Marcion, who he identified as one of the foremost leaders in the diverse and dangerous world of Gnostic thought.[7] In his writings against the Gnostics, Irenaeus emphasized the unity between the Old and New Testaments as a counterattack against the depleted canon of Marcion.[8] The way Irenaeus quotes Scripture and uses Scripture to interpret Scripture indicates that there was a generally accepted canon of Scripture in the second-century church.

2. Schaff, *History of the Christian Church*, 2:749–50.

3. St. Irenaeus, *Ancient Christian Writers, Proof of Apostolic Preaching*, ed. Joseph P. Smith, 41.

4. St. Irenaeus, *Ancient Christian Writers*, 44.

5. Brown, Harold O.J., *Heresies*, 43.

6. Only two of the works of Irenaeus survive: *Against the Heresies* and, the *Demonstration of Apostolic Preaching*.

7. Ancient Christian Writers, 16:22, 23.

8. Schaff, *History of the Christian Church*, 2:751–52.

The Trinity

As explained in the last chapter, Gnosticism taught that a lesser, rebellious god made the world and that the universe should never have been created in the first place. In response to this, Irenaeus argued that the one true God made the world and that all matter was inherently good. He wrote:

> There is only one God the Builder, he who is above every Principality and Authority and Dominion and Power; he who is the Father, God, Creator, Maker, Builder, made them by himself, that is, by his Word and Wisdom, namely, the heavens and the earth and sea, and all things that are in them.[9]

The "Word and Wisdom" of God refers to the Son, who is the Word of God, and the Holy Spirit, who is the Wisdom of God. Although the Father is the primary creator of all things, he created in cooperation with both the Son and the Spirit.

He also stressed the unity between the Father and the Son. The Son is the Word of God through whom the Father created and sustains the world, and it is the Son of God who took on human flesh. The Gnostics believed that matter was evil and that God would never take on human flesh and thus only appeared to be human. In response to this, Irenaeus emphasized that Jesus is the visible image of the invisible God. The theophanies of the Old Testament were manifestations of the Son of God who revealed the invisible God to humanity. Irenaeus believed that "the Son, was always coexisting with the Father," and it is through the Son that the Father revealed himself not only to humanity but to the various ranks of angels in heaven.[10] This same Son of God was truly born of the virgin Mary and indeed took on human flesh, and it is through Jesus Christ, the Holy Spirit is given.[11]

Irenaeus referred to the work of Jesus Christ as a "recapitulation" or a fresh start. The incarnation of Jesus Christ marked the beginning of the restoration of all that was lost in Adam because of sin. Through the incarnation, God was renewing his original plan for man and reversing the

---

9. Ancient Christian Writers, 65:2, 30.9.

10. Ancient Christian Writers, 65:2, 30.9.

11. Ancient Christian Writers, 16:31.

effects of the fall. The fruit of the incarnation is a renewed and intimate relationship between God and man.[12]

The Holy Spirit is the Wisdom of God, and it is by his power that the world was created. It was the Holy Spirit who spoke through both the prophets and the scriptures. He is the source of human life and created the image of God in man by breathing into them. Because of sin, man's innocence was lost, and the image of God was severely distorted. The Holy Spirit recreates that image in those who trust in Jesus Christ.

Although Irenaeus identified the three persons of the Trinity in his writings, he does not develop the deity or personality of the Holy Spirit, and yet he continually associated the Spirit with the Son of God.[13] He called the Spirit and the Son "the hands of God."[14] Even though he did not fully expand his doctrine of the Trinity, he affirmed both the deity of Jesus Christ and, through his writings, Irenaeus contributed to the fuller development of the doctrine of the Trinity in the fourth and fifth centuries.[15] Two of his great sentences that continue to be used in Christian theology are, "The Son of God [has] become a son of man," and "Jesus Christ, true man and true God."[16]

Man

Irenaeus taught that God created man in his own image and gave him the freedom to rule over the world. He intended that human beings should become more like God, but man used his freedom to sin against God, resulting in the loss of the likeness of God in him. All men died in Adam and bear the consequences of Adam's sin, but all who are in Christ benefit from the blessings that flow from Christ's obedient life.[17]

Irenaeus believed that human beings are a trichotomy, consisting of body, soul, and spirit. The body and the soul are associated with his life on earth, but the spirit can become like God. The Gnostics believed that only the body and soul could be saved, whereas Irenaeus taught that

12. Ancient Christian Writers, 16:36.

13. Ancient Christian Writers, 16:32.

14. Ancient Christian Writers, 16:35.

15. Brown, *Heresies*, 79.

16. Brown, *Heresies*, 84.

17. Brown, *Heresies*, 84.

body, soul, and spirit are all God's good creation and that the whole man was the subject of salvation.[18]

Apostolic Succession

Like other writers in his day, Irenaeus believed the succession of bishops in the church was proof that the established churches possessed the true gospel message and not the churches formed by Marcion and the Gnostics. Both the orthodox and the Gnostics claimed that their teaching was from the Lord. On the one hand, the Gnostics argued that secret knowledge was given to certain disciples and was handed on through them. On the other hand, Irenaeus reasoned that the gospel was preserved in the orthodox churches. The teachers of those churches could trace their line back to the apostles, a claim the Gnostics could not make. He believed the church had a united testimony, and this unity was seen in the cohesive testimony of the bishops. He believed that Scripture was the sole authority in determining correct theology, but he also believed it was to be interpreted according to the tradition of the church.[19]

Schaff summed up the last three books of Irenaeus *Against the Heresies* as follows:

> The last three books refute Gnosticism from the Holy Scripture and Christian tradition which teach the same thing; for the same gospel which was first orally preached and transmitted was subsequently committed to writing and faithfully preserved in all the apostolic churches through the regular succession of the bishops and elders; and this apostolic tradition ensures at the same time the correct interpretation of Scripture against heretical perversion.[20]

In his argument for apostolic succession, Irenaeus, unwittingly, set the stage for the rise of the Roman papacy. While he could not have anticipated the emergence of the modern papacy, his writings did contribute to its establishment. He wrote:

> In this way, we confound all those who in any way whatever, either because of an evil self-complacency, or of vain-glory, or of blindness and evil-mindedness, gather in unauthorized

18. Ancient Christian Writers, 16:33
19. Brown, *Heresies*, 80.
20. Schaff, *History of the Christian Church*, 2:752.

> assemblies. For with this Church [Rome], because of her greater authority, it is necessary that every Church, that is, the faithful who are everywhere, should agree, because in her the apostolic tradition has always been safeguarded by those who are everywhere.[21]

In the same section, he refers to the Roman church as "the most Ancient Church" founded by both the apostle Peter and apostle Paul. Because of its ancient and lofty origin, Christians everywhere should see the Roman church as an "ideal illustration" and follow her example.[22] He said that the Roman church is "a mirror of the universal church."[23]

Eschatology

Irenaeus adopted what is known as a chiliastic or millennial interpretation of the second coming of Christ. One early Christian leader who influenced the eschatology of Irenaeus was a man named Papias. According to Eusebius, Papias was influenced by a legendary unwritten account of the millennium. Eusebius wrote:

> Among them, he says that after the resurrection of the dead there will be a thousand-year period when the kingdom of Christ will be established on this earth in material form. I supposed that he got these notions by misunderstanding the apostolic accounts, not realizing that they had used mystic and symbolic language. For he was a man of very limited intelligence, as is clear from his books. Due to him, however, many church writers after him held the same opinion, relying on his early date: Irenaeus, for example, and any others who adopted the same views.[24]

Eusebius' words indicate that belief in a literal thousand-year reign of Jesus Christ on the earth was not necessarily the mainstream view of the church in the earlier centuries, but it does affirm that a literal interpretation of the millennial reign of Christ is of ancient origin.

21. Irenaeus, *Against Heresies*, 3.3.2.

22. Kelly, *Early Christian Doctrines*, 192.

23. Ferguson, *Everett, Church History*, 1:126.

24. Eusebius, CH, 3.39.

Tertullian (c.155–220)

Quintus Septimius Florens Tertullianus, more commonly known as Tertullian, was born in Carthage in North Africa around 160 AD. His father, a proconsular centurion, raised Tertullian in a pagan environment but made sure he received a good education in history, philosophy, literature, and rhetoric. He knew Latin and Greek, and the style of his writings would suggest he may have been trained as a lawyer.[25] As a young man, Tertullian lived the life of a self-indulgent sinner, and at some point, he got married and settled down, although his wife appears to have died at a young age. The date of his conversion to Christianity is unknown, but it took place sometime before 197 AD.[26]

One of the strange events in his life was his conversion to Montanism. Montanism began in the latter part of the second century and is named after its leader, Montanus. Montanus believed that the Holy Spirit was poured out on him and his prophetesses, and they represented the purest expression of Christianity in the world. The movement was called into question when a prophecy predicting that the heavenly Jerusalem would descend near Phrygia did not occur.

Around 206, Tertullian joined the movement, probably attracted to its promotion of rigorous living and its emphasis upon the presence of the Holy Spirit. Montanism embraced asceticism, prohibited remarriage, promoted fasting, forbade fleeing in times of persecution, and appeared to be more serious about holy living than the undisciplined catholic church. Tertullian supported them in their condemnation of the church's lenient attitude toward sin.[27]

Tertullian wrote extensively, and in the fifteen years between 196 and 212, he produced thirty books comprised of about fifteen hundred pages. His works can be divided into four major categories: apologetic, polemical, doctrinal, and practical, although some of his works could be placed in more than one category.

The first category is apologetic and includes those works written to defend Christianity in the face of pagan accusations against it. His most famous work is *The Apology,* in which he attacks the irrational beliefs of the Romans and defends the teaching and practice of the Christians as being rational and not worthy of persecution. He called upon the leaders

25. Gonzalez, *Story of Christianity,* 74.

26. *Encyclopedia of Ancient Christianity,* 3:716.

27. *Dictionary of the Christian Church,* "Montanism," 1107–8.

of the Roman Empire to look more carefully into Christianity's claims and allow Christians the opportunity to provide a proper hearing in defense of their faith. Included in this category are writings such as, *On Baptism*, in which he argues for the necessity of baptism against a group of Gnostics who denied its value.

The second category is Polemical. Tertullian wrote a five-volume book entitled *The Prescription Against the Heretics*, in which he dealt with the issue of Gnosticism and with Maricionism in particular. He identifies the old pagan philosophies as the seedbed of heresy, famously proclaiming:

> What indeed has Athens to do with Jerusalem? What concord is there between the Academy and the Church? What between heretics and Christians? Our instruction comes from the Portico of Solomon, who had himself taught that the Lord should be sought in simplicity of heart. Away with all attempts to produce a mottled Christianity of Stoic, Platonic, and dialectic composition! We want no curious disputation after possessing Christ Jesus, no inquisition after enjoying the Gospel! With our faith, we desire no further belief.[28]

Unlike Justin Martyr, who saw truth in ancient philosophy, and Clement of Alexandria and Origen, who embraced the methods and language of pagan philosophy to help them understand the Christian faith, Tertullian rejected it, believing that it was the source of heresy.[29]

The third category is doctrinal/theological. Probably Tertullian's most significant contribution to theology is his writing on the Triune nature of God. In his book *Against Praxeas*, he outlines his teaching on the Trinity. He is the first theologian to provide an in-depth discussion on the three persons in the Godhead and their relationship to one another.[30]

The fourth category is practical and would include more minor works like *An Exhortation to Chastity*, in which he advises against Remarriage. Also, *On Head-Coverings for Unmarried Girls* in which he gives reasons why a veil should be worn. He also wrote books that addressed monogamy, prayer, modesty, clothing, patience, fasting, and the Roman games.

---

28. Tertullian, *Prescription Against the Heretics*, ch.7.

29. Mike Aquilina, *Fathers of the Church*, 112.

30. *Encyclopedia of Ancient Christianity*, "Tertullian," 719.

Tertullian on the Trinity

Tertullian was the first writer to use the word Trinity to describe God.[31] He did not invent the concept of the Trinity but introduced technical language into Christian theology to help believers understand what the Bible teaches about the nature of God. His essential points in the defense of the triune nature of God are found in his important writing entitled, *Against Praxeas*. Although we do not know who Praxeas was, we can piece together his beliefs from the writings of Tertullian against him.

Praxeas affirmed that there was only one God, but in his desire to maintain the unity of God, he denied that there are three persons in the Trinity. He instead argued that the Father, Son, and Holy Spirit were the same person and were simply three modes in which God manifested himself. Sometimes God appeared as the Father, sometimes as the Son, and sometimes as the Holy Spirit, but there was no real distinction between the three.[32] On the other hand, Tertullian taught that God is a unified being, but there is a trinity within that unity. He offered several arguments to support his belief in the Trinity.

He argued that the doctrine of the Trinity was rooted in the gospel and was taught before the rise of the heretics, including Praxeas. He wrote, "whatever is first is true, whereas that is spurious which is later in date."[33] Any teaching that changes the doctrine of the Trinity as it had been received from the beginning is a perversion of the gospel. He argued that the heretics had no right to use the scriptures because only the orthodox churches could demonstrate that they possessed the scriptures from the beginning. Great churches like the ones in Rome and Antioch could trace their origins back to the apostles, and these churches agreed in their interpretation of the scriptures. The orthodox church alone was in possession of the scriptures, and only they had the right to interpret them.[34]

He also argued that the Son is the Reason or the Word that was with God from before the creation of the world. Even when God was alone, he was not truly alone because he had both Reason and the Word within himself.[35] Tertullian argued that the Wisdom spoken of in the book of

31. *Against Praxeas*, 4.

32. *Against Praxeas*, 2.

33. *Against Praxeas*, 2.

34. Gonzalez, *Story of Christianity*, 74.

35. *Against Praxeas*, 5.

Proverbs is the same as the Reason or the Word of God. At the time of creation, God sent forth his Word, who is both Reason and Wisdom, and through him created the world and all that is in it.[36] The Word is the only begotten of the Father and is thus equal with the Father. He shares in the Father's substance, and yet he is distinct from the Father.[37] Tertullian wrote, "The Word, therefore, is both always in the Father, as he says, "I am in the Father;" and is always with God, according to what is written, "and the Word was with God." and never separate from the Father, or other than the Father since "I am the Father are one."[38] He illustrated this truth in the following way, "For God sent forth the Word, as the Paraclete also declares, just as the root puts forth the tree, and the fountain the river and the sun the ray."[39] He compared the Father to the root of the tree, whereas the Son is the tree itself. The Father is the fountain, whereas the Son is the river that flows from the fountain. The Father is the sun, and the Son is the ray that emanates from the Sun. And just as the tree is not severed from the root and the fountain from the river, or the sun from the ray of light, so the Father is never severed from the Word, and yet they are distinct.

Tertullian reasoned that the names, Father and Son, prove that there is a distinction between them. If the Father and the Son are not distinct persons, then the title Father and Son make no sense. Tertullian reasoned this way:

> A father must needs have a son, in order to be a father; so like-wise a son, to be a son, must have a father. It is, however, one thing to have, and another thing to be. For instance, in order to be a husband, I must have a wife; I can never myself be my own wife. In like manner, in order to be a father, I have a son, for I never can be a son to myself and in order to be a son, I have a father, it being impossible for me ever to be my own father.[40]

He also argued that there are three distinct persons in the Trinity. Tertullian asserted that "the Father is one, and the Son one, and the Spirit

---

36. *Against Praxeas*, 6.

37. These are some of the verses Tertullian uses to support the unity and distinction between the Father and the Son: Col 1:15; Prov 8:22, 25; Ps 33:6; John 1:1, 3; Exod 20:7; Phil 2:6.

38. *Against Praxeas*, 8.

39. *Against Praxeas*, 8.

40. *Against Praxeas*, 9.

one, and that they are distinct from each other."[41] When speaking about the Holy Spirit, Tertullian continued to develop the illustrations of the tree and root, the fountain and the river, and the sun and the ray. He wrote, "Now the Spirit indeed is third from God and the Son; just as the fruit of the tree is third from the root, or as the stream out of the river is third from the fountain, or as the apex of the ray is third from the sun."[42] While it is true that there is a distinction between the three persons, the Son and the Holy Spirit are derived from the same source and thus share in the divine properties of the Father. Tertullian stated, "they are distinct, but not separate."[43] There is a plurality of persons in the Trinity but also a shared essence. All three persons are fully divine.

Origen of Alexandria (c.184–c.253)

Origenes Adamantius, more commonly known as Origen, was born to Christian parents around 184 AD in Alexandria, Egypt. Origen's father, Leonides, recognized his son's superior intellectual gifts early and provided him with a thorough Greek and biblical education. Believing that religious studies were of greater importance than all other topics, his father insisted that he pursue the study of the Bible with undivided devotion. Every day he was required to memorize Bible passages and repeat them aloud. Origen did not resent this, even though he was a child, but reveled in the study of God's Word. Leonides delighted in Origen's love of the Bible, considering himself blessed to have such a son given to him by God.[44]

While Origen was a teenager (c.202), persecution broke out against Christians during the reign of Septimius Severus. Many Christians were imprisoned, tortured, and executed for their faith, but it was particularly severe in Alexandria.[45] During this persecution Origen's father was arrested and thrown into prison. Rather than fighting for his father's release, Origen wrote to his father encouraging him to accept his martyrdom and not turn away from it. He was also possessed with a desire to be martyred for the faith, but his mother wisely hid her overly enthusiastic son's

41. *Against Praxeas*, 9.
42. *Against Praxeas*, 8.
43. *Against Praxeas*, 11.
44. Eusebius CH, 6.2.
45. Eusebius CH, 6.1.

clothing, forcing him to stay at home. His father was executed around 202.

As a result of Leonide's death, his family was plunged into a state of abject poverty. The state confiscated his father's property and left nothing for the support of his family. By the grace of God, Origen was welcomed into the home of a wealthy woman who cared for his physical needs. While under her care, he pursued his studies vigorously. His diligence paid off, and when he was only eighteen years of age, he became head of the catechetical school in Alexandria, the most famous Christian school in the Roman world at the time.[46] One reason for his appointment was the absence of teachers, many of whom fled during the persecution. Origen was very successful in his new position, instructing not only Christians but many pagan intellectuals as well. This resulted in great opposition and the catechetical school required military protection while Origen was teaching his students.[47]

As time went on, Origen became more ascetic in his lifestyle. He worked hard throughout the day while spending the nights studying the scriptures. He fasted, limited the number of hours he slept, and slept only on the floor. He refused to wear shoes, did not drink wine, and ate barely enough food to sustain his life. His lifestyle was so extreme that his friends became concerned about his health, but he refused to give way to their fears.[48] An example of his extreme asceticism was described by Eusebius:

> He took the saying, "There are those who have made themselves eunuchs for the kingdom of heaven's sake" [Matt 19:12] in too literal and absurd a sense and he was eager to fulfill the Savior's words and also to forestall all slander on the part of unbelievers (for, despite his youth, he held forth on religious matters before women as well as men), So he quickly carried out the Savior's word, trying to do so unnoticed by most of his students. But however much he wished it, he could not possibly hide such a deed.[49]

46. Aquilina, *Fathers of the Church*, 127.

47. Eusebius CH, 6.3.

48. Eusebius CH, 6:3.

49. Eusebius CH, 6.8.

Some believe that Origen did not castrate himself, but this was an accusation made against him by his enemies.[50] Whatever the truth may be, many of his students became as enthusiastic as he was for living the ascetic life, and some of them died as martyrs for the faith.[51] Origen's asceticism became a seedbed for the growth of monasticism in the fourth century.

His fame continued to grow and Demetrius, the bishop of Alexandria, likely jealous of Origen's success, began to slander him and oppose his ordination as a bishop. Despite this opposition, Origen was ordained by a group of Palestinian bishops. In response, Demetrius called a synod, stripped Origen of his priestly duties, and banished him from Alexandria.

After his banishment, Origen went to Caesarea, where he was graciously accepted by the bishops, who ignored the sentence passed against him. He taught in Caesarea but was also in demand as a teacher elsewhere. He taught and wrote extensively, producing upwards of six thousand written works by the end of his life. These works include sermons, commentaries on Scripture, apologetics, and other practical works, most of which have been destroyed or only survive in fragments or Latin translations.[52] Although he desired to return to his home city of Alexandria, he spent the rest of his life in Caesarea.

When persecution broke out in the year 250 under the reign of Emperor Decius, Origen was arrested and tortured to such an extent that he died from his wounds when he was sixty-nine years old. Eusebius described his sufferings as follows:

> In this persecution the evil demon attacked Origen, in particular, with all the weapons in his arsenal, making him endure chains and torture for the Word of Christ as he lay in irons in the depths of his dungeon. Day after day his legs were stretched apart four paces in the stocks, but he courageously endured threats of fire and every other torment devised by his enemies.[53]

The Romans tortured Origen, not because they desired his death, but his apostasy. As a leading Christian teacher, his denial of Christ would have a far-reaching impact on the church. But this was not to be.

---

50. Haykin, *Rediscovering the Church Fathers*, 70.

51. Eusebius, CH, 6.4.

52. *Dictionary of the Christian Church*, "Origen," 1193.

53. Eusebius 6.39.

When the emperor died, Origen was released from prison and expired a short time later, in 254 AD.

Origen was an exceptionally gifted man, possibly one of the most intellectually gifted men of his age. His name stands alongside Jerome as one of the greatest exegetes in the ancient world.[54] He mastered the Hebrew language and gathered together Greek and Hebrew manuscripts that he arranged in parallel columns, binding them together in one volume called the *Hexapla*.[55] It included the Hebrew text, a Hebrew text in Greek, four Greek translations, and the Septuagint. This was the first attempt to provide a critical edition of the Old Testament and certainly demonstrates Origen's high view of the text of the Bible.

He also produced a work entitled, *Against Celsus*, in which he provided a defense of the faith against the charges of Celsus that Christianity was an irrational religion. One other significant work is called *De Principiis* (First Principles), in which Origen sought to provide the first systematic theology in the history of the church. It was also in this work that he explained his method of biblical interpretation.

Biblical Interpretation

Origen is probably best remembered as a commentator and an interpreter of Scripture. He was the first scholar to systematically work his way verse by verse through large sections of the Old and New Testament.

Philo, the well-known Jewish philosopher who lived in Alexandria in the first century AD, was renowned for his heavy use of allegory when interpreting the Old Testament. As Christianity began to grow in Alexandria, many Christian leaders adopted his allegorical method. Origen, in particular, took it up and refined it. It is in his commentaries that we see the outworking of his method, a system of interpretation that has influenced the way many read the scriptures even up to the present.[56]

It is in the fourth book of *De Principiis* that Origen outlined his method of interpretation. He emphasized the fact that the Holy Spirit divinely inspired the Bible. Yet, he also believed the scriptures could be misunderstood if the right principles for interpretation were not used. He believed that each text of Scripture had three possible meanings, each

54. Crouzel, *Encyclopedia of Ancient Christianity*, 2:979.

55. Eusebius CH, 6.16.

56. Aquilina, *Fathers of the Church*, 127.

one corresponding with the three parts of the human being. First, the body is compared to the literal or historical interpretation. The historical is "a kind of covering and veil of spiritual truths."[57] Second, the soul is compared to the moral meaning of the text. And third, the spirit is likened to the allegorical/spiritual interpretation. The third category was most important in the mind of Origen, and it was the interpreter's job to dig out these spiritual riches from the text.

Origen believed that there was "hidden and secret meaning in each individual word."[58] Even every letter contained mysteries to be discovered. He considered that the historical interpretation of the text was vital, but he was most interested in finding the hidden spiritual mysteries.[59] Everything had a spiritual interpretation. The daughters of Lot who slept with their father; Sarah and Hagar, the wives of Abraham; Rachel and Leah, the wives of Jacob, all contain mysteries of the faith. The construction of the tabernacle was filled with spiritual meaning that is difficult or impossible to discover. He believed that all of Scripture contained hidden mysteries. He wrote, "All the narrative portion, relating either to the marriages, or to the begetting of the children, or to battles of different kinds, or to any other histories whatever, what else can they be supposed to be, save the forms and figures of hidden and sacred things?"[60]

This does not mean he rejected the historical interpretation. He believed that the Bible was filled with historical information that was critical for a right understanding of the Christian faith.[61] He wrote, "Let no one, however, entertain the suspicion that we do not believe any history in Scripture to be real . . . For the passages which hold good in their historical acceptation are much more numerous than those which contain a purely spiritual meaning."[62] Despite this, he would often give an overview of the text's literal meaning and then discard it, preferring a spiritual interpretation instead. He tended to ignore the influence of the human author on the text and looked for the spiritual meaning that the Holy Spirit had concealed there.[63] He would find hidden meanings in most

57. Origen, *De Principiis*, 4.1.14.

58. Origen, *De Principiis*, 4.1.7.

59. Gonzalez, *History of Christian Thought*, 1:211–12.

60. Origen, *De Principiis*, 4.1.9.

61. Haykin, *Rediscovering*, 84.

62. Origen, *De Principiis*, 4.1.19.

63. Crouzel, Encyclopedia of Ancient Christianity, 2:980.

passages which enabled him to sometimes stretch the text, like an elastic band, in whatever direction he wanted it to go. At other times he took the text in a hyper-literal way, such as his interpretation of Jesus' exhortation to cut off one's hand or to gouge out one's eye if it caused him to sin. It was his literal interpretation of this text that led him to castrate himself.[64]

Origen had other hermeneutical principles that guided him. For example, he believed in the rule of faith and sought to stay within the confines of the catholic interpretation of the Christian faith. He wrote,

> We shall endeavour, so far as our moderate capacity will permit, to point out to those who believe the holy Scriptures to be no human compositions, but to be written by inspiration of the Holy Spirit, and to be transmitted and entrusted to us by the will of God the Father, through His only-begotten Son Jesus Christ, what appears to us, who observe things by a right way of understanding, to be the standard and discipline delivered to the apostles by Jesus Christ, and which they handed down in succession to their posterity, the teachers of the holy Church.[65]

He did not view himself as doing theology on his own but within the context of the broader church community. He took seriously the way those who came before him understood the text and sought to stay within the boundaries of orthodoxy.

He also believed that the interpreter must be filled with the Holy Spirit. Apart from the work of the Spirit in the heart of a man, the scriptures will remain a closed book. The "deeper doctrines" have been placed in Scripture by the Holy Spirit, and only he can disclose them.[66] Origen stated it this way, "For God alone can burst the brazen gates by which they [the mysteries] are enclosed and concealed, and break in pieces the iron bolts and levers by which access is prevented to all those things which are written and concealed."[67]

Universalism

Origen certainly had some theological problems that led to his being rejected by later church councils. He taught that the soul was preexistent

64. Gonzalez, *History of Christian Thought*, 1:213, 214.

65. Origen, *De Principiis*, 4.1.9.

66. Haykin, *Rediscovering*, 86.

67. Origen, *De Principiis*, 4.1.23.

before being united with a body and was part of an earlier creation. He believed that all spirits were created equal and with the ability to exercise their will freely. At some point before the creation of this world, some spirits rebelled and became demons while others became rebellious souls trapped in a body. God created this present world and made physical bodies for our rebellious spirits as a place of testing. Origen even went as far as to suggest that reincarnation might be possible to bring people to higher levels of understanding. God's ultimate purpose is to enter back into harmony with God and all other beings.[68]

Because Origen believed that God planned to bring all things back into harmony with himself and one another, he embraced universal salvation. He suggested that everyone, including Satan and the demons, would be saved in the end. This belief led him to deny the eternal nature of hell. For Origen, hell was a place of purification, but it was not eternal, and everyone would ultimately be saved in the end.[69]

The Deity of Christ

While it is true that Origen believed in the triune nature of God and argued that both the Father and the Son are eternal, he was nevertheless guilty of what is known as subordinationism. Subordinationism is "teaching about the Godhead which regards either the Son as subordinate to the Father or the Holy Spirit as subordinate to both."[70] While acknowledging the deity of Christ, he relegated him to a lesser form of divine substance than the Father. Although Origen embraced the divinity of Christ, some of his followers took the next logical step and stripped Jesus of his deity, arguing that he was a mere man. Many believe this led to the rise of Arianism and the open assault upon the deity of Jesus Christ in the fourth century.[71]

Origen was condemned as a heretic at the fifth ecumenical council in Constantinople in 553. He is undoubtedly a controversial theologian whose theology is highly suspect in several areas, but we must appreciate the fact that he is rightly called the first systematic theologian in the history of the church and was not relying on the work of those who had

---

68. Gonzalez, *History of Christian Thought*, 220–21.

69. Gonzalez, *History of Christian Thought*, 222.

70. Marcus, *Der Subortinationanismus*, 1552.

71. McGrath, *Historical Theology*, 25.

gone before him. We interpret Scripture surrounded by mighty theological walls constructed over the centuries, but Origen lived in a time when those walls were only beginning to be built. He lived before any of the great ecumenical councils that defined and refined the church's teaching on the Trinity; the deity of Christ; the dual nature of Christ; the deity of the Holy Spirit, as well as many other key doctrines. He lived long before the Protestant Reformation and the proliferation of the many Christian Creeds that came out of the Reformation. He did not benefit from the thousands of commentaries on Scripture produced in the past four hundred years. It is easy to criticize Origen, but we must remember that we have two thousand years of theological reflection behind us to help inform our interpretation of Scripture. We should not lightly pass over his errors but we must appreciate more fully the time in history in which he lived and wrote. A bit of humility on our part is in order here.

Discussion Questions

1. Should the appearances of God in the Old Testament be understood as theophanies or Christophanies?

2. Is man a dichotomy or a trichotomy?

3. Discuss Tertullian's illustrations on the Trinity. Do they accurately reflect biblical teaching?

4. What are the strengths and weaknesses of Origen's method of interpretation?

Chapter 8

Persecution in the Third Century

Septimius Severus

SEPTIMIUS SEVERUS WAS BORN at Leptis Magna in 145 AD. The founder of the Severan dynasty, he became the Emperor of the Roman empire in 193 during a time of great disunity and upheaval. One of his first acts as emperor was to reorganize the administration of the empire to consolidate his own power. He dismissed the Praetorian Guard, who had become impossible to manage, replacing them with loyal men from his own Danubian legions. He then began to eliminate any rivals to the throne. He weakened the Roman Senate by appointing administrators from the equestrian class[1] who would be loyal to him rather than from the senatorial class. He additionally increased the soldiers' pay by twenty-five percent, cementing their allegiance to him, and also reduced the number of legions under a general's control, to prevent them from gaining sufficient power to rise up against him.[2]

Though Severus made some significant and needed changes to reestablish unity within the empire, his actions led to the persecution of the Christian church. During the earlier years of his reign, he left the Christians in peace. Synods and assemblies were freely held in different cities to discuss the issues of the day and there is no indication that the emperor resisted the work of the church. However, this tolerant attitude

1. The equestrian class was one rung below the senatorial class on the social ladder. By appointing them as administrators he undercut the authority of the Roman senators.

2. Gomez, *Encyclopedia of the Ancient Roman Empire*, 292.

was short-lived.[3] As part of his unifying agenda, the emperor sought to establish the worship of the Unconquered Sun as the religion of the empire. People could worship whatever gods they wanted to as long as they recognized the Unconquered Sun as the chief among the gods.[4] This has been described as "a form of pagan monotheism."[5]

This presented a problem for both Jews and Christians. Both groups refused to acknowledge any god, except the God of the Jewish and Christian scriptures, which brought them into direct conflict with the Roman authorities. In 202, in response to their obstinacy, Severus sought to destroy both Judaism and Christianity by making it illegal to convert to either of these religions. This persecution resulted in the death of many Christians, including Origen's father, and Irenaeus.[6] Eusebius informed us that there were large numbers of Christians, particularly in Alexandria, who were martyred during the reign of Septimius Severus. He described the persecution as "a fierce blaze [where] countless numbers received the crown of martyrdom."[7] Christians were subject to various forms of torture and execution, including burning, beheading, boiling tar poured slowly over various parts of the body, and other gruesome forms of cruelty.[8] One of the most moving accounts of martyrdom during this persecution was that of Perpetua and Felicitas.

The Martyrdom of Perpetua and Felicitas[9]

Perpetua and Felicitas were two of five catechumens[10] who were arrested and thrown into prison, presumably for disobeying the new law against conversion to Christianity. Perpetua's father sought to persuade her to abandon the faith with threats of violence, but she would not budge in her commitment to her Saviour. This does not mean that she was not anxious about her situation. She said that she was filled with fear because of the darkness of her prison, the ill-treatment of the soldiers, and the

3. Siniscalco, "Septimius Severus, Emperor," 3:539.

4. Gonzalez, *Story of Christianity*, 83.

5. Mathisen, *Ancient Roman Civilization*, 365.

6. Gonzalez, *Story of Christianity*, 83.

7. Eusebius, CH, 6.1.

8. Eusebius, CH, 4.4–5.

9. *Passion of SS. Perpetua and Felicity*.

10. A catechumen is a professing Christian who received teaching in preparation for baptism.

heavy concern of caring for her infant child who was with her in the cell. While she languished in jail, she asked God to reveal to her whether or not she would be martyred for the faith or set free. Having received a vision from God, she was convinced that it was God's will that she give up her life for the sake of the gospel. She, consequently, gave up all hope of living any longer in this world and set her mind on the surety of her impending execution.

After the order was given that Perpetua and her companions were to be put on trial, her father came to her again and begged her to renounce her faith and not to disgrace their family. She felt sad for her father but committed herself to the will of God. Her father went away with a heart filled with grief.

On another day, Perpetua and her companions were taken out of prison and put on trial. Once again, Perpetua's father came to her and tried to convince her to "perform the sacrifice" and to have mercy on her child. Hilarian, the Procurator, also tried to persuade her to sacrifice to the emperor by appealing to her familial relationships. He said, "Spare your father's grey hairs; spare the infancy of the boy. Make sacrifice for the emperor's prosperity." Perpetua could not be persuaded and said, "I am a Christian," at which point the Procurator had her father beaten in her presence. While she felt deep sorrow for her father's sufferings, she would not budge in her commitment to Christ. Because of her stubbornness, she and her companions were condemned to be thrown to the wild animals.

Perpetua and her friends were taken back to their prison. Their hearts were filled with joy, and they spent much time in prayer together. As the day of their execution was approaching, Perpetua's father made one final attempt to persuade his daughter to recant. He pulled hair from his beard while weeping and wailing in her presence. Although she continued to feel sorry for her father, she was unmoved in her commitment to her Saviour.

Felicitas, one of the companions of Perpetua, was eight months pregnant when she was arrested. She was unhappy because she might not be able to die with her friends in the amphitheater, but would have to wait until the baby was born. Her companions united in prayer three days before their execution. Immediately after they prayed, Felicitas went into labour and delivered a baby girl who was subsequently given to a Christian woman to raise.

The night before they were to be thrown to the wild beasts, Perpetua had a vivid dream in which she was taken to the amphitheater where she defeated a great Egyptian warrior in battle. After the violent encounter, she was given a branch and it was said to her, "Daughter, peace be with you." She then said, "…and I began to go with glory to the gate called the Gate of Life." After waking up, she realized that she was not destined to fight wild beasts but was fighting against the devil, and she would be triumphant and enjoy a sweet victory.

When the day of their execution arrived, the faithful band of disciples was filled with joy at the prospect of leaving this world in such a glorious manner. As they entered the theatre, they looked at Hilarian the Procurator and said to him, "You judge and God judges you." In response to these words, the crowd was enraged and cried out that they should be scourged before being thrown to the wild animals. The women were joyful because they were allowed to enter into the sufferings of their Lord.

Saturninus and Revocatus, two of the male companions, were the first to suffer. They faced a leopard and then a wild bear. After this, Saturus, a third male disciple, was tied to a wild boar, and although the animal dragged him about, he came out of this ordeal unharmed. Even when they tied him up to be attacked by the bear, the bear did not touch him. He was then presented to the leopard who bit Saturnus, causing a fatal wound.

Perpetua and the women were set before a wild cow prepared for the day and were severely mauled. Although the wild beast threw them about, Perpetua was more anxious with covering up her nakedness out of concern for modesty and pinning up her hair because she reasoned that a martyr should not go to her death with disheveled hair. Surviving their encounter with the wild cow, they were gathered together with the others who were still alive. After a final kiss, they were struck down with the sword. And so, Perpetua, Felicitas, and their brave companions gave their lives in faithfulness to their Lord and Saviour, Jesus Christ. The record of their martyrdom ends with these words:

> O most valiant and blessed martyrs! O truly called and elected to the glory of Our Lord Jesus Christ! Which glory he that magnifies, honors and adores, ought to read these witnesses likewise, as being no less than the old, to the Church's edification; that these new wonders also may testify that one and the same Holy Spirit works ever until now, and with Him God the Father

Almighty, and His Son Jesus Christ Our Lord, to Whom is glory and power unending forever and ever. Amen.

The emperor Septimus died in Britain in the city of York in 211. His final words were, "Anything else to do? Give it here?"[11] Upon his death, his son, Caracalla (r. 198–217) became emperor, the persecution subsided, and the Christians enjoyed peace for almost fifty years until Decius came to the throne.

Emperor Decius (r. 249–51)

Decius became emperor in 249 and ruled for only two years. Shortly after becoming emperor, he declared war on the Christians by initiating the fiercest and first empire-wide persecution the church had experienced to date. Like Emperor Severus, Decius sought to use religion as a unifying force for the empire. He commanded that every citizen demonstrate his loyalty by offering a sacrifice to the gods. In exchange, they would receive a certificate that read, "I have always sacrificed to the gods, and now, according to the order, I have made sacrifice and libation, and tasted the victim's flesh."[12] This order presented a serious problem for the Christians.

Christians responded to this order in one of three ways. First, out of fear, many professing Christians apostatized and offered the sacrifice to save their own lives. Eusebius said that some "ran eagerly, as if to show that they had never been Christians."[13] Some Christians resisted for a time, but under pain of torture, they renounced their faith. Second, some bribed officials who gave them certificates showing that they offered the sacrifice, but they actually didn't.[14] Third, many Christians would not compromise the faith and suffered greatly for their faithfulness to the Lord.[15] Fabian, the bishop of Rome, was one of the earliest martyrs. He was killed sometime before January 20, 250.[16]

The persecution was most intense in the city of Alexandria. Eusebius described the suffering of the Christians in graphic detail:

11. Mathisen, *Ancient Roman Civilization*, 345.

12. Mathisen, *Ancient Roman Civilization*, 352.

13. Eusebius, CH, 6.41

14. *Letters of St. Cyprian*, Intro. 32.

15. Cyprian, *Lapsed, The Unity of the Catholic Church*, Intro. 4.

16. *Letters of St. Cyprian*, Intro. 25.

First, they seized an old man named Metras and ordered him to blaspheme. When he refused, they beat him with clubs, stabbed his face and eyes with pointed reeds, took him to the suburbs, and stoned him to death. Then they led a believer named Quinta to the temple of idols and tried to make her worship. When she turned away in disgust, they tied her feet and dragged her across the city over the rough pavement, beating her while she was being bruised by the big stones, and stoned her to death at the same place. They all rushed in a group to the houses of the godly and attacked, plundered, and looted their own neighbors, stealing the more valuable possessions and burning the cheaper, wooden items in the streets, making the city look as if it had been overwhelmed by enemies. The brethren gradually yielded and cheerfully endured the plundering of their possessions, and I do not know of anyone who has denied the Lord, with one possible exception.[17]

Further to this, Christians had their teeth knocked out, they were burned in fire, their bones were broken, and their limbs were torn from their bodies. Some were placed on camels and beaten with sticks as they were paraded through the streets, while others were beheaded or thrown to wild beasts. Many languished in prison, having their skin scraped with sharp objects and viciously whipped till their flesh was torn open, yet they remained faithful. After describing many of these horrors, Eusebius wrote, "Need I speak of the multitudes who wandered across deserts and mountains, dying from hunger, thirst, cold, disease, robbers, and wild beasts?"[18]

In 251, Decius was killed in battle and the Christians rejoiced, seeing this as God's judgment upon him.[19] After his death, Gallus (r. 251–53) became emperor and while he did not completely stop the persecution, it was less severe under his reign. Despite the brief respite enjoyed by the Christians, persecution was renewed a few years later under the reign of Emperor Valerian.

17. Eusebius, CH, 6.41.

18. Eusebius, CH, 6.42.

19. Mathisen, *Ancient Roman Civilization*, 352.

Emperor Valerian (r. 253–60)

When Valerian became the emperor in 253, he seemed to be favorably disposed toward Christians. Eusebius wrote, "his earlier conduct was mild and friendly to God's people; no emperor before him was so kindly displaced toward them, not even those said to have been Christians, as he clearly was in receiving them in close friendship at the start."[20] Despite this promising beginning he was led astray by ungodly counsel and initiated a terrible persecution against the Christians.

At this time, the leaders of the church were commanded to give up Christianity and follow the Roman gods. It was believed that if the leaders abandoned the faith, other Christians would follow them in their apostasy. Most church leaders refused to give up their faith, and they were either exiled, imprisoned, or executed. Those sent into exile were not permitted to have church meetings and were forbidden from visiting Christian cemeteries. In most cases, the leaders sent into exile continued to preach the gospel and large assemblies of people gathered around them. Even many unbelievers who first persecuted them were converted and became Christians. In this way, the gospel was preached in areas where it was previously unknown. Many Christian leaders concluded that God was the one who exiled them so they could preach the gospel to these new communities of people.[21]

Not only the leaders were persecuted during this time. Eusebius quoted a letter of Dionysius, a Christian leader who reported on the persecution:

> It is unnecessary to name our people, since they are numerous and unknown to you. Only know that men and women, boys and patriarchs, girls and old ladies, soldiers and civilians, every race and every age, some suffering scourging and fire, others the sword—all conquered in the struggle and have received their crowns.[22]

In 260, Valerian was taken captive by the Persian king Shapur I, also known as Shapur the Great, and was made a slave. His son, Gallienus, became emperor and immediately ended the persecution against

20. Eusebius, CH, 7.10.

21. Eusebius, CH, 7.11.

22. Eusebius, CH, 7.11.

the Christians.[23] The Christians would enjoy a time of relative peace for the next forty years.

Novatianism

Immediately following the Decian persecution, the church was confronted with a new question: What should be done with lapsed Christians, that is, Christians who had denied the faith under the threat of torture, imprisonment, and even death? With the threat of persecution gone, many lapsed Christians wanted to be received back into the church. This issue resulted in a great schism that threatened the unity of the church.

One prominent leader in this debate was Cyprian, the Bishop of Carthage from 249–58. Cyprian was born into a wealthy family sometime around 200 in the city of Carthage. He became a successful pagan rhetorician and enjoyed all the comforts of this world. He was converted to Christianity around 246 and subsequently sold his property, gave the money to the poor, and took a vow of chastity. From this point on, he devoted himself to an ascetic life. He passionately studied the scriptures and the teachers of the church.[24]

Although he was a young believer, his natural giftedness was recognized, and he was appointed the bishop of Carthage only two years after his conversion. In 249, the persecution under Emperor Decius broke out and Cyprian went into hiding, not out of fear, but love for his congregation. He continued to lead and encourage the church through the writing of regular letters. In 251, after the persecution subsided, he returned to Carthage and his first sermon was on the issue of "the lapsed." In this sermon, he addressed the question of what to do with lapsed Christians.[25] One is impressed when reading the sermon by the compassion Cyprian had for the church of God and for those who fell away during the persecution. He said,

> My heart bleeds with each one of you, I share the weight of your sorrow and distress. I mourn with those that mourn, I weep with those that weep, with the fallen I feel I have fallen myself. My limbs too were struck by the arrows of the lurking foe, his angry sword pierced my body too. When persecution rages, the

23. Eusebius, CH, 7.13.

24. Schaff, *History of the Christian Church*, 2:843–44.

25. Cyprian, *Lapsed*, Intro. 3.

mind of none escapes free and unscathed: when my brethren fell, my heart was struck and I fell at their side.[26]

In spite of his compassion for the people, he rebuked those who immediately turned away from the faith even before the persecution broke out. Just the threat of persecution and the thought of being arrested was enough for many professing Christians to renounce their faith. Numerous believers willingly offered the required sacrifice to the emperor and could therefore not claim that they submitted against their will. Cyprian does not hold back when describing the spiritual travesty of offering the sacrifice:

> Could a servant of God stand there and speak—and renounce Christ, whereas it was the world and the devil he had renounced before? Was not that altar, where he was going to his death, in fact his funeral pyre? When he saw that altar of the devil, smoking and reeking with its foul stench, should he not have fled in terror, as from the place where his soul must burn? Poor fellow, why bring any other offering or victim for the sacrifice? You yourself are the offering and the victim come to the altar; there you have slain your hope of salvation, there in those fatal fires you have reduced your faith to ashes.[27]

It would have been better if those who offered the sacrifice withdrew from society and went into hiding, waiting out the persecution rather than to have offered the sacrifice to preserve their own lives. Cyprian said that their love of the things of this world and their unwillingness to leave their homes and properties compelled them to offer the soul-damning sacrifice.

Cyprian was much more sympathetic to those who denied the Lord under pain of punishment. The first man denied the Lord at the thought of torture, but the second man denied the Lord while being tortured. Cyprian described the second man in this way,

> My purpose was firm, my faith strong, and long did my soul struggle resolutely with the pain of the tortures. But as the ferocity of the cruel judge flared up again, I was already exhausted when first I was lashed with whips, then beaten with truncheons, then stretched on the rack, then ploughed with hooks, then burnt with the fire, till I lost heart from the struggle; it was my physical weakness that gave way, it was not my spirit

26. Cyprian, *Lapsed*, Chapter 4.

27. Cyprian, *Lapsed*, 8.

but my flesh that cracked under the pain. Such a plea may truly avail for forgiveness, such a defense deserves our pity.[28]

In some cases, those who denied the Lord during their suffering, recanted, were rearrested and remained faithful to the Lord in their second round of torture.

Cyprian was less sympathetic towards those who did not offer the sacrifice but managed to secure a certificate by bribing an official. He viewed the possession of the certificate as "a confession of apostasy."[29] Even though the man did not offer the sacrifice, his certificate implied that he did. He may be able to escape the judgement of men, but he would not escape the judgement of God, who will condemn him for his public denial of Jesus Christ.

Cyprian called on those who denied the Lord to confess their sin to God and repent of their wicked actions. He called for repentance that was prolonged and in accord with the gravity of their sin. He wrote,

> You must beg and pray assiduously, spend the day sorrowing and the night in vigils and tears, fill every moment with weeping and lamentation; you must lie on the ground amidst clinging ashes, toss about chafing in the sackcloth of mourning; having once been clothed with Christ, refuse all other raiment now; having supped with the devil, choose rather now to fast; apply yourself to good deeds which can wash away your sins, be constant and generous in giving alms, whereby souls are freed from death...[30] To him who prays with all his heart, to him who mourns with tears and sighs of true repentance, to him who by good works of persevering charity pleads to the Lord for mercy on his sin—to such He can extend His mercy.[31]

Cyprian held out hope for the man who denied his Lord in the face of persecution. The one who recognized the seriousness of his sin, the shame associated with it, and truly repented would rise up from his knees forgiven and renewed in the strength of the Lord. Faith would be revived in his heart, and he would enter once again into the battle as a faithful soldier of Jesus Christ. He would be restored to the church's fellowship and bring joy to the hearts of God's people.

28. Cyprian, *Lapsed*, 13.

29. Cyprian, *Lapsed*, 27.

30. Cyprian, *Lapsed*, 35.

31. Cyprian, *Lapsed*, 36.

Cyprian called a synod to settle the question concerning what should be done with the lapsed. They came to three main conclusions. First, it was decided that those who obtained certificates through bribery but did not offer the sacrifice would be immediately welcomed back into the fellowship of the church. Second, those who did offer the sacrifice would remain outside the church until their deathbed. The only exception to this rule was if another persecution broke out, providing them the opportunity to demonstrate the genuine nature of their repentance. Third, those who offered the sacrifice and showed no remorse for their action were barred from ever being reconciled to the church.[32]

Some opposed Cyprian's leadership, calling him a coward because he ran away and hid during the persecution. They questioned his authority as a bishop to speak on the issue of the lapsed. Whether or not there was any cowardice in the heart of Cyprian we cannot know for sure, but it should be noted that on September 4, 258, Cyprian was martyred during the Valerian persecution, demonstrating that he was not the coward many claimed him to be.

Novatian (c.200–258), a prominent leader in the church of Rome, opposed Cyprian and those who adopted his position. Novatian was a polarizing character who has elicited both praise from his admirers and condemnation from his critics. On the one hand, he has been described as "a man of unblemished, though austere character, considerable biblical and philosophical learning, speculative talent, and eloquence."[33] On the other hand, Eusebius described him as a man filled with contempt, pride, and stupidity.[34] He was also depicted as "a deceitful, cunning and savage beast."[35] However one views the man, his influence is undeniable.

In 251, a man named Cornelius was elected as the bishop of the Roman church, a position that Novatian appears to have desired. There was a small group that voted for Novatian, but the majority supported Cornelius. Cornelius sided with Cyprian, adopting a more lenient approach to dealing with the lapsed, but Novatian and his followers argued that those who gave up the faith in times of persecution should not be allowed

32. Gonzalez, Justo, L., *Story of Christianity*, 89.

33. Schaff, *History of the Christian Church*, 2:850.

34. Eusebius, CH, 6.43.

35. Schaff, *History of the Christian Church*, 2:852.

back into fellowship. This disagreement led to the establishment of a rival church under his leadership that claimed to be the pure church of God.[36]

The Novatianists grew like wildfire leading to the development of a network of smaller congregations. They called themselves "Cathari," which means "pure ones," and viewed the catholic church as having compromised its purity by allowing the lapsed to re-enter. To join the Novatianist church, you had to be re-baptized because your first baptism was considered illegitimate. As time progressed, they took strict positions on other moral issues as well. If you were in a second marriage or committed a particularly heinous sin after baptism, like murder, adultery, or apostasy, you were barred from the church for life.[37]

Novatianists were persecuted until 326 when Emperor Constantine granted them the freedom to worship, build their own churches, and own burial grounds. Despite this new freedom, they were continually bullied by catholic leadership in various places. In 428, they were being persecuted by Nestorius, and in 429, the bishop of Rome stripped them of their church buildings. By the seventh century, their influence was waning, and they were reabsorbed into the catholic church.[38]

Initially, the catholic church held out an olive branch to the Novatianist bishops, seeking to win them back to the fold. Canon 8 of the Council of Nicaea[39] provided the conditions that must be met for a Novatianist to be received back into the church.

> Concerning those who call themselves Cathari, if they come over to the Catholic and Apostolic Church, the great and holy Synod decrees that they who are ordained shall continue as they are in the clergy. But it is before all things necessary that they should profess in writing that they will observe and follow the dogmas of the Catholic and Apostolic Church; in particular that they will communicate with persons who have been twice married, and with those who having lapsed in persecution have had a period [of penance] laid upon them, and a time [of restoration] fixed so that in all things they will follow the dogmas of the Catholic Church.[40]

---

36. Vogt, "Novatian," *Encyclopedia of Ancient Christianity*, 2:934.

37. *Eerdmans' Handbook To The History of Christianity*, 78.

38. *Eerdmans' Handbook To The History of Christianity*, 78.

39. The Council of Nicaea was the first great ecumenical council of the church. It met from May to August in 325 AD.

40. Percival, "Canons of the 318 Holy Fathers," 19–20.

This requirement for readmittance into the church emphasizes that the schism between the catholics and the Cathari was not over Christian theology. It is important to remember that Novatian was an orthodox believer and held to the basic tenets of the Christian faith, although his doctrine of the Trinity was inadequate.

Novatian wrote an important work on the Trinity in which he argued for the deity of Christ and the distinctness of the Father and the Son. While attempting to refute Sabellianism,[41] Novatian overly emphasized the distinction between the Father and the Son, and in doing so, he made the Son inferior to the Father. While not denying the eternal nature of the Son, like Origen, he leaned heavily toward subordinationism.[42] He also affirmed that the Holy Spirit is God, but he made the Spirit inferior to both the Father and the Son. Although he recognized the triune nature of God, along with Origen, Novatian is seen by some as unwittingly preparing the way for the rise of Arianism.[43]

Discussion Questions

1. Was Cyprian right to flee during the Decian persecution?

2. How should the church deal with those who sin grievously in the church?

3. Do you think Cyprian or Novatian was right in their approach to the lapsed?

4. Study the following texts: Matt 5:11, 44; 10:23; 1 Cor 4:12. How should Christians respond in times of persecution?

41. See definition of Sabellianism in Appendix 1.
42. See definition of Subordinationism in Appendix 1.
43. Gonzalez, *History of Christian Thought*, 236.

Chapter 9

The Persecution of Emperor Diocletian

Emperor Diocletian (r. 284–305)

DIOCLETIAN BECAME EMPEROR AT a time of great political instability. Invasions, rebellions, and short-lived emperors, some ruling for only a few months before being assassinated, were common during the decades leading up to his rule. Many believed the Roman Empire was in a state of rapid and irreversible decay. Diocletian, a seasoned soldier and capable administrator was precisely the kind of leader needed to restore peace and stability in the empire. When he ascended the throne, he immediately began reorganizing the empire into administratively manageable sections. In 286, Diocletian appointed his friend Maximian co-emperor and gave him authority to rule the western half of the empire while Diocletian continued to rule over the eastern half. In 293, he divided it further into four sections, appointing Galerius and Constantius Chlorus as rulers over the newly created regions. The new political structure, known as the tetrarchy, was organized with Diocletian and Maximian as Augusti (senior emperors) and Galerius and Constantius Chlorus as Caesars (junior emperors). When an Augusti died or retired, one of the Caesars would become an Augusti and then appoint a Caesar to serve under him, thereby providing a smooth transition of power. Although each of these men ruled over a quarter of the empire, Diocletian retained ultimate authority over the other three. This arrangement worked well during Diocletian's reign.[1]

1. *Encyclopedia of the Ancient Roman Empire*, 306.

Diocletian built new roads and forts along the borders to further stabilize the empire, increased the number of legions from thirty-nine to sixty, and enlarged the military by approximately thirty percent. He also reformed the tax system to make it more equitable for the people and profitable for the imperial treasury. He reduced the authority of local governors by centralizing power in his own hands and the hands of his fellow tetrarchs.[2]

With this new administrative arrangement, the empire enjoyed a time of peace and prosperity, and initially, there was no indication that the church would be persecuted during Diocletian's reign. Christians were allowed to be governors of provinces, church leaders were honoured, there were large Christian gatherings, and enormous spacious buildings were constructed to house the worshipers. Even servants within the emperor's household and members of his own family were allowed to practice the faith. There was no indication that the worst empire-wide persecution ever experienced by the Christians was about to be launched.[3]

All the public appearances of the emperor were highly choreographed to make a lasting impression and increase his prestige in the minds of the people. Unlike previous emperors, Diocletian appeared in public wearing a lavish crown and jewelry. He was luxuriously dressed and forbade anyone from wearing purple except the emperors. Anyone who approached him was required to prostrate themselves before him and kiss the hem of his robe.[4]

Despite these extravagant public displays of royal power, Diocletian believed in the traditional Roman gods and vigorously sought to re-establish their influence throughout the Roman Empire. Because of this, religions like Manichaeism and Christianity posed a threat to his religious agenda. In an attempt to suppress Manichaeism, he ordered that lower-class Manicheans be executed and sent higher-class ones to work in the mines. After dealing with the Manichean threat, he turned his energy toward the Christians.[5]

Eusebius lived during Diocletian's reign and provided an eyewitness account of the events. He believed the persecution was a divine judgement upon the church because of its unfaithfulness to God. He recorded

2. *Encyclopedia of the Ancient Roman Empire*, 308–10.

3. Eusebius, CH, 8.1.

4. *Encyclopedia of the Ancient Roman Empire*, 310.

5. *Encyclopedia of the Ancient Roman Empire*, 310–11.

that before the persecution broke out, there was a great deal of pride, laziness, division, and infighting amongst the Christians. Eusebius wrote:

> Church leaders attacked church leaders and laymen formed factions against laymen, while unspeakable hypocrisy and pretense reached their evil limit. Finally, while the assemblies were still crowded, divine judgment, with its accustomed mercy, gradually started to intervene...those who were supposed to be pastors, unrestrained by the fear of God, quarreled bitterly with one another and only added to the strife, threats, jealousy, and hate, frantically claiming the tyrannical power they craved. Then it was that the Lord in his anger humiliated his daughter Zion.[6]

The persecution was initially encouraged by Galerius, one of the four tetrarchs, who began harassing Christians in the military. Those refusing to swear allegiance to the Roman gods were stripped of their rank and expelled from the military. The wider persecution began in 303 when Diocletian and the other tetrarchs enacted a series of laws directed against the Christians. Constantius, the tetrarch who ruled over Gaul, Britain, and Spain, was favourably disposed toward the Christians and sought to protect them. Nevertheless, churches were destroyed, and Christians were martyred in Spain and Britain during this time.[7]

Throughout the empire, Christians were commanded to abandon their Christian beliefs and submit to the traditional gods of Rome. Church buildings were demolished, the scriptures were burned, Christians who held high positions were removed from office, and anyone who refused to deny the faith was imprisoned. While in prison, every means possible was used to force them to offer sacrifices to the gods.[8] Eusebius provided a graphic description of the suffering experienced by faithful believers at this time:

> Each was subjected to a series of various tortures: one was scourged mercilessly, another racked and scraped to death. People emerged from the ordeal in different ways: one man would be shoved at the loathsome, unholy sacrifices and dismissed as if he had sacrificed when he had not; another who came nowhere near any such abomination but was said to have sacrificed would leave in silence at the falsehood. Still another, half dead, would be discarded as a corpse, while a man who had sacrificed

6. Eusebius, CH, 8.1.

7. Schaff, *History of the Christian Church*, 2:67.

8. Eusebius, CH, 8.2.

willingly was nevertheless dragged a long distance by his feet. One man would shout at the top of his voice that he had not sacrificed and never would, while yet another would proclaim that he was a Christian and glory in the Saviour's name. These were silenced by a large band of soldiers, who struck them on the mouth and battered their faces. The overriding goal of the enemies of godliness was to appear to have accomplished their purpose.[9]

Eusebius described a variety of cruel methods by which Christians were persecuted for their faith. Some were whipped and had salt and vinegar poured into their open wounds. Hot irons were applied to different parts of the body and in this way, the body was slowly roasted to inflict the greatest amount of pain. Others were beheaded and many others were butchered with the sword. Some were burned in the fire while others were tied up and thrown into the sea to drown. Others were thrown to the wild beasts to be devoured in the amphitheater. Even dead bodies were dug up and tossed into the sea to prevent anyone from honouring them at their graves.[10] He went on to speak about the sufferings of Christians in Egypt.

> Women were tied by one foot and swung high in the air, head downward, by machines, their bodies totally naked without a stitch of clothing-the most shameful, cruel, and inhuman of all spectacles for onlookers. Others died fastened to trees: they bent down their strongest branches by machines, fastened one of the martyr's legs to each, and then let the branches fly back to their natural position, instantly tearing apart limbs of their victims. This went on not for a few days but for some whole years. Sometimes ten or more, at times more than twenty were put to death, or thirty, or almost sixty; at other times a hundred men, women, and little children were condemned to a variety of punishments and killed in a single day.[11]

Eusebius provided many more detailed accounts of the suffering experienced by Christians during this dark time. In the face of this great suffering, vast numbers of Christians remained faithful to the Lord and became martyrs for the faith. As in previous persecutions, many denied the faith when threatened with imprisonment, torture, and loss of life.

9. Eusebius, CH, 8.3.
10. Eusebius, CH, 8.6.
11. Eusebius, CH, 8.9.

In 305, Diocletian contracted a dreadful disease that appears to have affected his mental abilities. Because of this he resigned his position as emperor and went to live out his final days in a small town named Spalatum. He died in 312.[12] Maxentius also retired at the same time.

Galerius, who instigated the persecution against the Christians in the first place, became the supreme ruler in the empire. He continued to harass the Christians until he was struck with a deadly disease that ravaged his body. This sickness led to a reversal of his policy on persecuting Christians. On April 30, 311, Galerius issued a decree to end the persecution. By his order, Christians were to be released from prison, allowed to rebuild their churches, perform their religious rights, and commanded to pray for the prosperity of the Roman Empire.[13] Despite this reversal in official policy, Galerius died shortly after the decree was issued. Not surprisingly, the Christians saw this as a judgment from the Lord for his actions against God's people.

The persecution unleashed against the Christians was the last great attempt of paganism to destroy its rival for dominance in the Roman world. It was the greatest and most widespread persecution ever experienced by the church. It has been rightly said:

> All former persecutions of the faith were forgotten in the horror with which men looked back upon the last and greatest… the fiendish cruelty of Nero, the jealous fears of Domitian, the unimpassioned dislike of Marcus, the sweeping purpose of Decius, the clever devices of Valerian, fell into obscurity when compared with the concentrated terrors of that final grapple, which resulted in the destruction of the Roman Empire and the establishment of the Cross as the symbol of the world's hope.[14]

Although Galerius' edict put an end to persecution, the precarious status of the Christian church within the empire remained unchanged until Constantine, the first Christian emperor, rose to power.[15] As the first Christian emperor, Constantine legalized Christianity (up to this time it was only a tolerated religion) and paved the way for its dominance in much of the world for the next sixteen hundred years.

12. Eusebius, CH, 8.13.

13. Eusebius, CH, 8.17.

14. Schaff, *History of the Christian Church*, 2:64–65.

15. Mathisen, *Ancient Roman Civilization*, 389.

Discussion Questions

1. What changes did Diocletian introduce to address the decades-long political instability of the Roman Empire?

2. Why were Christians seen as a threat to the empire, which resulted in their persecution?

Chapter 10

Emperor Constantine
and the Council of Nicaea

AFTER THE DEATH OF emperor Galerius in 311, a power struggle broke out between the four tetrarchs. The western portion of the empire was divided between Constantine and Maxentius. Constantine, the son of Constantius Chlorus, ruled Britain and Gaul and Spain, while Maxentius, the son of Maximian, and son-in-law of Galerius, ruled Italy and much of North Africa. The eastern portion of the empire was divided between Licinius and Maximinus. Licinius ruled over Pannonia (parts of western Hungary and eastern Austria), while Maximinus ruled Asia Minor, Syria, and Egypt.[1]

In 312, Maxentius and Maximinus (also known as Maximin) formed a secret alliance, which compelled Constantine and Licinius to ally with one another as well. Maxentius, who was stationed in Rome, promoted a policy that resulted in the persecution of Christians. Constantine was favourably disposed toward the Christians and believed it was necessary to remove Maxentius from office. He led his army into Italy and marched on Rome. Eusebius believed that God raised Constantine up and incited him to wage war against Maxentius as a judgment upon Maxentius for his persecution of the Christians.[2] Maxentius brought his army out to meet Constantine at Milvian Bridge on October 28, 312.

The night before this famous battle, Constantine claimed that while he was praying during midday he saw the sign of the cross in the sky

---

1. Eusebius, CH, 285.
2. Eusebius, CH, 9.9.

130

above him with the words, "Conquer by this" inscribed on it.[3] When he went to sleep that night he asserted that the Lord appeared to him and told him to make a likeness of the sign as a means of protection for his army.[4] The next morning, Constantine immediately had the image created. Eusebius described it:

> Now it was made in the following manner. A long spear, overlaid with gold, formed the figure of the cross by means of a transverse bar laid over it. On the top of the whole was fixed a wreath of gold and precious stones; and with this, the symbol of the Saviour's name, two letters indicating the name of Christ by means of its initial characters, the Letter P being intersected by X in its center: and these letters the emperor was in the habit of wearing on his helmet at a later period.[5]

Under this new vision-inspired standard, Constantine battled and defeated Maxentius who drowned in the Tiber River. With Maxentius' defeat and death, Constatine became sole ruler of the western portion of the empire.

Meanwhile, in the eastern empire, Maximinus, like Maxentius, had also subjected the Christians to terrible persecution. Eusebius wrote:

> The men endured fire, sword, and nailings; wild beasts and submersion in the sea; branding and cutting off of limbs; stabbing, gouging out of eyes, and mutilation of the whole body; and, in addition, starvation, chains, and the mines. They preferred to suffer for the faith rather than transfer to idols the reverence due to God. As for the women, inspired by the divine Word, they showed themselves as manly as the men. Some were subject to the same ordeals as the men and won the same prizes for valor; others, while dragged away to seduction, surrendered their spirits to death rather than their bodies to dishonor.[6]

The relationship between Lucinius and Maximinus rapidly deteriorated and war broke out. On April 30, 313, their armies met at the battle of Tzirallum, and Maximinus was soundly defeated, resulting in Lucinius becoming the sole ruler of the eastern empire. With this the Tetrarchy

---

3. Eusebius, *Life of Constantine*, 2.28.

4. Eusebius, *Life of Constantine*, 2.29.

5. Eusebius, *Life of Constantine*, 2.31.

6. Eusebius, CH, 8.14.

ended and the Roman Empire was ruled by two emperors, Constantine in the west and Lucinius in the east.

Persecution came to an end and Christians throughout the empire were free to practice their faith. The Edict of Milan was signed in February 313, by Constantine and Licinius, only weeks before the defeat of Maximinus. The Edict legalized Christianity but did not make it the sole religion of the empire. It wasn't until the reign of Emperor Theodosius (r. 379–95) that Christianity would become the state religion.

This arrangement on ruling the empire worked well for several years, but Licinius was not content with the agreement. Even though Constantine had given his sister to Licinius in marriage, Licinius began to plot against his brother-in-law. Not only did he desire to overthrow Constantine; he also set out to destroy the Christian faith. Sometime after 317, he dismissed the Christians from his household. He then gave the order that all soldiers who refused to offer the sacrifices were to be stripped of their rank. He also ordered the execution of the more prominent bishops. To add insult to injury, some of their bodies were cut up and thrown into the sea for fish food. Many churches were either destroyed or locked up so that people could no longer worship in them. Numerous Christians were sent to work in the mines, and countless others fled to the wilderness to find safety until the persecution ended.[7]

Constantine went to war with Licinius and defeated him at the Battle of Chrysopolis in 324. Constantine later ordered that Licinius be executed for his crimes. The empire once again was united under one emperor, who was greatly loved and respected by the people. Many believed he was raised up by God to punish the persecutors of Christianity and to fully establish the Christian faith throughout the empire. During his reign, the Christians experienced a level of freedom never enjoyed before.[8]

Shortly after these events, Constantine passed several edicts to compensate the Christians who had suffered under Licinius' reign. Those who had fled into the wilderness were encouraged to return to their homes, and those who had lost property were compensated. Christians who were sent to the mines were released, and those who had lost their military rank were reinstated. Whatever injustice that was endured was

7. Eusebius, CH, 10.8.
8. Eusebius, CH, 10.8.

to be made right.[9] Church lands, including cemeteries and buildings, were returned to the church.[10]

Although he was not raised by Christian parents, Constantine openly proclaimed himself to be a Christian after he defeated Maxentius at Milvian Bridge. As a Christian emperor, he believed that he was God's instrument for the establishment of the Christian faith throughout the Roman world. Eusebius wrote:

> Accordingly, beginning at the remote Britannic ocean, and the regions where, according to the law of nature, the sun sinks beneath the horizon, through the aid of divine power I banished and utterly removed every form of evil which prevailed, in the hope that the human race, enlightened through my instrumentality might be recalled to a due observance of the holy laws of God, and at the same time our most blessed faith might prosper under the guidance of his almighty hand.[11]

Constantine's conversion brought dramatic change for Christianity in the empire. At his order, existing church buildings were repaired and enlarged, and new buildings erected where necessary. All expenses were paid out of the imperial treasury. Constantine was especially zealous to make Constantinople a Christian city. Eusebius wrote:

> Being filled, too, with Divine wisdom, he determined to purge the city which was to be distinguished by his own name from idolatry of every kind, that in the temples of those falsely reputed to be gods, nor any altars defiled by the pollution of blood: that there might be no sacrifices consumed by fire, no demon festivals, nor any of the other ceremonies usually observed by the superstitious.[12]

Not only were churches flourishing and idolatrous temples destroyed, but for the first time since the inception of the church, the entire household of the emperor was entrusted to the care of deacons and ministers. Christian priests were exempt from paying taxes, and Sunday was declared a day of worship and was set aside as a special occasion for prayer. Constantine himself performed devotions on that day and encouraged all his subjects to do the same. The soldiers were also urged

9. Eusebius, *Life of Constantine*, 2.20.

10. Eusebius, *Life of Constantine*, 2.39, 40.

11. Eusebius, *Life of Constantine*, 2.28.

12. Eusebius, *Life of Constantine*, 3.28.

to take the day off and attend worship services.[13] One motivation behind these changes was Constantine's belief that he was God's chosen instrument for the establishment of the Christian faith.

This new favoured position of Christianity is considered by some to be a glorious victory for the Christian faith. One writer described Constantine's victory at Milvian bridge as "a military and political victory of Christianity over heathenism."[14] Eusebius heaped excessive praise on the emperor in his work, *The Life of Constantine.*

> Like a faithful and good servant, did he act and testify, openly declaring and confessing himself the obedient minister of the supreme King. And God forthwith rewarded him, by making him ruler and sovereign, and victorious to such a degree that he alone of all rulers pursued a continual course of conquest, unsubdued and invincible, and through his trophies a greater ruler than tradition records ever to have been before. So dear was he to God, and so blessed; so pious and so fortunate in all that he undertook, that with the greatest facility he obtained the authority over more nations than any who had preceded him, and yet retained his power, undisturbed, to the very close of his life.[15]

Others are unconvinced that Christianity's victory over heathenism was good for the church. They believe it marked the beginning of the church's descent into compromise and spiritual decline. As the favoured religion, Christianity attracted many to the church, not because they were converted, but because they saw political and social advantage in being part of the growing movement. For the first three hundred years, the vast majority of church members were Christians, but now a large number of professing Christians were half-hearted, politically ambitious, self-serving sinners who never truly abandoned their pagan beliefs.[16] This led to lukewarm commitment, lower standards of Christian living, the introduction of many pagan practices into Christian worship, and political pressure in shaping religious belief.[17] As we will see in chapter twelve, Monasticism was one response to the spiritual decline of the church.

Many view this new relationship between church and state as paving the way for the rise of Roman Catholic hierarchical Christianity with

13. Eusebius, *Life of Constantine*, 4.18–20.

14. Schaff, *History of the Christian Church*, 3:28.

15. Eusebius, *Life of Constantine*, 1.6.

16. Shelly, *Church History in Plain Language*, 96.

17. Ferguson, *Church History*, 182.

its spiritual totalitarian spirit that dominated the western world for over a thousand years.

Although Emperor Constantine was a professing Christian, he was also pragmatic and desired peace and unity within the empire. He sought to rule fairly over both Christians and pagans allowing each to live in peace and freedom. Eusebius wrote;

> My own desire is, for the common good of the world and the advantage of all mankind, that thy people should enjoy a life of peace and undisturbed concord. Let those, therefore, who still delight in error, be made welcome to the same degree of peace and tranquillity which they have who believe.[18]

Despite this attempt at tolerance, Constantine clearly favoured Christianity. It has been rightly said that "without persecuting paganism [he] weighted the scales of neutrality strongly in favour of Christianity,"[19] He agreed with Diocletian that religion could unify the empire, but he thought that Diocletian chose the wrong religion.[20] Constantine was confident that this policy would ultimately lead many pagans to abandon their idolatry and embrace the Christian faith. Constantine believed Christianity could be the glue that united and held the empire together. One can only imagine how distressed he was when he became aware of a serious theological issue that threatened to tear the church apart.

The Arian controversy and the Council of Nicaea

The controversy came to light when Arius (256–336), a senior pastor in Alexandria, denied the deity of Jesus Christ. Arius argued that if the Son was truly a son then he must have had a beginning. He rejected the eternal nature of the Son and taught that there was a time when the Son did not exist. His teaching spread like wildfire throughout the empire. Eusebius said, "that a mighty fire was kindled as it were from a little spark."[21] Something needed to be done to put out the fire before it burned through the entire church. Or, to put it another way, the teaching of Arius was like fast-spreading cancer that infected the entire body of the church. A

---

18. Eusebius, *Life of Constantine*, 2.56.

19. Barrow, *Romans*, 183.

20. Mathisen, *Ancient Roman Civilization*, 391.

21. Eusebius, *Life of Constantine*, 2.61.

quick and decisive response needed to be made to stop the cancer from spreading further and doing more internal damage to the body of Christ.

The Egyptian bishops moved quickly to silence Arius by deposing him at an Egyptian synod in 323. Despite this attempt, Arius' teaching continued spreading, garnering support from many quarters of the church. Lay people, deacons, presbyters, and even some bishops, including Eusebius, Bishop of Berytus (not Eusebius the historian), embraced his teaching. The issue became so divisive that the emperor himself was compelled to intervene.

Constantine wrote to Alexander, the bishop of Alexandria, and Arius calling upon both sides to settle the issue, which the emperor believed to be a "small and very insignificant question,"[22] and come to an agreement on the matter for the sake of unity in the church and the empire.[23] Despite this feeble attempt at a resolution, the controversy continued to grow, so the emperor took action and called a council of bishops to decide the issue. This pivotal meeting, known as the Council of Nicaea, was the first ecumenical council of all the Christian churches. Although local councils were a well-established institution in the church, this was the first council that gathered bishops together from the broader church community.

This is also the first time that a political power called a council of the church and it marked the beginning of a relationship between church and state that would continue unabated for the next twelve hundred years, until the time of the Protestant Reformation.[24] As one writer put it, "The age of persecution was over and the age of Christendom—Christianity as a religion favored by government—had begun."[25] The state now had a say in the affairs of the church and the church began to call upon the state to help resolve disputes within the church.

The council gathered on May 20, 325 and it included approximately two hundred and fifty bishops from different regions of the empire.[26] Eusebius described the gathering as follows:

22. Eusebius, *Life of Constantine*, 2.71.

23. Eusebius, *Life of Constantine*, 2.64.

24. Although many of the Protestant Reformers supported a strong relationship between the church and the state, this relationship began to slowly unravel in the sixteenth century. Reformation groups like the anabaptists, and the Baptists taught a separation between church and state that eventually took hold in the western world.

25. Ferguson, *Church History*, 187.

26. Eusebius, *Life of Constantine*, 3.8.

> In effect, the most distinguished of God's ministers from all the churches which abounded in Europe, Lybia, and Asia were here assembled. And a single house of prayer, as though divinely enlarged, sufficed to contain at once Syrians and Cilicians, Phoenicians and Arabians, delegates from Palestine, and others from Egypt; Thebans and Libyans, with those who came from the regions of Mesopotamia. A Persian bishop too was present at this conference, nor was even a Scythian found wanting to the number. Pontus, Galatia, and Pamphylia, Cappadocia, Asia, and Phrygia, furnished their most distinguished prelates; while those who dwelt in the remotest districts of Thrace and Macedonia, of Achaia and Epirus, were notwithstanding in attendance. even from Spain itself, one whose fame was widely spread took his seat as an individual in the great assembly. The prelate of the imperial city was prevented from attending by extreme old age; but his presbyters were present, and supplied his place.[27]

One weakness of the council was the lack of representation from the western church. Most of the bishops were from the eastern regions of the empire.

Since many attending the council bore the marks of persecution on their bodies, a poignant reminder of the recent suffering Christians had endured at the hands of the government, it must have been a surreal experience to have the Roman emperor pay all their expenses.

The council was essentially comprised of three groups: those firmly convinced of the Arian position; those gathered around Alexander of Alexandria in vigorous opposition to Arianism; and those who were generally orthodox, but sympathetic to Arianism, likely because they did not perceive its danger for the church. Surprisingly, the majority of bishops attending were sympathetic to Arianism, and only a minority held to a well-defined doctrinal position.

After a prolonged debate, to the shock and dismay of the Arians, the council voted in favour of a creed that affirmed the deity of Christ and condemned the Arian position as heresy. Because of the mixed nature of the group, only a minority of the bishops stood firm in wanting to condemn Arius' views. The majority desired a compromise solution in order to preserve the unity of the church and allow it to move on to other matters. The turning point came when Eusebius of Nicomedia (not Eusebius the church historian), representing Arius, made his views clearly known. He thought that an unambiguous statement of the Arian position would

27. Eusebius, *Life of Constantine*, 3.7.

solicit all the support needed to see their views accepted. He was wrong. When he put forward the view that the Word or Son was no more than a creature, many of the bishops reacted with anger. Some cried out, "You lie!" "Blasphemy!" "Heresy!" Eusebius was shouted down, and we are told that his speech was ripped from his hand, torn into pieces, and trampled on the ground. The majority were now ready to condemn Arius' doctrine.

Following lengthy and laborious discussions, the council produced what is known as the Nicene Creed. It became the measure of orthodoxy for both the western and eastern branches of the church. It also provided the foundation on which all future councils based their doctrinal authority. The creed ratified by the council is as follows:

> We believe in one God, the Father, the almighty, the maker of all things seen and unseen. And in one Lord Jesus Christ, the Son of God; begotten from the Father; only-begotten–that is, from the substance of the Father God from God; light from light; true God from true God; begotten not made; of one substance with the Father; through whom all things in heaven and on earth came into being; who on account of us human beings and our salvation came down and took flesh, becoming a human being he suffered and rose again on the third day, ascended into the heavens;' and will come again to judge the living and the dead. And in the Holy Spirit.[28]

To reinforce the statement, the framers of the confession put under a curse all who denied the truth of the eternal divine nature of the Son.

> As for those who say that "there was when he was not," and "before being born he was not," and "he came into existence out of nothing," or who declared that the Son of God is of different substance or nature, or is subject to alteration or change—the catholic and apostolic church condemns these.[29]

This anathema marks the beginning of a long history of attaching anathemas to doctrinal formulations as a means of excluding those who would not subscribe to the statement.

Only Arius and two other bishops refused to subscribe to the Nicene confession, resulting in their excommunication from the church and banishment to Illyria.[30] The banishment of the Arians marked the

---

28. McGrath, *Christian Theology Reader*, 7.

29. McGrath, *Christian Theology Reader*, 7.

30. "Nicaea," *Encyclopedia of Ancient Christianity*, 909.

beginning of state enforced banishments over doctrinal issues and set a dangerous precedent for the future. Despite this formal doctrinal victory, Arianism continued to spread and influence people for several more centuries. Nevertheless, the long-term influence of the Nicene creed is much greater and has provided the foundation of orthodoxy for over sixteen hundred years of Christian history.[31]

One controversy that continues to be discussed to the present is the question of Constantine's faith. Was Constantine's faith genuine? Did he convert to the Christian faith for religious or political reasons? Did he really believe that Christianity was the truth, or did he merely recognize the growing force of Christianity and seek to manipulate it for his own political ambition? Maybe he saw the disastrous attempt by Diocletian to reinstitute the worship of the old Roman gods and learned from it. He wasn't going to make the same mistake so he embraced Christianity and promoted it rather than oppressing it.

Those who argue that Constantine was not a genuine believer point to several irregularities in his life. Constantine approved the building of a temple in honour of his own family that was cared for by a pagan priest. He continued to honour the Unconquered Sun, the most important god in the Roman pantheon, and he issued coins that had both Christian and pagan symbols engraved on them.[32] He also kept the title *Pontifex Maximus* as chief priest and head of the state religion for his entire life. It is an interesting fact that Emperor Constantine was not baptized until the end of his life. In 337 when he was sixty-five years of age he was baptized by Eusebius of Nicomedia, the Arian bishop. Some argue that he delayed his baptism because he did not want to put himself under the authority of the Christian church.

Others argue that despite these inconsistencies, the faith of Constantine was genuine. The contradictions can be explained as decisions made by an emperor who was attempting to rule over a vast empire that included divergent opinions on matters of religion. His compromise was out of political necessity to help satisfy his large number of pagan subjects.[33] Concerning his baptism, Constantine might have delayed it for political reasons, or he might have waited because he erroneously believed that baptism would wash away all his past sins, enabling him to

31. Dowley, *Eerdmans' Handbook to the History of Christianity*, 135.

32. Mathisen, *Ancient Roman Civilization*, 393.

33. Dowley, *Eerdmans' Handbook to the History of Christianity*, 130.

enter into the kingdom of God when he died.[34] It was not uncommon at this time for people to delay their baptism until the end of their lives to avoid being punished for mortal sins (a gravely sinful act).[35] Constantine died a few days after his baptism on May 22, 337 and his remains were buried in the church of the Holy Apostles in the city of Constantinople.

Only God knows the true heart of a man, but one thing can be said for certain, the favour that Emperor Constantine showed Christianity permanently altered the life of the church. It was during the reign of Constantine that the simplicity of Christian worship became more ostentatious and staged. The use of incense was introduced at this time. Elaborate processionals now marked the beginning of the worship service. Pastors began wearing more extravagant clothing, choirs were formed and the entire service began to feel more like a religious performance than an act of worship. Massive richly decorated buildings were erected, replacing the ordinary places of worship the Christians were accustomed to. The average person in the pew became an observer rather than a participant in the worship service.[36]

Discussion questions

1. What relationship, if any, should the church and state have with one another?

2. What do the following biblical texts tell us about the church's responsibility to the state? (Acts 4:18–20; Rom 13:1–7; 1 Tim 2:1–4)

3. Was the victory of Christianity over paganism a positive or negative development?

4. What is acceptable and what is unacceptable in Christian worship services?

34. Schaff, *History of the Christian Church*, 3:35.
35. Dowley, *Eerdmans' Handbook to the History of Christianity*, 130.
36. Gonzalez, *Story of Christianity*, 125.

Chapter 11

Athanasius of Alexandria
(295/300–373 AD)

ATHANASIUS WAS A CONTROVERSIAL character who is praised by some as an example of selfless leadership, while others reduce him to the level of a modern-day gangster.[1] Frances Young emphasized the fact that although the traditional history of Athanasius puts him in a good light, there is another side that does not portray him in such a favourable light.[2] Some have suggested that his election as bishop was illegal and that he had a "pitiless streak in his character and that he resorted to violence to achieve his own ends…"[3] C.S. Lewis was much more positive when he wrote,

> His epitaph is Athanasius *contra mundum*, "Athanasius against the world." We are proud that our own country has more than once stood against the world. Athanasius did the same. He stood for the Trinitarian doctrine, "whole and undefiled," when it looked as if all the civilized world was slipping back from Christianity into the religion of Arius—into one of those "sensible" synthetic religions which are so strongly recommended today and which, then as now, included among their devotees many highly cultivated clergymen. It is his glory that he did not move with the times; it is his reward that he now remains when those times, as all times do, have moved away.[4]

Whatever one's opinion of Athanasius, it is universally recognized by all that he was one of the most influential men of the fourth century,

1. Esler, *Early Christian World*, 1102.
2. Young, *Nicaea to Chalcedon*, 67.
3. Young, *Nicaea to Chalcedon*, 67.
4. Athanasius, *On the Incarnation*, 16.

permanently influencing the life and theology of the Christian church up to the present.

In terms of physical appearance, Athanasius was probably a short, dark-skinned Egyptian man which can be assumed from his enemies' nickname for him, "the black dwarf." He was described as, "a young man of puny stature, but with a face of singular beauty and animation."[5] Schaff wrote, "Athanasius, like many great men, was very small of stature, somewhat stooping and emaciated by fasting and many troubles, but fair of countenance, with a piercing eye and a personal appearance of great power even over his enemies."[6]

His Early Years and education

Athanasius was born sometime between 296 and 299 AD in the city of Alexandria. His parents were of the wealthy class and held a high rank in society, enabling them to provide a good classical education for their son. He was trained in the classics, the scriptures, and the church fathers.[7] In 303, while he was still a child, severe persecution broke out against the Christians, particularly in the city of Alexandria. This had a profound affect on his spiritual development and approach to the Christian faith, especially concerning martyrdom. In his book *On the Incarnation*, Athanasius referred to the dramatic change in people's lives who became Christians. Before their conversion, they were afraid of death, but after their conversion, they faced death gladly. He wrote:

> Is it a feeble demonstration of the victory over it [death] wrought by the Savior, when boys and young girls in Christ despise this present life and practice dying? For by nature human beings are afraid of death and of the dissolution of the body. But this is most amazing, that one who has put on the faith of the cross scorns even things according to nature, and is not afraid of death because of Christ.[8]

This was not mere rhetoric on the part of Athanasius. As a child, he saw Christian men, women, and children dragged away and executed for their faith. Possibly some of his own friends were among the children who

5. Bright, *Age of the Fathers*, 78.

6. Schaff, *History of the Christian Church*, 3:888.

7. Schaff, *History of the Christian Church*, 3:886.

8. Athanasius, *On the Incarnation*, 28.

laid down their lives for the saviour. This experience prepared Athanasius to stand firm in the face of the persecution he encountered throughout his entire adult life. It also deepened his faith in the power of Christ's resurrection to change the lives of those who trust Jesus for salvation.

Athanasius was trained in the Alexandrian School, which was also the school of Clement, and Origen. He came under the influence of Alexander (250–328), Bishop of Alexandria (313–28), and was deeply impacted by his teaching. There is a story told about Athanasius' introduction to the school.

> The Bishop, on the anniversary of the martyrdom of his predecessor, Peter, was expecting some clergy to dinner after service in a house by the sea. Out of the window, he saw some boys at play on the shore: as he watched, he saw that they were imitating the sacred rites of the church. Thinking at last that they were going too far, he sent some of his clergy to bring them in. At first his enquiries of the little fellows produced an alarmed denial. But at length he elicited that one of them had acted the bishop and had baptized some of the others in the character of the catechumens. On ascertaining that all details had been duly observed, he consulted his clergy, and decided that the baptisms should be treated as valid, and that the boy-bishop and his clergy had given such plain proof of their vocation that their parents must be instructed to hand them over to be educated from the sacred profession. Young Athanasius accordingly, after a further course of elementary studies, was handed over to the bishop to be brought up, like Samuel, in the Temple of God.[9]

The reliability of this story is uncertain, but if nothing else, it points to the fact that Athanasius was from a very young age destined to serve the church.[10]

Athanasius was ordained a deacon in 319 while he was still in his early twenties. He accompanied Alexander to the Council of Nicea in 325. Although a witness to the council's deliberations, and serving as an advisor to his bishop, because he was a deacon, he did not have authority to vote on any issues.

9. Schaff, and Henry Wace, *Athanasius*, xiv.

10. Schaff, *History of the Christian Church*, 3:886.

Bishop of Alexandria

Alexander, the bishop of Alexandria died on April 17, 328. Athanasius suspecting that he would be installed as the next bishop fled to the desert to hide. He had no desire to hold such a high office in the church. Several weeks later he emerged from the desert and submitted to the wishes of the church to ordain him as bishop. Some argue that despite Athanasius' attempt to go into hiding, he actually desired the position and was behind the move to have himself appointed. Certainly, Alexander valued the great gifts of Athanasius and wanted him to be his successor. Athanasius was not yet thirty years of age and was considered too young to be elected bishop.[11] Whatever the case may be, Athanasius was appointed as bishop of Alexandria on June 8, 329, and remained in that position for the rest of his life.

When Athanasius became the bishop of Alexandria he did not retire into a picturesque, pastoral setting where he quietly cared for his flock. His days were not filled with enjoyable luncheons with parishioners or in hours of uninterrupted study. His pastoral career was filled with danger, exile, and theological dissension. The city of Alexandria was not a small hamlet, but a bustling city that attracted people from all over the empire. Rich and poor alike were drawn to the city because of the opportunities it provided for its inhabitants. The city was the seat of the central government for all of Egypt. It was a place filled with material wealth, as well as a wealth of new ideas. The port of the city was the door to trade with the Asian and African world and the imported goods from Africa, Ethiopia, India, and Sri Lanka would enter the Roman Empire through this harbor. Many of the goods that passed through Alexandria were crops like fruits, nuts, wheat, and papyrus which were used in the production of writing tablets.[12]

Because Alexandria was an influential city, the church in Alexandria was also influential. The bishop of the Alexandrian church held great sway over the wider church as seen in the sixth canon of the council of Nicaea:

> The bishop of Alexandria shall have jurisdiction over Egypt, Libya, and Pentapolis. As also the Roman bishop over those subject to Rome. So, too, the Bishop of Antioch and the rest over those who are under them. If any be a bishop contrary to the

11. *Encyclopedia of Ancient Christianity*, 1:274.

12. Petterson, *Athanasius*, 1–3.

judgment of the Metropolitan, let him be no bishop. Provided it
be in accordance with the cannons by the suffrage of the majority, if three object, their objection shall be of no force.[13]

It was not long after becoming the bishop that Athanasius was confronted with the growing threat of Arianism. Although Arius and other
Arian teachers were sent into exile after the council of Nicaea, they had
since returned and were freely teaching in the churches. Athanasius was
especially qualified to provide a rigorous response.

Athanasius was one of the great theologians of his generation, but
his theology was not what we might call "ivory tower theology." That is,
his theology was pastoral in nature and was hammered out on the an-
vil of theological controversy, not fine-tuned in the halls of theological
academia. As one historian wrote, "his interest is practical and religious
rather than speculative or academic."[14] Another said that Athanasius approached the mystery of Christ, "not as a theologian, but as a believing
soul in need of a Saviour."[15] His writings are saturated in Scripture and he
freely quoted from the Bible, often employing biblical imagery.[16] Because
Athanasius wrote in response to the pastoral concerns of his generation
and sought to deal with what he viewed as the heretical opinions of his
day, one will look in vain to find a systematic theology in his writings.[17]

Athanasius was fiercely devoted to the Nicene definition of the
Christian faith. Immediately after becoming bishop, he traveled throughout Egypt teaching and strengthening the churches and the monasteries
against both the Meletians[18] and the Arians. He spent his entire ministry
defending the Nicene Creed and fighting against those who were seeking doctrinal compromise with the Arians. Because he was such an able
defender of the Nicene position, he was considered the greatest threat
to the establishment of Arianism in the empire. For this reason, many
Arian bishops wanted him silenced and used their influence against him.
Because he refused to allow Arians into the church he was removed from

13. Schaff and Wace, *Seven Ecumenical Councils*, 14–15.

14. Gonzalez, *History of Christian Thought*, 293.

15. Robertson, "Introduction to St. Athanasius," NPNF, xiv.

16. Brogan, "Athanasius," *Dictionary of Major Biblical Interpreters*, 129.

17. Gonzalez, *Christian Thought*, 292.

18. The Meletians like the Novatianists, split from the church over the question of
the lapsed, and took a hard-line approach to those who lapsed in times of persecution.
See appendix 1 for a fuller definition of Meletians.

office in 335 and exiled to Trier, in Gaul, until the death of Emperor Constantine I in 337.

Constantine I was succeeded by his three sons, Constantine II, Constans, and Constantius, who divided the empire between them. During the reign of the three brothers, Athanasius was allowed to return to Alexandria and resume pastoral care over his flock. Not long after the political arrangement between the three brothers, Constantine II was killed in battle while attempting to gain control over Constans' territory. As a result of his death, Constans became the ruler over the entire western empire. Constans supported the Nicene Creed, while his brother Constantius who ruled in the east was pro-Arian. Eusebius, Bishop of Constantinople, and an Arian supporter called a Synod in Antioch in 339 which resulted in Athanasius being exiled a second time. He went to Rome where he spent seven years between 339 and 346. Even though he was exiled from Alexandria, the people of his congregation were devoted to him and Arianism was unable to make inroads into the Nicene community. Gonzalez wrote:

> Of all the opponents of Arianism Athanasius was most to be feared. The reasons for this were not to be found in subtlety of logical argument, nor in elegance of style, nor even in political perspicacity. In all these areas, Athanasius could be bested by his opponents. His strong suit was in his close ties to the people among whom he lived, and in living out his faith without the subtleties of the Arians or the pomp of so many bishops of other important sees. His monastic discipline, his roots among the people, his fiery spirit, and his profound and unshakable conviction made him invincible.[19]

In 343 Constans and Constantius called an ecumenical council to examine the accusations against Athanasius. He was declared innocent of all charges, and in 347 he returned to Alexandria.

In 353, Constantius II became the sole ruler of the Roman Empire. As emperor, Constantius sought a middle road between the Arians and the supporters of the Nicene Creed, but Athanasius would not agree. The emperor called a council in 353 that met at Arles, in Gaul, and another one in 355 in Milan, resulting in Athanasius being banished in 356 for the third time. He left Alexandria and went to live among the Monks in the desert.

---

19. Gonzalez, *Story of Christianity*, 174.

Constantius died in 361 and was succeeded by Julian. The new emperor was a pagan and did not care about promoting the prosperity of the church. Under his brief reign, Athanasius returned to Alexandria but this was to be short-lived. Within only a few brief months Julian had Athanasius exiled for the fourth time because of his success at winning pagans to Christ through his preaching. There is a humorous account of his departure:

> He bowed his head to the storm and prepared to leave Alexandria once more. His friends stood round lamenting their loss. "Be of good heart," he replied, "it is only a cloud, and will soon pass away." He took a Nile boat, and set off toward Upper Egypt, but finding that he was tracked by the government officers he directed the boat's course to be reversed. Presently they met that of the pursuers, who suspecting nothing asked for news of Athanasius. "He is not far off" was the answer, given according to one account by Athanasius himself.[20] Another account says that his reply to the question, "Have you seen Athanasius?" was "yes, he is just ahead of you, and if you hurry you shall overtake him." Soon the ship was far ahead of Athanasius.[21]

Emperor Julian died in 363 and Jovian became emperor. Even though the new emperor was a Christian, he was not interested in participating in church affairs. Under his reign, Athanasius was allowed to return from exile.

After the death of Jovian, Valentinian I became emperor and put his brother Valens in charge of the eastern portion of the empire. Valens supported the Arian cause and Athanasius was once again banished from Alexandria in 365. He was reinstated in 366 and spent the next seven years of his life serving his church in Alexandria until his death on May 2, 373.

Athanasius the writer

Athanasius was a prolific writer and most of his writing took place during the years he spent in exile. One of the greatest struggles in his life was the ongoing theological war against Arianism and the vast majority of his works were written in defense of the orthodox Nicene faith.

20. Schaff, "Athanasius," *Nicene and Post-Nicene Fathers*, 4:iix.
21. Schaff, "Athanasius," *Nicene and Post-Nicene Fathers*, 4:iix.

His importance is primarily in his Christological writings in which he defended the belief that God took on human flesh in the person of Jesus Christ. He emphasized the unity between the Father and the Son,[22] the divine nature of the Son,[23] and the Son as an uncreated being.[24][25] His writings helped to stop the forward advance of Arianism, ensuring victory for the Nicene faith.[26]

Athanasius identified three principles for the right interpretation of Scripture. First, the interpreter must be living a holy life. Second, the passage must be interpreted within its context. The interpreter needed to know the time, place, and purpose of a text if he was to understand it properly.

> When he was interpreting a biblical passage, Athanasius argued that it is imperative that the interpreter consider the "time" (pre-incarnation, incarnation or present glorification), the "person" (the pre-incarnate Son, the incarnate Word or the glorified Son) and the purpose (salvation) to which the biblical author is referring.[27]

Third, the passage must be interpreted in the light of the teaching of the "scope of Scripture." He meant by this, the theological unity of the Bible that was faithfully handed down by the church Fathers. He rejected the teaching of the Arians because he believed them to be unholy and irreligious men. They ignored the context of Scripture and they turned away from the teaching of the church Fathers. Because they disregarded these principles, they were unable to properly interpret the scriptures.[28]

His most famous and influential book is entitled *On the Incarnation* in which he laid out his basic theological position on the nature of Jesus Christ. Although this treatise is not directed specifically at the Arians, it is a clear defense of an orthodox Nicene understanding of the nature of the Son of God. His purpose in writing the book was to prove both the

22. Some of his favorite texts were (Matt 10:40; 11:27; 28:19; John 5:17, 23; 10:30, 38; 14:6, 9–10; 1 Cor 8:6).

23. (Matt 16:16; John 1:1, 14, 18:8:58; 10:33; 1 Cor 1:24; 2:8; Phil 2:6, 7; Heb 1:2–3; 13:8).

24. (John 1:3; 3:35; 16:15; 17:10; Rom 8:29; Col 1:16–17; Heb 1:4).

25. Brogan, "Athanasius," 130.

26. Ferguson, *Church History*, 206.

27. Brogan, "Athanasius," 132.

28. Brogan, "Athanasius," 131.

human and divine nature of the Word of God or as he put it, "the God Word." Athanasius believed that "the God Word" is of the same essence as the Father and existed from all eternity. He is coequal, coeternal, and consubstantial with the Father. This same eternal Word took on human flesh and died on behalf of sinful humanity that God might restore us to life. He wrote, "For since through human beings death had seized human beings, for this reason, again, through the incarnation of the God Word there occurred the dissolution of death and the resurrection of life…"[29] Through the death, burial, and resurrection of Jesus Christ, sinful men who turned away from God could once again know and have a relationship with him.

Athanasius identified two serious consequences of denying the deity of Jesus Christ. First, if Jesus was merely a creature it would be impossible for him to save human beings from their sin because it is impossible for one creature to save another. Athanasius believed that if Jesus was to secure salvation for his people, he must be divine. Second, the Christian church would be guilty of idolatry because Christians regularly worship Jesus Christ. If he is not God, to worship him would be the ultimate form of blasphemy. Athanasius wrote a letter to Bishop Adelphius of Onuphis in which he denied that Christians are guilty of idolatry when they worship Jesus:

> We do not worship a creature. Far be the thought. For such an error belongs to heathens and Arians. But we worship the Lord of Creation, Incarnate, the Word of God. For if the flesh also is in itself a part of the created world, yet it has become God's body. And we neither divide the body from the Word and worship it by itself, nor when we wish to worship the Word do we set Him far apart from the flesh. But knowing, as we said above, that "the Word was made flesh," we recognize Him also as God come in the flesh.[30]

Another very popular book of Athanasius was entitled the *Life of St. Antony*. Through this biography, he promoted monasticism, believing it to be one of the highest forms of Christian living. Athanasius held a high view of the ascetic life and spent a considerable amount of time living with the monks in the desert. We will look at the life of St. Antony in chapter twelve on monasticism.

29. Athanasius, *On the Incarnation*, 10.
30. Aquilina, *Fathers of the Church*, 155.

The importance of Athanasius in the defense of Nicene orthodoxy cannot be overstated. He almost singlehandedly stood against the overwhelming tide of Arianism that threatened the church during his day, and he has been rightly referred to as the "father of orthodoxy."[31] The fact that he was exiled five times demonstrates the fear that his influence engendered in the minds of the most powerful political and religious leaders of the early to mid-fourth century. His life is an ongoing example of faithful, sacrificial, and fearless service to the church of Jesus Christ.

Discussion Questions

1. How important is it to consult the early church Fathers when interpreting Scripture?

2. What can we learn from the stubborn refusal of Athanasius to compromise with the Arians?

3. What kind of pressures to compromise doctrine does the church experience today?

4. What kind of pressures to compromise do you experience in your personal life and ministry?

31. Schaff, *History of the Christian Church*, 3:886.

Chapter 12

The Monastic Movement

THE EARLY MONKS

"When we awaken each day, we should think that we shall not live till evening; and again, when about to go to sleep we should think that we shall not awaken."[1]—ANTONY

EMPEROR CONSTANTINE LEGALIZED CHRISTIANITY in 313 AD with the proclamation of the Edict of Milan. Because of this new legal status for the Christian faith, it became advantageous to be a member of the church. The church received a large influx of people at this time, not because they came to see the truth of the Christian faith but to gain the social and political advantages membership afforded. This rapid inflow of new members brought wealth, luxury, pomp, and greater power for the church. Church leaders began to live in large houses and their personal wealth and influence skyrocketed. Bishops became advisors to the emperor and Christians served in the most powerful offices in the Roman Empire. Many people considered this a new and wonderful day for the Christian church, while others believed it was spiritually devastating. The rapid growth of the church resulted in lukewarmness and compromise. Men sought leadership in the church, not because they loved the flock of God, but for the political clout they would enjoy. Devout Christians who were serious about following Jesus were distressed at the increased worldliness of the church and believed that a great apostasy was taking place. Monasticism arose in response to this situation.

1. Athanasius, *Life of St. Antony*, 36.

Monasticism was an ascetic movement that began in the late third and early fourth century AD. Ascetic monks lived a life of extreme self-denial, choosing not to participate in many legitimate pleasures including, marriage, having possessions, wealth, and other bodily comforts. Unlike Gnosticism, which taught all matter is evil, the early ascetics believed they were renouncing that which was good, for the sake of obtaining that which is better.[2] They did not believe that marriage, wealth, or food was inherently evil but were a hindrance in the pursuit of greater things. Many who embraced the monastic life withdrew from society to live as hermits in desert caves, or in communities with other men or women who embraced asceticism as the Christian ideal.

Paul of Thebes (c.226/227–c.341)

There is an ongoing debate about who the first monk was to take up the solitary monastic life. Jerome (342–420), who wrote a treatise on the life of Paul of Thebes said that Paul was the first man to become an ascetic monk. Athanasius (296–373) wrote the biography of Antony and claimed that Antony was the first solitary monk. While a definite answer is not likely, what we can say is that both Paul and Antony stood at the beginning of a movement that would change the face of Christianity up to the present.

Paul was born around 226 AD into a wealthy home. His parents died young, leaving him a large inheritance. He received good training and was educated in both Greek and Egyptian. When he was fifteen years of age during the persecution of Emperor Decius (249–251) and Emperor Valerian (253-260), he fled and went into hiding with his sister and her husband. However, his brother-in-law planned to betray Paul, so he went to the desert to hide and wait until the persecution subsided.[3] Unexpectedly, Paul embraced life in the desert, eventually making his way to a cave that was allegedly the site of a minting operation during the time of Marc Antony (83–33 BC) and Cleopatra (69–30 BC). Believing that God led him to this location, he took up residence there and committed himself to a life of prayer and ascetic living.[4]

---

2. Ferguson, *Church History*, 1:228.

3. *Life of Saint Paul of Thebes*, Chaper 4.

4. *Life of Saint Paul of Thebes*, Chapter 4.

When Paul was one hundred and thirteen years of age, Antony, who was also living in the desert at the time, came to visit him in his cave. There is a humorous story told about their first meal together:

> As they were speaking, they saw a raven coming to rest in the branches of the tree. It gently flew down and placed a whole loaf of bread before their wondering eyes before flying off again. How marvelous!" said Paul. "the kind and most merciful Lord for the last sixty years has been sending me half a loaf of bread. And now because of your coming He has sent His servants a double measure!" They gave thanks for the works of the Lord and sat down by the side of the sparkling spring. From then until evening time they had an argument about who should break the bread. Paul said that the guest should do so, Anthony said the elder should. At last they came to a compromise, that each should take hold of one end of the loaf and pull, with the result that each would have a portion of the loaf in his hands. Each of them then drank a little water lying face downwards, after which they spent the night in a vigil, offering God the sacrifice of praise.[5]

Paul was an old man and he knew that his death was imminent. He asked Antony to go and fetch a cloak that was given to him by Athanasius. He wanted to be wrapped in the cloak and buried in it after he died. While Antony was gone, Paul passed away and when Antony came back to the cave, he saw the dead man on his knees with his hands stretched out as though he was praying. Antony wrapped his body in the cloak and dragged the lifeless corpse out of the cave. He did not have a shovel and wondered how he was going to bury the body. Allegedly, two lions showed up, and pawing at the earth they dug a hole large enough for the body. After the lions departed, Antony buried Paul. The life of Paul ends with these challenging words:

> To conclude this little work, let me ask those who do not know the extent of their inheritance, who live in marble halls, and who make sure that an only son will benefit from all their wealth, whether this geronda (Spiritual leader) ever lacked anything in his nakedness. You drink from precious goblets, he was satisfied with his cupped hands, you wear tunics of golden thread, his clothing was rougher than that of your meanest slave. But to him in his deepest poverty the gates of paradise were opened, you with your gold will inherit hell. He, naked, was clothed with

5. *Life of Saint Paul of Thebes*, Chapter 9.

Christ, you in your silks have lost Christ's covering. Paul, buried in barren dust, will rise again in glory, you vaunting yourselves in sumptuous tombs, will burn with all your works. I beg you, share, share out at least some of your cherished riches. Why are your dead entombed in golden shrouds? How is it that your ambition is not slaked even in midst of the tears of mourning? Do you imagine that the bodies of the dead will not rot if wrapped in silk? Whoever you are that reads this story, I beg that you will remember Jerome, a sinner, who if the Lord were to give him a choice, would much prefer the tunic of Paul with all its merit than the purple of kings and their kingdoms.[6]

Whether or not the story of Paul of Thebes is entirely true (it is difficult to believe that the two "grave-digging lions,"[7] is a credible account) is not the point. If nothing else the story illustrates the simple faith and ascetic living of the early solitary monks. They lived in caves, ate simple food, wore rough clothing, denied themselves all earthly pleasure, and spent much of their time in prayer and meditation. As difficult as this kind of life was, Paul was the first of a growing number of men and women who saw desert living as the only real choice in the face of a corrupt and compromised church.

Antony

The *Life of Antony* is a remarkable book and if even half of what is told of Antony is true, one would conclude that he was an outstanding Christian man. Athanasius held Antony in high regard and considered that "for monks the life of Antony is an ideal pattern of the ascetical life."[8] Athanasius knew Antony well, was familiar with his lifestyle, and was thus well suited to write his biography.

Antony was of Egyptian descent and enjoyed the privileges of being raised in a wealthy, Christian family. He was taught the Christian faith from his youth and appears to have been a good student who was obedient to his parents. Although surrounded by affluence, Antony preferred a simple life, content with what was given to him. Antony's parents died when he was between eighteen and twenty years of age, leaving him with the responsibility of caring for his sister. Not long after the death of

6. *Life of Saint Paul of Thebes*, Chapter 14.

7. Schaff, *History of the Christian Church*, 3:181.

8. Athanasius, *Life of St. Antony*, 10, 17.

his parents, he was walking to church and meditating on Acts 4:34–35, "There was not a needy person among them, for as many as were owners of lands or houses sold them and brought the proceeds of what was sold and laid it at the apostles' feet, and it was distributed to each as any had need" (ESV). He was impressed with the early church's practice of selling one's goods and bringing the money to the apostles for distribution to the needy. He was also impressed with the willingness of the apostles to leave all that they owned and follow the Saviour. Upon arriving and entering the church, he heard Matt 19:21 being read, "If you would be perfect, go, sell what you possess and give to the poor, and you will have treasure in heaven; and come, follow me." Believing this to be a direct message from God, he immediately gave away his sizable farm and wealth, keeping only enough to care for the physical needs of his sister. On another occasion while he was attending church, he heard the words of Matt 6:34, "Therefore do not be anxious about tomorrow, for tomorrow will be anxious for itself. Sufficient for the day is its own trouble." In response to this scripture, he gave away the rest of his money and put his sister in a convent to be cared for. His sister remained a virgin for her entire life, eventually becoming a leader among the other women.

At first, Antony began to live outside the village not far from his house and sought to develop a life of rigid discipline. He continued working to provide food for himself and to make enough money to give to people in need. He often prayed and visited godly men to receive advice on how to live a spiritual life. He sought to incorporate into his life the best of what he saw in other men. The local villagers were impressed with Antony's commitment to the spiritual life, calling him "God's Friend."[9] Although Antony was determined to live an ascetic life he was often tempted to forsake his new life and return to his former one. Referring to the devil's temptations Athanasius wrote, "he tried to make him desert the ascetic life by putting him in mind of his property, the care of his sister, the attachments of kindred, the love of money, the love of fame, the myriad pleasures of eating, and all the other amenities of life."[10] He also claimed that the devil tempted him in various other ways even taking on the shape of a woman in an attempt to lead him astray. The spirit of lust is said to have appeared to him in the form of a boy and spoke to him in a human voice. Despite these temptations, Antony remained steadfast in

9. Athanasius, *Life of St. Antony*, 4.

10. Athanasius, *Life of St. Antony*, 5.

his determination to live the life of a hermit. Recognizing the danger of temptation Antony determined to live an even stricter life by denying himself all luxurious food, sweet drinks, and regular sleep. When he did sleep, he slept on a mat or the ground. He ate once a day and sometimes he ate every other day or even every third or fourth day. His diet consisted of bread, salt, and water. He would not indulge any bodily pleasure but sought to live a life of complete simplicity and solitude. He prayed, fasted, and filled his mind with thoughts of Christ and holy things. Athanasius wrote,

> The enemy would suggest filthy thoughts, but the other would dissipate them by his prayers; he would try to incite him to lust, but Antony, sensing shame, would gird his body with his faith, with his prayers and his fasting. The wretched Devil even dared to masquerade as a woman by night and to impersonate such in every possible way, merely in order to deceive Antony. But he filled his thoughts with Christ and reflected upon the nobility of the soul that comes from Him, and its spirituality, and thus quenched the glowing coal of temptation."[11]

In his battle against temptation, Antony moved further away from his village and had himself locked in a tomb. He arranged to have food delivered to him by a friend every few days. While living in the tomb Antony claimed that he was attacked by the devil with great severity. He spoke of demons appearing in the form of animals to frighten him from his chosen path. He recalled:

> All at once the place was filled with the phantoms of lions, bears, leopards, bulls, and of serpents, asps, and scorpions, and of wolves; and each moved according to the shape it had assumed. The lion roared, ready to spring upon him, the bull appeared about to gore him through, the serpent writhed without quite reaching him, the wolf was rushing straight at him; and the noises emitted simultaneously by all the apparitions were frightful and the fury shown was fierce.[12]

Immediately following this terrible struggle Antony received a vision from the Lord and a promise of help and support in his struggle against the enemy.

11. Athanasius, *Life of Antony*, 5.
12. Athanasius, *Life of Antony*, 9.

When he was around thirty-five years of age, Antony left his tomb and went to the mountains, to find a more secluded place in which to live. He claimed that while traveling through the desert the devil tempted him with physical manifestations of silver and gold placed on the path in front of him. He resisted these temptations and eventually found an old fort in which he took up residence. He refused to see or meet with anyone but had bread lowered into his chamber from time to time by a trusted friend. It is said that he was tormented by demons while in that place, but God gave him the strength to overcome them. After nearly twenty years of living as a solitary monk, he came out of the fortress and began teaching and healing people of their sicknesses. He taught the people to call upon Christ and serve him rather than the things of this world. His influence was so great that many people chose to abandon the world and become hermits. The mountains and the deserts were now filled with monks and Antony was considered their father and shepherd. They would sometimes gather together in the same place and ask Antony to teach them, which he was more than willing to do. On one occasion, he exhorted his fellow monks:

> So, children, let us not grow weary nor think that we are toiling a long time or that we are doing something great. For the sufferings of this present time are not worthy to be compared with the glory to come that shall be revealed to us. Neither let us look back upon the world and think that we have renounced great things. For even the whole world is a very trifling thing compared with all of Heaven. Accordingly, if we should be lords of the whole earth and renounced the whole earth, this would again mean nothing as compared with the Kingdom of Heaven… therefore, let none of us have even the desire to possess riches. For what does it avail us to possess what we cannot take with us? Why not rather possess those things which we can take along with us—prudence, justice, temperance, fortitude, understanding, charity, love of the poor, faith in Christ, meekness, hospitality? Once we possess these we shall find them going before us, preparing a welcome for us in the land of the meek.[13]

With similar words on other occasions, he encouraged his brethren in their pursuit of the ascetic life.

Although Antony preferred solitary desert life, he did come out of hiding when it was in the best interest of the church to do so. During the

13. Athanasius, *Life of Antony*, 17.

persecution under Emperor Maximinus (r. 235–38), he travelled to the city of Alexandria to comfort and encourage those being oppressed. He went into the courtroom and publicly supported the accused who stood before the judge. He walked with the condemned Christians as they were taken out to be martyred, and remained with them until their execution. The judge was disturbed by the boldness of the monks and ordered that no monk was allowed in the courtroom or the city. Antony ignored the order and fearlessly showed up at court the day after the order was given. He must have been a sight to behold. Not only was he a legend in the minds of the people, but many of them had never seen him before. They only knew him through the many stories that were told about the allusive holy man who lived alone in the wilderness. His clothing was a hairy dress, his visage was emaciated, and his untamed, ethereal presence would have left a deep and lasting impression on the people. Antony was hoping to be arrested and martyred for the faith but was disappointed when this did not happen. So, when the persecution ended, he went back to live in his solitary cell in the wilderness. He continued to live the life of self-denial and described his daily practices as follows:

> He fasted continually, his clothing was hair on the inside while the outside was skin, and this he kept to his dying day. He never bathed his body in water to remove filth, nor did he as much as wash his feet or even allow himself to put them in water without necessity. No one ever saw him undressed, nor did anyone ever look upon his bare body till he died and was buried.[14]

People continued coming to Antony seeking prayer and healing. He is credited with having performed many miraculous healings, but he was unhappy that he was not left alone to pursue his life of solitude. He went further into the desert to live in a very secluded area. He found a place on a mountain that had clean water and few date palms. He also received bread from the occasional traveller. He continued to struggle against the powers of darkness, but they were unable to turn him away from his life as a monk. As always, people sought him out in the desert and he was obligated to speak with them. He would give the same message to every monk who found him:

> To place their confidence in the Lord and to love Him, to keep themselves from bad thoughts and pleasures of the flesh, and not to be seduced by a full stomach, as is written in Proverbs.

14. Athanasius, *Life of Antony*, 47.

They should flee conceit and pray continually, sing Psalms before sleeping and after, commit to heart the commandments enjoined in the Scriptures, and hark back to the deeds of the saints, that the soul by keeping in mind the commandments might train itself on the example of their zeal.[15]

Antony appears to have been a gracious man with an agreeable personality but he refused to have fellowship with heretics in the church. He spoke against the Meletian schismatics, Manichaeans, and especially the Arian heresy which "was the worst of all and a forerunner of the Antichrist."[16] He believed that fellowship with those who held to any of these opinions would be harmful to the soul. Some of his final words before he died were, "do not go near the Meletian schismatics, for you know their wicked and unholy teaching. Have nothing to do with the Arians, for the irreligion of these is plain to everyone."[17] On one occasion, the Arians said that Antony held the same views as they did, so he came down from his mountain and appeared before the bishops of the church to set the record straight. He publicly denounced the teaching of the Arians and reaffirmed his belief in the deity of Jesus Christ. Antony believed that Arians were not Christians and their teaching was a lie of the devil. He wrote, "only defile not yourselves with the Arians. This their teaching is not of the Apostles, but of the demons and their father, the Devil. Indeed, it is sterile and unreasonable, and it lacks right sense—like the senselessness of mules."[18] This delighted the people and the entire city of Alexandria came to see Antony. More people were converted to Christianity in a few short days than in an entire year of regular ministry. Shortly thereafter he went back to his home in the mountain.

His view of not remaining too long with others could be summed up with a simile he used when speaking with a military general. "Just as fish exposed for any length of time on dry land die, so monks go to pieces when they loiter among you and spend too much time with you. Therefore, we must [go] off to the mountain as fish to the sea. Otherwise, if we tarry, we may lose sight of the inner life."[19] Although he desired solitude, he often left his mountain home to teach the humble, rebuke the

15. Athanasius, *Life of Antony*, 52.

16. Athanasius, *Life of Antony*, 69.

17. Athanasius, *Life of Antony*, 89.

18. Athanasius, *Life of Antony*, 82.

19. Athanasius, *Life of Antony*, 85.

proud, and defend the innocent. Antony's fame was legendary. Philosophers sought him out in the wilderness. Christian emperors wrote him letters seeking a reply. Judges listened to his wisdom. Scores of ordinary people went to him for healing and young and old men alike wanted him to teach them the ascetic life. Through his influence hundreds, even thousands of monk cells were established in the desert.

Antony lived a long and fruitful life, dying at one hundred and four years of age. He was afraid that after he died, his body would be wrapped and placed in an ornate tomb and given great honour so he instructed the two monks who were staying with him in the latter years of his life to take his body and bury it in a hidden place. Some of his final words were "Live as though dying daily." He died shortly thereafter and, as requested, was buried in an unmarked grave.

Pachomius (292–348)

Pachomius was the first monk to establish a communal monastery and through his influence the monastic movement continued to change and grow. While he possessed a deep appreciation for the solitary life, he believed that he was called by God to establish a place where men could serve God together with a less demanding form of asceticism than what was practiced by the solitary monks.

Pachomius was an Egyptian who was raised in a pagan home. From his youth, he adopted a rigorous lifestyle and committed himself to regular fasting. His parents were pagans who took their son to the idol sacrifices and made sure that he was educated in Egyptian wisdom. At twenty years of age (c.312 AD) he was conscripted into the army and sent away to serve the martial concerns of the empire. As a new recruit, he was treated poorly, sometimes not even having enough to eat and drink. On one occasion some local people took pity on him and his companions and brought them food and water. He found out that they were Christians and he was strangely attracted to their teaching and way of life. When he was alone, he prayed to God:

> "O Almighty God, Who made heaven and earth," he said, "if Thou wilt hearken to my prayer and show me how to order my life according to Thy holy name, and free me from my oppressive shackles, then I pledge myself to Thy service all the days

of my life. I will turn my back on the world and cleave only to Thee."[20]

From this moment on he sought to live a holy life, resisting the worldly temptations that he faced as a soldier.

After he was released from the military, he went to the village of Chinoboscium where he became a catechumen and was baptized. He gave himself fully to the Christian life and was determined to live his life as a monk. He heard about a man named Palaemon who lived in a remote part of the desert, so he went and asked if he could live with him and learn the ascetic life. Palaemon at first resisted, but sensing the sincerity of Pachomius he welcomed him and taught him the life of abstinence and prayer. They also worked together weaving baskets to make money to meet their own needs and the needs of others. Their diet was made up of bread, salt, and water.

After a while, Pachomius went to a small town called Tabennisi in upper Egypt. In response to a vision he received from the Lord, he established a monastery in that place. Palaemon joined him and made a pact that they would never leave one another as long as they lived. Not long after this pact was made, Palaemon, who had wasted away because of his meager diet died, leaving Pachomius to pursue the life of asceticism alone.

After the death of his fellow ascetic, Pachomius' brother came and joined him in Tabennisi. He and his brother expanded the building they were living in and built other dwelling places to accommodate the men who they believed would come to live with them. Not long after, his brother died and he was alone again. Later, another man named Hieracapolon came to him and encouraged his heart. Sadly, he too died and Pachomius was alone once more. And yet, he was not discouraged in his pursuit of a holy life but continued to grow in confidence and dedication to the ascetic life.

After a time, others began to arrive at the monastery and were welcomed into the growing community of monks. The rules that governed their lives were reasonable, allowing for sufficient food, drink, rest, work, friendship, and prayer. Although life in the monastery was rigorous and demanding, it was more comfortable than the life of a solitary monk. Monks who struggled with physical infirmities were required to do less work, while those who were stronger were expected to do more.

20. Baker, trans., *Life of Saint Pachomius*, Chapter 4.

Pachomius, like Antony, detested heretics and he was particularly disgusted with Origen who he believed to be "a blasphemous traitor." His biography says:

> Just as poisoners disguise a bitter taste with honey, so did Origen bedaub the poison of his erroneous opinions with a most heavenly ability to write well, and so disseminated his pernicious doctrines among those who did not know any better. So Pachomius was careful to warn all the brothers not merely to refrain from reading any of Origen's commentaries, but also to pay no heed to anyone who had read them. It is said, that on one occasion he picked up a volume of Origen's and threw it into the river. If it weren't for the fact that I know that it contains the holy Name of God," he said as he did so, "I would have consigned all those outpourings of blasphemy to the flames!"[21]

On another occasion, while speaking with some church leaders who read Origen's works, he said:

> Before God I say to you that anyone who reads Origen and agrees with his depraved opinions will be sent to the lowest parts of Hell, where his inheritance will be worms and outer darkness, where the souls of the wicked suffer eternal punishment...cast all the books of Origen in the river lest you be cast into the river of fire.[22]

While it is true that the writings of Origen contain some very serious theological errors that should be condemned,[23] modern scholars tend to be a bit more gracious in their opinion of his contribution to Christian thought.

The fame of Pachomius continued to spread far and wide and many sick people came to him seeking prayer and healing. It is alleged that he healed people of various illnesses, cast out demons, and performed other wonders by the power of the Holy Spirit. Many men and women were helped through the ministry of Pachomius and he was instrumental in establishing other monasteries and did much to promote the monastic

---

21. Baker, trans., *Life of Saint Pachomius*, Chapter 25.

22. Baker, trans., *Life of Saint Pachomius*, Chapter 42.

23. For example, Origen believed in the pre-existence of souls and in universal salvation. He also taught that Satan and his host of demons would be saved in the end. While Origen affirmed the divine nature of Christ, his views on the "eternal generation" of the Son led some who came after him to reject of deity of Christ and the Triune nature of God. Many believe that Arianism is the fruit of his views in this matter.

life. Two days before Pachomius died he spoke some final words to his fellow monks:

> Beloved brothers, I am about to enter into the path the Fathers have trodden before me, for I hear the Lord calling me hence. But you, remember all the teachings you have heard from me again and again. Be watchful in prayer and sober in all you do. Have nothing to do with the sects of Meletius, Arius, Origen, or any others who set themselves up against the precepts of Christ. Keep to the company of those who fear the Lord and are able to assist you in pursuit of a holy life and provide your souls with spiritual comfort. I am now ready to be delivered, and the time of my departure is at hand (2 Tim.4:6).[24]

He died on May 9, 348 and his disciples buried him in the mountain where he first began his monastic journey.

Conclusion

There are a few important observations to be made about early Monasticism. First, some people might think that the early monks were biblically illiterate, but this was not always the case. Many of the monks were orthodox men who understood and affirmed the Nicene creed and were able to clearly articulate it. Antony was a man who saturated himself in the scriptures. Athanasius wrote, "he was so attentive at the reading of the Scripture lessons that nothing escaped him: he retained everything and so his memory served him in place of books."[25] After the conversion of Pachomius, it is said that "from then on he was inflamed with desire for God and pierced by the saving dart of divine love, which impelled him to give himself entirely to the disciplines and precepts of God."[26] Both Antony and Pachomius came out of the desert from time to time to defend the Christian faith against the heretics and they were committed to helping their followers to understand the Christian message, as they understood it. Their lives were extreme and at some points misguided, but many of these men were genuine believers who were committed to living a life for God and in service to his people. Second, the visions and trances

---

24. Baker, trans., *Life of Saint Pachomius*, Chapter 51.

25. Athanasius, *Life of St. Antony*, 3.

26. Baker, trans., *Life of Saint Pachomius*, Chapter 6.

experienced by the desert monks are interpreted in different ways. Some argue that these were the product of extreme deprivation. One historian wrote:

> The prolonged loneliness and the shortage of food and sleep fostered hallucinations as well as growth in spiritual awareness of God...Many of the visions, trances and strange experiences of the desert hermits have obvious psychological explanations (for example, the appearance of the devil as a seductive woman could be the result of repressed sexual feelings).[27]

Schaff, the great church historian, held a similar view:

> The monastic demonology and demonomachy is a strange mixture of gross superstitions and deep spiritual experiences. It forms the romantic shady side of the otherwise so tedious monotony of the secluded life, and contains much material for the history of ethics, psychology, and pathology.[28]

Others are convinced that these were genuine divine and Satanic experiences and that the visions and trances cannot be explained away on psychological grounds alone. Third, while a person might admire the incredible resolve needed to live the life of an ascetic, there is no biblical example to support the solitary monastic life. Elijah and John the Baptist are often cited as examples, but there is no reason to believe that either of these men went into the desert, lived alone, sustaining themselves on a diet of water, salt and bread, and cutting themselves off from human contact and interaction with the world around them. Although Jesus spent time alone to commune with his Father, and on at least one occasion he spent forty days in the desert alone, he is more often seen eating and drinking in the homes of friends, family, and others. Both men and women traveled with Jesus as he preached the gospel and he enjoyed good and pure relationships with both men and women. Most of the apostles had wives and children, and they spent their lives preaching the gospel and establishing Christian communities throughout the Roman empire. There are no examples in the New Testament, that would support the extreme lifestyle adopted by the early ascetics. The Christian life is lived out in the context of community. The church is described as

---

27. Smith, "Christian Ascetics and Monks," *Eerdmans' Handbook to the History of Christianity*, 205–6.

28. Schaff, *History of the Christian Church*, 3:170.

a body made up of many parts and each of those parts has a role to play within the body of Christ. Schaff sums it up nicely:

> There is more virtue in the temperate and thankful enjoyment of the gifts of God, than in total abstinence; in charitable and well-seasoned speech, than in total silence; in connubial chastity, than in celibacy; in self-denying practical labor for the church, than in solitary asceticism, which only pleases self and profits no one else.[29]

Discussion Questions

1. Were the monks right to retreat to the desert to live out their Christian lives?

2. How do you interpret the following verses: Acts 4:34–35; Matt 19:21; Matt 6:34?

3. What can we learn from the devotion of these early monks?

4. How would you interpret the visions, temptations, and dreams of the solitary monks?

5. Is the monastic life a legitimate form of the Christian life?

6. Read the following passages: 1 Tim 4:1–5; Col 2:16–19; 1 Cor 7:32–40. What do these passages teach about the ascetic life?

7. Are Elijah, Elisha, and John the Baptist examples of the ascetic life? Is it right to pattern the Christian life on the lives of these men?

---

29. Schaff, *History of the Christian Church*, 3:172.

Chapter 13

The Monastic Movement

TWO GREAT MONASTICS

Before the rising of the sun, they rise, hale and sober, sing as with one mouth hymns to the praise of God, then bow the knee in prayer, under the direction of the abbot, read the holy Scriptures, and go to their labors; pray again at nine, twelve, and three o'clock; after a good day's work, enjoy a simple meal of bread and salt, perhaps with oil, and sometimes with pulse; sing a thanksgiving hymn, and lay themselves on their pallets of straw without care, grief, or murmur. When one dies, they say: 'he is perfected;' and all pray God for a like end, that they also may come to the eternal sabbath-rest, and to the vision of Christ."[1]—(Chrysostom describing the life of fourth-century monks living in Antioch)

Basil of Caesarea[2]
(c.330–379 AD)

BASIL WAS BORN IN Caesarea in Cappadocia in eastern Asia Minor in 330 AD, into a wealthy and deeply religious family. He came into the world only four years before the city of Constantinople was proclaimed the new capital of the Roman Empire and seventeen years after Christianity was declared a legal religion. He was born five years after the Council of Nicaea produced the famous Nicene Creed, but before the creed enjoyed

---

1. Schaff, *History of the Christian Church*, 3:169.
2. Also known as "Basil the Great."

166

widespread acceptance in the church. The Arian controversy began in 319, only ten years before his birth, and Basil would spend a good portion of his life defending the Nicene faith against it. Needless to say, Basil was born during a time of significant theological and political upheaval.[3]

Basil trained in rhetoric, literature, mathematics, and philosophy as a young man, studying at Caesarea, then Constantinople and Athens. He was also taught the Christian faith by his devout grandmother, Macrina, a woman held in high regard throughout the Christian community. His education would ensure that he would enjoy a long and lucrative career as a teacher. While studying in Athens, he met Gregory of Nazianzus (330–389), who became a lifelong friend. They were known for "their diligence and success in work; their stainless and devout life; and their close mutual affection. Everything was common to them. They were as one soul."[4] Basil, his younger brother Gregory of Nyssa (ca. 320–95), and Gregory of Nazianzus are known as the Cappadocian Fathers and were great defenders of God's Triune nature and the Nicene faith.

Basil left Athens after completing his studies and returned to Caesarea in 356 to begin his teaching career. Under the influence of his sister Macrina, he underwent a spiritual transformation and was determined to abandon his teaching vocation and commit himself to the ascetic life. After making this decision, he was distressed over the years he spent studying pagan literature. He wrote:

> Much time had I spent in vanity, and had wasted nearly all my youth in the vain labour which I underwent in acquiring the wisdom made foolish by God. Then once upon a time, like a man roused from deep sleep, I turned my eyes to the marvellous light of the truth of the Gospel, and I perceived the uselessness of "the wisdom of the princes of this world, that come to naught." I wept many tears over my miserable life, and I prayed that guidance might be vouchsafed me to admit me to the doctrines of true religion.[5]

Although Basil mourned his classical education, his early training prepared him for his future work as a pastor and teacher. Having been trained in rhetoric, he was thoroughly equipped to preach the gospel with eloquence and power. It also helped him to become an effective writer.

3. Schaff, *History of the Christian Church*, 8:xiv.

4. Schaff, *Prolegomena*, xv.

5. Basil, Letter 223.2.

After his father died in 358, Basil abandoned his career ambitions, was baptized, and committed himself to the ascetic life. After spending a short time in Syria and Egypt visiting different ascetics and monastic communities, he took up residence in Annesi near Neocaesarea in Pontus and became a hermit. At some point, his brother Gregory of Nyssa and their friend Gregory of Nazianzus came to live with him, and they founded a monastic community. Basil went on to establish cenobitic[6] monastic communities for both men and women throughout Cappadocia. He also developed the monastic rule that would become the standard for monastic living throughout the eastern church.

Basil did not stay long in the monastery but went back to Caesarea, where he was ordained in 364 and appointed bishop in 370. When he was ordained, Valens was emperor of the Roman Empire and fully supported the Arian cause. Basil, on the other hand, was theologically orthodox and held to the Nicene Creed. He provided strong and effective leadership against Arianism and persuaded many church leaders and laymen to embrace the Nicene faith. It was only a matter of time before these two influential men entered into conflict with one another. The emperor was unhappy with Basil's influence and sought to have him removed from office but could not do so because of the popularity of Basil's ministry. It is striking that Basil's power and influence were so great that even the emperor did not have the courage to remove him from office. There is an interesting story told about Basil and the emperor. The emperor commanded that Basil be brought to Antioch, questioned by the prefect, and urged to accept the emperor's faith. Basil refused to change his theological position and was imprisoned. While he was in prison, the emperor's child became sick. Dominica, the child's mother, went to the emperor and told him that she believed the sickness was a chastisement from God for how poorly Basil was treated. The emperor sent for Basil, and the conversation between them went as follows:

> The emperor after a little reflection sent for Basil, and in order to prove his faith said to him, "If the doctrine you maintain is the truth, pray that my son may not die." "If your majesty should believe as I do," replied Basil, "and the church should be unified, the child shall live." To these conditions the emperor would not agree: "God's will concerning the child will be done then," said

6. "Cenobitic" is a monastic tradition that emphasised community life.

Basil; as Basil said this the emperor ordered him to be dismissed; the child, however, died shortly after.[7]

The emperor believed that the death of his son was God's punishment upon him, and from that day forward, he left Basil alone. Basil's refusal to pray for the emperor's son illustrates his absolute commitment to the Nicene faith and his unwillingness to give any ground to the Arian cause. This resolve is seen in his response to the prefect's death threat if Basil did not embrace the emperor's faith. He said:

> My determination will be the same to-morrow as it is to-day; for since I am a creature I can never be induced to worship that which is similar to myself and worship it as God; neither will I conform to your religion, nor to that of the emperor. Although your distinction may be great, and although you have the honor of ruling no inconsiderable portion of the empire, yet I ought not on these accounts to seek to please men, and, at the same time, belittle that Divine faith which neither loss of goods, nor exile, nor condemnation to death would ever impel me to betray.[8]

Basil continued his struggle against Arianism until he died in 379. In 381, only two years after his death, the church fully embraced the Nicene faith at the Council of Constantinople, and Arianism rapidly declined in influence. The Council also expanded and revised the Apostles' Creed to include a fuller definition of the Holy Spirit. The Constantinopolitan Creed is as follows:

> We believe in one God, the Father Almighty, Maker of heaven and earth, and of all things visible and invisible; And in one Lord Jesus Christ, the Son of God, the Only-begotten, Begotten of the Father before all ages, Light of Light, Very God of Very God, Begotten, not made; of one essence with the Father; by whom all things were made: Who for us men and for our salvation came down from heaven, and was incarnate of the Holy Spirit and the Virgin Mary, and was made man; And was crucified also for us under Pontius Pilate, and suffered and was buried; And the third day He rose again, according to the scriptures; And ascended into heaven, and sits at the right hand of the Father; And He shall come again with glory to judge the living and the dead, Whose kingdom shall have no end. And we believe in the

7. Socrates, *Ecclesiastical History*, 4.26.

8. Sozomen, *Ecclesiastical History of Sozomen*, xvi.

> Holy Spirit, the Lord, and Giver of Life, Who proceeds from the Father, Who with the Father and the Son together is worshipped and glorified, Who spoke by the Prophets; And we believe in one, holy, catholic, and apostolic Church. We acknowledge one Baptism for the remission of sins. We look for the Resurrection of the dead, And the Life of the age to come. Amen.[9]

Basil was a striking character, and he carried himself with confidence and determination. Schaff described him as he would have looked in middle age:

> He was now in the ripe prime of life, but bore marks of premature age. Upright in carriage, of commanding stature, thin, with brown hair and eyes, and long beard, slightly bald, with bent brow, high cheek bones, and smooth skin, he would shew in every tone and gesture at once his high birth and breeding, the supreme culture that comes of intercourse with the noblest of books and of men, and the dignity of a mind made up and of a heart of single purpose.[10]

Basil was the central figure in eastern monasticism, and his rules for monastic living are still followed by the Eastern Orthodox Church today. Although Pachomius was the first monk to establish monastic communities, his monasteries were loosely connected to the church, and the abbot possessed ultimate authority within the monastery. Basil's monasteries were less independent, and he made sure that they functioned in cooperation with the broader church community. The local bishop, not the abbot, possessed supreme authority in the monastery. Basil believed that a person could only obey the commandment of Christ in relationship with other people and viewed solitary monasticism as an inferior form of Christian living. He wrote, "caves and rocks are always ready for us, but the help we get from our fellow man is not always at hand."[11] Believing that the monastery should be the center of social care and evangelism, he emphasized the responsibility of the monks to care for strangers, the sick, and the poor. He often wrote on social justice, in which he argued for the rights of the poor. He rebuked the rich for their love of money and mercilessly condemned them for their lack of concern for the underprivileged. When preaching on Matthew 19:16–22, he said:

9. *Orthodox Wiki,* "Nicene-Constantinopolitan Creed."
10. Schaff, *Prolegomena,* xxiv.
11. Basil, Letter 150.4.

Tell me, what better service do silver-encrusted tables and chairs or ivory-inlaid beds and couches provide than their simpler counterparts? Yet for their sake the rich do not respond to the poor, not though thousands should come to their door crying with piteous voices. Indeed, you refuse to give anything, insisting that it is impossible to satisfy the needs of those who beg of you. You profess this to be true with your tongue, but your hand gives you the lie; silently, your hand bears witness to the falsehood, flashing as it does with the jewels from your ring. How many could you have delivered from want with but a single ring from your finger? How many households fallen into destitution might you have raised? In just one of your closets there are enough clothes to cover an entire town shivering with cold. You showed no mercy; it will not be shown to you. You opened not your house; you will be expelled from the Kingdom. You gave not your bread; you will not receive eternal life.[12]

Basil practiced what he preached. When he was the Bishop of Caesarea, he constructed a hospital, a school, and a program to help relieve the suffering of the poor.[13] He preached multiple sermons against hoarding money and warned those guilty of materialism that God would severely judge them for their greed.

While Basil is known for his love for the poor, he was equally, if not more concerned with people's spiritual lives. He often preached and wrote on Christian ethics, doctrine, and lifestyle, seeking to instruct the people of God in holy living. He preached practical sermons addressing issues like anger, humility, fasting, and self-denial. He also preached doctrinal sermons covering topics like the Trinity, faith, the Holy Spirit, humanity, sin, evil, and the holiness of God. He also refuted error and wrote against Sabellians, Anomoeans, and the Pneumatomachians.[14]

Above all, Basil was a pastor. His writings are not as theological as his friend Gregory of Nazianzus but are no less profound. Along with Apollinaris (310–90), bishop of Laodicea, Athanasius, the bishop of Alexandria, and Gregory of Nazianzus, he was instrumental in the final demise of Arianism.[15] He wrote more on the doctrine of the Holy Spirit than any previous writer and made a crucial contribution to the

12. St. Basil the Great, *On Social Justice*, 49.

13. Smith, *Basil the Great*, 71.

14. See appendix 1 for definitions of Sabellians, Anomoeans, and Pneumatomachians.

15. Sozomen, *Ecclesiastical History of Sozomen*, 6.22.

development of the doctrine of the Trinity.[16] He also assisted in putting monasticism on a solid footing, helping to remove some of the harsher elements associated with it. Basil of Caesarea certainly does merit the title, Basil the Great.

Jerome (c. 342–420 AD)

Jerome was born around 342 AD in the town of Stridon, located in the Roman province of Dalmatia (modern Croatia). His family were land-owners and appear to have been relatively wealthy. When he was around twelve years old, his parents sent him to Rome, where he studied under a famous grammarian named Aelius Donatus. After he completed his studies with Donatus, he went to a Roman school of rhetoric. Jerome excelled in his studies and was well on his way to enjoying a successful political career. He was baptized while he lived in Rome.

Although little is known about Jerome's early life, it appears he left Rome around 367 to seek his fortune in Trier, Germany. At this time, under unknown circumstances, he came under the spell of the monastic ideal. He became convinced that asceticism was the most excellent form of Christian living. He went to Italy, joined an ascetic group in Aquileia, and spent much of his time recopying the writings of Tertullian, Cyprian, and Hilary.[17] In 373, Jerome left Aquileia and went to Antioch to continue his studies. While there, he had a dream in which the Lord told him, "You are a Ciceronian, not a Christian." He took this as a message from the Lord, abandoned his study of pagan literature, and retreated to the Syrian desert to become a monk. It appears that Jerome may have participated in sexual sin as a student, and retreating to the desert did not enable him to rid his heart of sexual temptation. He wrote:

> How often when I was living in the desert, in the vast solitude which gives to hermits a savage dwelling-place, parched by the burning sun, how often did I fancy myself among the pleasures of Rome! …now, although in my fear of hell I had consigned myself to this prison, where I had no companions but scorpions and wild beasts, I often found myself amid bevies of girls. My face was pale and my frame chilled with fasting; yet my mind was burning with desire, and the fires of lust kept bubbling up

16. Gonzalez, *History of Christian Thought*, 308.
17. *Encyclopedia of Ancient Christianity*, 398.

before me when my flesh was as good as dead. Helpless, I cast myself at the feet of Jesus.[18]

Jerome denied himself of every imaginal physical pleasure. He spent weeks on end living in a state of extreme self-denial in an attempt to suppress the sexual lust he struggled with so profoundly. He counseled young people to avoid wine as you would avoid a deadly poison because passion is fuelled with the consumption of wine.[19] Despite his struggles, Jerome committed himself to study Greek, Hebrew, and Latin, the trinity of theological languages, in the fourth century. In 379, he went to Constantinople and was likely ordained as a priest at this time and was in the city during the Council of Constantinople in 381. While in the city, he became friends with both Gregory of Nazianzus and Gregory of Nyssa.[20]

In 383, he went to Rome and served as secretary to the Roman bishop, Damasus. After the death of Damasus in 385, Jerome left the city, never to return. He finally settled in Bethlehem, where he provided leadership for a monastery. During this extended period of time, Jerome completed his translation of the scriptures into Latin and produced multiple commentaries on the scriptures. He continued to live and work in Bethlehem until he died in 419 or 420.

There are several reasons why Jerome is an important figure in the history of the church. First, he directed his substantial linguistic knowledge and skill to translate the scriptures into Latin. While visiting Rome, the bishop of Rome asked him (without an official mandate)[21] to prepare a definitive Latin translation of the Bible. Recognizing the problems with the present translations, Jerome committed himself to a total overhaul of these earlier translations. His attitude toward his work is revealed in the following quote:

> I am not so stupid as to think that any of the Lord's words either need correcting or are not divinely inspired; but the Latin Manuscripts of the Scriptures are proved faulty by the variations which are found in all of them. My aim has been to restore them to the form of the Greek original, from which my critics do not deny that they have been translated.[22]

18. Jerome, Letter 22.7.

19. Jerome, Letter 22.8.

20. *Letters of St. Jerome*, 7.

21. *Encyclopedia of Ancient Christianity*, 399.

22. Jerome, Letter 27.

Jerome translated the Old Testament directly from Hebrew and not Greek. After twenty-two years of part-time labour, his translation was complete in 405/406. The Latin Vulgate was the most outstanding and longest-lasting contribution that Jerome offered to the church. It has been rightly said, "It is not possible to understand the influence of the Bible through the centuries unless we know the traditional Greek and Latin translations."[23] Just as C.H. Spurgeon is known as "The Prince of Preachers," Jerome is known as "The Prince of Translators." Second, Jerome was a leader in asceticism, and he popularized monasticism in the western church. He held a high view of solitary monasticism and often wrote in praise of monks who lived in extreme circumstances.[24] He described the monks scattered throughout the Egyptian desert as "heaven's family on earth."[25] He called the desert "the fairest city of all…a veritable paradise."[26] When urging a friend to return to his life of monasticism, he wrote, "O desert of Christ, burgeoning with flowers! O solitude, in which those stones are produced of which in the Apocalypse the city of the great king is constructed! O wilderness that rejoices in intimacy with God!"[27] These and many other praises of desert living are scattered throughout Jerome's letters. Third, Jerome influenced the church's understanding of Mary, the mother of Jesus. Jerome held a very high view of single life and believed the only value of marriage was to bring more virgins into the world. He argued for the perpetual virginity of Mary in his treatise, *Against Helvidius*.[28] His defense of Mary's perpetual virginity rested in the following: Joseph was only assumed to be Mary's husband; the brothers of Jesus were really his cousins, not the biological children of Mary; and virginity was better than marriage. His view has influenced the church's view of Mary and human sexuality which continues to the present.

Jerome's writings also contributed to the elevation of the Bishop of Rome to the place of the universal vicar of Christ. When writing to Damasus, the bishop of Rome, he said,

> I speak with the successor of the fisherman and the disciple of
> the cross. Following none but Christ as my primate, I am united

---

23. *Encyclopedia of Ancient Christianity*, 399.

24. Jerome, Letter 3.4, 5.

25. Jerome, Letter 3.1.

26. Jerome, Letter 2.1.

27. Jerome, Letter 14.2.

28. Schaff, NPNF, *Against Helevidius*, 6:334–46.

in communion with Your Beatitude—that is, with the chair of
Peter. Upon that rock I know the church is built. Whoever eats a
lamb outside this house is profane.[29]

Jerome's statement reveals that as early as the fourth century the
bishop of Rome was considered, at least by some, to enjoy an elevated
status in the church. Jerome also called upon the bishop of Rome to settle
theological disputes and was ready to accept his word as fixed truth.[30]
The seeds were being planted that eventually grew into the full-bloomed
modern papacy.

Jerome was the most learned and influential Christian leader of the
later fourth century. He is one of the most distinguished scholars in the
church's history and one of the most outstanding Bible translators of all
time. He contributed much to the growth and spread of monasticism,
especially in the western Latin-speaking church. Along with Augustine,
Ambrose, and Gregory the Great, Jerome is recognized by Roman Catholicism as one of the church's four great doctors.

The Problems of Monasticism

While those who embraced monasticism did so with the desire toward
greater piety and devotion to Christ, it did present some serious problems. First, monasticism promoted a twisted view of human sexuality
and marriage. Jerome believed that Adam and Eve were virgins while in
paradise and that marriage and sex were introduced after the fall of man.
He taught that marriage was an inferior state to celibacy, and even within
marriage, celibacy should be the norm. He believed that the value of marriage is that it produces more virgins in the world and that Christian
mothers should rejoice if their daughters choose a celibate life over marriage.[31] He wrote, "death came through Eve, but life has come through
Mary."[32] By this, he was saying that sex came through Eve, but virginity
came through Mary. When God expelled Adam and Eve from the garden, Jerome said they were expelled "from the paradise of virginity." He
also wrote, "in paradise Eve was a virgin, and it was only after the coats

29. Jerome, Letter 15.2.
30. Jerome, Letter 19.1.
31. NPNF 6, Jerome Letter 22.20.
32. NPNF 6, Jerome Letter 22.21.

of skins that she began her married life."[33] Even more strikingly, he said, "no gold or silver vessel was ever so dear to God as is the temple of a virgin's body."[34] Basil said that "widowhood is inferior to virginity."[35] Many statements of this type can be found in the writings of the early church. It might be better to say that monasticism was the fruit and not the cause of a distorted view of virginity, sex, and marriage. Nevertheless, monasticism was instrumental in promoting many of these erroneous views in the church. Second, monasticism led to the abandonment of normal, healthy relationships. When a man or a woman moved to the desert or entered a monastery, they separated themselves from mainstream society and most, if not all, social relationships. Pachomius refused to meet his sister when she came to him because he feared it would interfere with his separation from the world. Even laughter, a normal part of human relationships, was discouraged by Basil, who wrote, "it is clear for the faithful soul there is never a time for laughter."[36]

Positive Contributions of Monasticism

While the strict monastic life did lead to many erroneous teachings regarding proper Christian living, it did however provide some positive influences to the church. First, monasteries brought order and devotion to a compromised church. After emperor Constantine legalized Christianity in 313, many people flooded into the church, resulting in a watered-down and lukewarm Christianity that demanded little in the way of devotion. Monasticism provided a way for zealous Christians to escape the spiritual lethargy of the church and commit themselves to a life of service to Jesus Christ. While it is true that some monks went to extremes in their commitment to the monastic ideal, many lived disciplined and holy lives that were a rebuke to the compromised church.[37] Second, monasteries were centers of evangelism, education, and material support for the community and travelers who needed somewhere to stay. Although Basil was a bishop, he supported the monasteries and encouraged monks to

33. NPNF 6, Jerome Letter, 22.19.

34. NPNF 6, Jerome Letter, 22.23.

35. NPNF 8, Basil Letter, 199.18.

36. BASIL; SILVAS, A. *The Rule of St. Basil in Latin and English: A Revised Critical Edition* (Collegeville, Minnesota: Liturgical Press, 2013), Question 53.

37. Gonzalez, *Story of Christianity*, 146–47.

become deeply involved in meeting the community's needs around them. Many poor people would have starved and many physical needs would not have been met if not for the monasteries. Third, monasteries copied and preserved ancient manuscripts. Many manuscripts would be lost if not for the monks' devotion in copying and preserving these documents for the benefit of future generations. Many New Testament Greek manuscripts would have been destroyed if they had not been preserved in the libraries of the monasteries. While countries were at war and empires and nations were being forged, many monasteries were ignored and left unmolested to do their work in peace.

Someone might argue that the positive contributions made by monasticism outweigh any adverse effects it had on the world. While it is true that God has used monasticism to do some wonderful things, monasticism is not necessarily the reason for that blessing. Schaff wrote,

> It is not monasticism, as such, which has proved a blessing to the church and the world; for the monasticism of India, which for three thousand years has pushed the practice of mortification of all the excesses of delirium, never saved a single soul, nor produced a single benefit to the race. It was Christianity in monasticism which has done all the good, and used this abnormal mode of life as a means for carrying forward its mission of love and peace. In proportion as monasticism was animated and controlled by the spirit of Christianity, it proved a blessing while separated from it, it degenerated and became a fruitful source of evil.[38]

The Bible is our final source of faith and practice. All traditions and rituals should be weighed against the teaching of Scripture. There is no evidence that first and second-century Christians separated themselves from the world to live as hermits or in cloisters. The Christians, both men, and women lived their lives within the wider society. They associated with their unbelieving neighbours, sought to live holy lives, and preached the gospel to the entire community in which they lived. *The Epistle to Diognetus,* mentioned in chapter 5, described the life of the early Christians,

> Christians are not distinguished from the rest of mankind by either country, speech, or customs; the fact is, they nowhere settle in cities of their own; they use no peculiar language; they

---

38. Schaff, *History of the Christian Church,* 3:174–75,

cultivate no eccentric mode of life…while they dwell in both Greek and non-Greek cities, as each one's lot was cast, and conform to the customs of the country in dress, food, and mode of life in general, the whole tenor of their way of living stamps it as worthy of admiration and admittedly extraordinary…they marry like all others and beget children; but they do not expose their offspring. Their board they spread for all, but not their bed. They find themselves *in the flesh*, but do not live *according to the flesh*. They spend their days on earth, but hold citizenship in heaven. They obey the established laws, but in their private lives they rise above the law.[39]

This quote makes it clear that Christians were ordinary citizens who were distinguished, not by their separation from the society in which they lived but by the way they lived within that society.

Discussion Questions

1. Are Christians required to deny themselves of certain types of food?

2. Is celibacy a higher form of Christian living than marriage?

3. Has the Protestant church failed to appreciate the value of choosing to live a celibate life in service to Jesus?

4. Is there a place for monasteries in today's world? If no, why not? If yes, how should they be organized?

39. *Epistle to Diognetus*, 5.

Chapter 14

John Chrysostom (c.347–407)

John Chrysostom was born sometime between 340 and 354 AD in Antioch, the city where the followers of Jesus were first called Christians.[1] He was born into a wealthy family and received a good quality education. His father, a military commander in Syria, was named Secundus, and his mother's name was Anthusa.[2] His father died when John was only a child, and there is no evidence that he ever became a Christian.[3] On the other hand, his mother was a fervent believer and sought to instill Christianity into her children's lives.[4] As a young man, Chrysostom studied under a pagan classical scholar named Libanius, who was distressed when Chrysostom became a Christian. When asked who would succeed him, Libanius said, "John, if only the Christians had not stolen him from us."[5] Upon completing his studies, John became a rhetorician and lawyer and was on the path to a prosperous political career until he unexpectedly abandoned his profession and went into the Christian ministry.[6]

When Chrysostom was twenty-seven years old (c.369–70), Meletius, bishop of Antioch (361–81), recognized John's superior mental and spiritual qualities and became his mentor. Meletius taught him the Christian faith and then baptized him.[7] Shortly after Chrysostom's bap-

1. Acts 11:26.

2. Palladius, *Dialogue on the Life of St. John Chrysostom*, 34, 35.

3. Schaff, *Chrysostom*, NPNF, 9:5.

4. Schaff, *Chrysostom*, 5.

5. Schaff, *Chrysostom*, 6.

6. Schaff, *Chrysostom*, 6.

7. Palladius, *Dialogue on the Life of St. John Chrysostom*, 35.

tism, Meletius ordained him to the office of lector. In this position, he was responsible for the public reading of Scripture but was not allowed to preach or officiate at the Lord's Supper.[8]

Chrysostom was unhappy with life in the city but could not leave because he was responsible for the care of his aging mother. Following her death, he went to live as a hermit in the mountains for four years, spending his time hauling rocks up from the sea and building living quarters for other hermits. In this way, he sought to suppress his youthful temptations and desires. After four years of hard labour, he lived alone in a cave for an additional two years, where he devoted himself to the ascetic life. He was not idle during this time but spent many hours committing the scriptures to memory.[9] His pursuit of asceticism did not have a positive impact on his life. He became stern and severe and was more prone "to irritability, rather than to modesty."[10] His life of extreme austerity seriously damaged his health, and after two years, he moved back to the city of Antioch.[11] After five years of serving in the church, he was ordained a deacon in 381 by Meletius. While he was a deacon, Chrysostom probably wrote his most famous work, *On the Priesthood*, where he gives practical teaching on the duties of priests and bishops. He was ordained a priest in 386 by bishop Flavianus, who succeeded Meletius as bishop of Antioch in 381.

Even though he was now a priest, he continued to live an ascetic life. He often ate only vegetables and never drank wine because of its ill effects on his body. Schaff described him as having "an emaciated frame, a large, bald head, a lofty, wrinkled forehead, deep-set, bright piercing eyes, pallid, hollow cheeks, and short, gray beard."[12] He certainly did not fit into the higher society of Antioch. It has been rightly said that "the thin, shriveled, stunted figure, the bald head, the mean dress, would have seemed out of place amid the gorgeous personages who had been wont to exchange amenities with the ex-senator Nectarius."[13] Much of the starkness in his physical appearance was undoubtedly a result of his austere lifestyle.

8. Schaff, *Chrysostom*, 7.

9. *Encyclopedia of Ancient Christianity*, 2:430.

10. Socrates, *Ecclesiastical History*, 139.

11. Palladius, *On St. John Chrysostom*, 35.

12. Schaff, *Chrysostom*, 16.

13. Bright, *Age of the Fathers*, 2:37.

For the next twelve years, Chrysostom preached in the city of Antioch, enjoying a far-reaching and influential ministry. Antioch was one of the greatest cities of the Roman Empire, and the bishop held enormous sway over the people. His oratorical gifts emerged quickly, and he very rapidly became a famous preacher. In fact, Chrysostom is considered by many to be one of the greatest, if not the greatest, preacher in the history of the Christian church. The epithet "Chrysostom" means "golden-mouth" and appears to have been applied to him in the later fifth century and is an excellent testimony to his eloquence displayed in the pulpit.[14] Libanius, the Syrian, said that he "surpassed all of the age."[15] The crowds that gathered to hear him were so large and compressed that Chrysostom had to warn the people of the presence of pickpockets who would take advantage of this potentially lucrative situation.[16] Of course, such popularity was bound to get a person into trouble, especially one with the convictions of this lion-hearted preacher.

While there were divisions in the church at Antioch, Chrysostom's real trouble began when Constantinople, the capital of the Roman Empire, showed interest in him becoming Archbishop of that city. Some might consider this a great privilege and an opportunity to influence larger numbers of people for the gospel, however it would lead to his ultimate downfall. On September 27, 397, Nectarius, bishop of Constantinople, died after serving as Archbishop for sixteen years. The first question to be considered upon his death was, "who would take his place?" The bishopric of Constantinople was by far one of the most influential and powerful positions in all of Christendom. The man who held this office would preside over a great body of clergy, have influence over the churches of Thrace, Asia, and Pontus, live in luxurious surroundings, provide hospitality for the great men and women of the empire, and have the ear of the emperor himself. Many men sought the office because of the privileges it afforded, something that Chrysostom could not understand.[17] However, he did admit that he struggled with ambition, which was one reason he feared high office in the church.[18] While he did not seek the Archbishopric of Constantinople, he was chosen for the position

---

14. Bright, *Age of the Fathers*, 2:27.

15. Sozomenus, *Ecclesiastical History of Sozomen*, 2:399.

16. Schaff, *Chrysostom*, 11.

17. Bright, *Age of the Fathers*, 2:28.

18. Chrysostom, *On the Priesthood*, 82.

and compelled to accept it.[19] After a thriving ministry in Antioch, he was spirited out of the city under cover of darkness so as not to upset the people of the city who wouldn't take kindly to the removal of such a popular leader. He was consecrated bishop of the church of Constantinople on February 26, 398. His consecration brought him into the very heart of Byzantine politics and all the political machinations that came with it. His years in Antioch would be considered a treat compared to the troubles that awaited him in the empire's capital.

After his installation as bishop, he immediately began to bring about many necessary reforms in the church. He first sought to eliminate the sexual immorality that was rife amongst the clergy. The clerics sought to hide their improprieties by claiming to live with a woman as brother and sister or have women come into their homes as housekeepers to cover up their true purpose. Chrysostom considered this practice to be a greater sin than the sin of brothel-keeping because the clergy were supposed to be the mouthpieces of God.[20] John not only reproved the lifestyle of the clergy but also had some of them ejected from office.[21] While the clergy supported John's installation as bishop, they rapidly turned against him, some becoming his mortal enemies.[22] It didn't help that he tended to be harsh and rude to those with whom he disagreed.[23]

Though many biographies on Chrysostom's life tend to highlight his angry outbursts and his disproportionate use of harsh language, his writings as a whole present a different picture. They reveal a man who lived a well-adjusted life, and his teaching is evenly balanced, showing concern for the practical day-to-day issues in the life of his parishioners. Even though he spent his earlier years as a monk, he was not unaware of the harsh realities of life for the average person and spent much time teaching people how to live a life that was pleasing to God.[24] After his initial attempt to reform the lifestyle of the clergy, he began to focus on the laymen. He mentions two sins in particular that he considered especially grievous: greed and purse watching (those who are addicted to wealth). He condemned the unbridled pursuit of wealth and encouraged people

---

19. Bright, *Age of the Fathers*, 2:29.

20. Palladius, *On St. John Chrysostom*, 38.

21. Sozomen, *Ecclesiastical History of Sozomen*, 401.

22. Socrates, *Ecclesiastical History*, 139.

23. Socrates, *Ecclesiastical History*, 140.

24. Malingrey, *John Chrysostom*, 432.

to be content with the wages they received. It is important to note that he did not denounce these behaviours as a self-righteous Pharisee but believed it was necessary to tear down what he viewed as a corrupt building, before constructing another one on the firmer foundation of righteousness.[25] He criticized the circus, theater, and public entertainments, especially when his own congregation chose them over attendance at church.

Empress Eudoxia was displeased with Chrysostom's popularity among the people and his influence over her husband. She considered him rigid and uncompromising in his views on sin. She was also offended on more than one occasion with his stinging rebukes from the pulpit. During one preaching service, he cried out, "Again Herodias is raging, again she is dancing, again she demands the head of John on a platter,"[26] and on another occasion, he compared her to Jezebel, the evil queen in ancient Israel.[27] These were provocative comparisons that were bound to receive a harsh response from the empress. She became a great and powerful enemy of Chrysostom and was instrumental in his ultimate downfall.[28]

He scrutinized the financial records, concluding that there were unnecessary disbursements of cash that were of no advantage to the church. He sought to eliminate all unnecessary future expenses, including excessive amounts of money spent on the episcopal household. Not only did he attack the pleasure-seeking lifestyle of the people, but he also sought to get his own house in order. He sold all the luxurious furniture and everything designed as a display of wealth, giving the money to the hospital, as well as building other hospitals and financially supporting a staff to provide medical care for the community.[29] He also used his personal income to help various charities. His emphasis on charity however, was not all good because it tended to increase the number of people begging around the churches and in public places, presumably because the rich were more generous to beggars in response to the appeals of Chrysostom.[30]

Following these reforms, he sought to reorganize the widows who served as deaconesses in the church, urging them to abandon luxurious

25. Palladius, *On St. John Chrysostom*, 38, 39.

26. Schaff, *Chrysostom*, 14.

27. Schaff, *Chrysostom*, 13.

28. Schaff, *Chrysostom*, 12.

29. Palladius, *On St. John Chrysostom*, 39.

30. Schaff, *Chrysostom*, 13.

living and embrace a more modest lifestyle. He also advised some of the widows to remarry to avoid dishonouring the Lord.[31] The stinging nature of his appeals is seen in the following exhortation, "You gray-haired women! At your age, why do you compel yourselves to make your bodies young again, wearing curly locks of hair upon your foreheads like common whores? You outrage the rest of the free women, beguiling all you meet, some of you even widows to boot."[32]

Chrysostom introduced other changes, including the establishment of regular prayer times, which proved beneficial to the life of the church and the city. Palladius wrote concerning these changes, "The very color of the city was changed to piety; everyone looked bright and fresh with soberness and Psalm-singing."[33] While Chrysostom's rapidly implemented reforms enjoyed early success, not all were pleased, especially those who served in the church for prestige, pleasure and financial gain rather than for the good of the people.

Several church leaders sought to stir up trouble for Chrysostom. Unable to find any real accusation against him, they turned to Theophilus, bishop of Alexandria, known for his deceptive and shrewd ways. From the very beginning, Theophilus resented John because he wanted to promote his own man, Isidore, to the episcopal office in Constantinople.[34] The character of Theophilus is seen in his treatment of some local monks who were banished from Egypt over a theological dispute. The monks confronted Theophilus and demanded a reason for his ill-treatment of them. Palladius briefly described this interaction, "he [Theophilus] regarded them like a dragon with bloodshot eyes. He glared like a bull. With his temper beyond control he was at first livid, then sallow, and then smiling sarcastically. He snatched the pallium (a piece of cloth hanging over the shoulder) from the aged Ammonius and twisting it around his neck he inflicted blows upon his jaw, making his nose bleed with his clenched fists, and kept crying out: Anathematize Origen, you heretic!"[35] Elsewhere Palladius calls him a "crooked serpent."[36] It was this man who turned his mind toward the destruction of Chrysostom.

<hr>

31. Palladius, *On St. John Chrysostom*, 39.

32. Palladius, *On St. John Chrysostom*, 52.

33. Palladius, *On St. John Chrysostom*, 40.

34. Socrates, *Ecclesiastical History*, 138.

35. Palladius, *On St. John Chrysostom*, 44.

36. Palladius, *On St. John Chrysostom*, 46.

The monks who were treated in such a despicable way eventually made their way to Constantinople, to seek the help of Chrysostom. Chrysostom, thinking he could reason with Theophilus, wrote him a letter, asking that he reconsider his treatment of these men and receive them back into his fold, but he refused. The interactions between the two men increased in fervour until Theophilus declared open war against Chrysostom. The distressed monks, sensing no other option, appealed to empress Eudoxia to resolve the issue. She responded by summoning Theophilus to Constantinople, so the problem could be finally settled.[37] A provincial synod was called in 403 AD, known as the Synod of Oak, during which there were many fabricated charges leveled against Chrysostom. Chrysostom was summoned to appear at the Synod, but he refused, even after the emperor himself commanded him to attend. The council decided to depose him in August 403, but almost immediately, riots broke out in the city to protest his removal. Along with the riots, there was a great earthquake that struck terror into the heart of the empress. She immediately sent envoys to bring Chrysostom back to the city as quickly as possible.[38]

Theophilus was not happy with the reinstatement of Chrysostom and leveled new charges against him. The enemies of Chrysostom misled the emperor, and so he commanded him to leave his church. Not wanting to appear to have abandoned his post, Chrysostom said to the emperor, "I have received this church from God our Savior for the care of the salvation of my people and I cannot abandon her. But if you desire this (for the city belongs to you) then expel me by force so that I may defend myself on the grounds that I went by your command rather than that I abandoned my charge."[39] Sozomen said that the renewed call for Chrysostom's removal came from empress Eudoxia. The empress erected a silver statue of herself not far from the church called "Hagia Sophia" with great fanfare. Chrysostom was not impressed and condemned her from the pulpit. The empress was determined to get rid of John once and for all.

After much unrest in the churches of Antioch, Chrysostom was once again condemned and expelled from Constantinople. Shortly after, the church was set on fire and burned to the ground. Many believed that God himself started the fire as a judgment against those wicked men that

---

37. Palladius, *On St. John Chrysostom*, 49.

38. Theodoret, *The Ecclesiastical History of Theodoret*, 3:5.34.

39. Palladius: *On St. John Chrysostom*, 61.

attacked Chrysostom, while others accused Chrysostom of setting the fire before leaving the city.[40] Many of those who supported John were arrested, thrown into prison, and forced to condemn him.[41] Soldiers took Chrysostom to Bithynia and then to a town in Armenia called Cucusus,[42] described as "the most deserted place in the world."[43] After this, while enroute to an even more remote location, Pityus, a deserted area on the eastern shore of the Black sea, John, whose "emaciated body being as though it were an apple turning ripe in the sun on the topmost branch of the tree," died.[44] His death took place on September 14, 407. His remains were eventually brought back to Constantinople and buried in the church of the Apostles on January 27, 438.[45]

Insights from the Life and Times of Chrysostom

The life of Chrysostom provides valuable insight into the relationship between church and state in the later fourth and early fifth century. After the death of Nectarius, emperor Arcadius summoned John and ordered the bishops to appoint him as Archbishop of Constantinople. This act certainly demonstrates the influence the emperor had over church appointments in the city.[46] The ecclesiastical influence of the emperor dates back to Constantine the Great, who believed that the survival of the empire depended upon unity in the church. He used imperial power to promote this unity, seen most clearly in the calling of the First Council of Nicaea over which he presided. The emperor provided for the needs of the bishop using state funds, certainly a first in the church's history.[47] Constantine's actions set a precedent that future emperors would follow, but not without regular eruptions of conflict with church leaders. Chrysostom, for example, believed that the church was superior to the state and that the emperor did not have administrative authority over the life of the

40. Palladius, *On St. John Chrysostom*, 67–68.

41. Sozomen, *Ecclesiastical History of Sozomen*, 413.

42. Palladius, *On St. John Chrysostom*, 69.

43. Malingrey, *John Chrysostom*, 430.

44. Palladius, *On St. John Chrysostom*, 72.

45. Malingrey, *John Chrysostom*, 430.

46. Theodoret, *Ecclesiastical History of Theodoret*, 3:5.27.

47. Speros, *Byzantium and Europe*, 24.

church.[48] This would certainly explain, in part, why Chrysostom was so free in his criticism of the civil authorities. He believed that government officials were to live in submission to the church's teaching, and if they did not, they should be called out for their disobedience. His boldness in condemning empress Eudoxia for her extravagance was probably rooted not in arrogance but a deep-seated belief that the gospel message applied to everyone in society, from the lowliest peasant to the emperor himself. Notwithstanding, Chrysostom's two exiles reveal the state's power over the church through its willingness to intervene in church business if they believed the state's power was under threat.

Second, it is important to note that Innocent, the bishop of Rome, could not influence the proceedings against Chrysostom. When he received word of what happened to John, he was "extremely indignant" and condemned the actions taken against him.[49] The fact that the bishop of Rome was still in contact with Chrysostom demonstrated that he was in fellowship with many bishops of the eastern church. Nevertheless, his inability to influence the proceedings against Chrysostom and persuade the bishops to support him demonstrates that the bishop of Rome was not recognized as having Papal authority in Constantinople in the fourth century. Although the church was still officially united, the rift between the western and eastern branches of the church was already developing. The great schism in 1054[50] permanently divided Christianity into the Roman Catholic church in the west and the Greek Orthodox in the east.

Third, the attempt of Theophilus to install a man of his choosing in the Archbishopric; his failure to do so, and his hatred for Chrysostom reveal a struggle between the See of Alexandria[51] and the See of Constantinople for pre-eminence in the Eastern church. If Theophilus could put someone of his own choosing in Constantinople, he could wield incredible influence over the church. His failure to do so was a source of great bitterness which he unleashed on Chrysostom, leading to the eventual banishment and death of this great preacher of the Christian faith. The

48. *Oxford Dictionary of Byzantium*, 2:456.

49. Malingrey, *John Chrysostom*, 456.

50. The Great Schism took place over the authority of the pope in Rome, which was not recognized in the east and the filioque (and from the Son) that was inserted into the Nicene Creed. The Filioque asserted that the Holy Spirit proceeded from both the Father and the Son. The Greek Orthodox Church argues the Holy Spirit proceeds only from the Father.

51. The see is the seat of church authority.

conflict between the See of Alexandria and the See of Constantinople grew in the fifth century as Constantinople grew in political importance. Political power had shifted from Rome to Constantinople and gave the Archbishop of Constantinople greater influence over the church. Many were arguing that Constantinople, not Rome, should be in the position of ecclesiastical prominence.[52] Alexandria, Antioch, Jerusalem, Rome, and Constantinople represent the five most important ecclesiastical centers in the fourth century, each one vying for greater influence in the church. This struggle, however, came to an end when Alexandria, Antioch, and Jerusalem fell to the Muslims in the seventh century AD, leaving only Rome and Constantinople, both of which eventually went their separate ecclesiastical ways.

John Chrysostom lived during a time of great political and ecclesiastical upheaval. The simplicity of the first-century church gave way to a complex organization that pervaded every aspect of society. During the first decades of the Christian church, the state barely recognized her existence. By the later third and early fourth century, Christianity had become the official religion of the Roman Empire. The affairs of the church were now the affairs of the emperor. Many unscrupulous characters sought to fill the powerful bishoprics, not out of concern for the spiritual life of the people but in the pursuit of wealth, power, and influence. John Chrysostom, despite his self-professed desire for influence, appears to have been motivated by a deep concern for the purity of the church. His book *On the Priesthood* demonstrates a profound passion for the integrity and spiritual effectiveness of the clergy. His sermons are richly illustrated to help people understand the Bible more clearly. While it is true that he did possess a somewhat stubborn spirit and his language was offensive and sharp, at least based on today's standard for public discourse, his heart was large, and his love for the church and society was genuine. Chrysostom's theological battles, and the struggles with Theophilus in particular, are not evidence of a haughty spirit or a desire for conflict. They reveal instead the heart of a man convinced of the rightness of his principles. If we seek to understand Chrysostom in the context in which he lived, we can forgive him for some of his glaring faults while recognizing the greatness of his person and the ongoing influence that he still has within the Christian church.

52. Speros, *Byzantium and Europe,* 36, 37.

Discussion Questions

1. What stands out to you in the life of Chrysostom? Why?

2. How should we deal with those who disagree with us theologically?

3. Read *On the Priesthood* and discuss its contents with a fellow Christian.

Chapter 15

Augustine of Hippo (354–430)

"Those who look for joys outside themselves become empty, they pour out their substance on 'things visible and transitory,' they lick shadows and their minds starve."—St. Augustine

Augustine is without question the most influential theologian in the history of the church. His influence not only pervades the Roman Catholic Church but all the branches of Protestantism as well. Martin Luther and John Calvin, and a great many other sixteenth-century Protestant reformers were deeply influenced by his theology, in particular his soteriology. It has been rightly said, "on any short list of those who shaped Western civilization, Augustine's name must appear."

Augustine was born during a time of great upheaval within the Roman Empire. Celtic aggression was increasing at the northern borders as the barbarians advanced deeper into Roman territory, while internal political struggles weakened Roman rule, threatening its very existence. Augustine lived during these tumultuous years and was deeply affected by the sack of the city of Rome by Alaric, king of the Visigoths on August 24, 410 AD. This glorious, and so it was thought, eternal city, was destroyed. This was truly an earth-shattering event for those who witnessed it and Augustine, whose mind was deeply affected by the incident, produced what many believe to be his greatest work, *On the City of God*. In this vast work of twenty-four books, Augustine compared the fleeting nature of the kingdoms of this world to the permanency of the kingdom of God.

When Augustine was forty-four years old, he wrote the *Confessions*, a record of his personal testimony. Much of what we know about his life is found in this book and it is essential reading for those who want to know the theology and spirituality of Augustine. The *Confessions* has been rightly described as follows:

> They are a sublime composition, in which Augustine, like David in the fifty-first Psalm, confesses to God, in view of his own and of succeeding generations, without reserve the sins of his youth; and they are at the same time a hymn of praise to the grace of God, which led him out of darkness into light, and called him to service in the kingdom of Christ.[1]

It is the most edifying of all his works and the most popular of his writings.

Aurelius Augustinus was born November 13, 354 AD in an insignificant village named Tagaste in the province of Numidia in North Africa (modern-day Algeria). His father Patricius was a pagan, but his mother Monica was a devout Christian woman. His father was a small landowner, who was heavily taxed, enjoying only a modest income from his hard labour. Despite the family's financial hardships, Augustine's father recognized his son's intellectual gifts and sacrificed much in every way to provide his son with an education that would enable him to enter a higher social and economic class. Not only did His father recognize his son's intellectual abilities, but Augustine as well came to see his own superior intelligence. When he was twenty years of age, he read Aristotle's book entitled *Categories* and unlike many men who needed the help of other scholars to understand it, Augustine was able to grasp its intricate concepts on his own. He was surprised, when he began teaching, that even his brightest students expended a great deal of mental energy to understand the subjects that he mastered with ease.[2] This was a source of pride for him.

Augustine began his general education at the primary school in his hometown, but despite his intellectual giftedness he did not like school, and would not have studied if he had not been forced.[3] In his book entitled The *Confessions of Saint Augustine*, he portrayed himself as an ordinary child who did well at school, but did not particularly enjoy it. He spoke of being beaten when he was slow to learn, and he often began his day with the prayer that God would keep him from being beaten at

1. Schaff, *Nicene and Post-Nicene Fathers*, 1:3.

2. Augustine, *Confessions*, 4.6.28–30.

3. Augustine, *Confessions*, 1.4.19.

school that day.[4] Although he did not relish studying, he did love Latin, but, considered the study of Greek a form of punishment.[5] He attributed his love of Latin to the encouragement he received in acquiring it as compared to the threats and punishments he received from teachers if he did not learn Greek.[6] Although he did not always enjoy his studies, he excelled beyond his peers. He was even praised for his progress by his fellow students.[7] Later in life, Augustine expressed appreciation for the benefit he had received from these studies, although he did not recognize their value at the time.

The religious training of Augustine started from infancy. He was taught the gospel from his youth and said that the name of Christ was precious to him from the time he was a young child.[8] He was a catechumen,[9] although he was not converted and baptized till much later in his life. His mother Monica was deeply concerned for his soul, but his father, a non-Christian, influenced him away from the Christian faith.

Although Augustine was not conscious of his sinfulness when he was a child, he eventually came to understand the depth of his own depravity. Through his reflection on Scripture, he came to believe that even infants were sinful in the sight of God. He wrote, "I was conceived in evil, and my mother sheltered a sinful me in her womb."[10] While Augustine did not remember his infancy, he recognized that his sinful tendencies appeared immediately after he was born. He acknowledged that his ability to sin developed as he learned to speak and to express his sinful nature more freely. He confessed that when he was a child, he sinned by disobeying his parents and teachers, loving sports and victories, and amusing himself with games rather than his school work. He wrote, "I sinned, then, when as a boy I preferred those empty to those more profitable studies, or rather loved the one and hated the other. 'One and one, two'; 'two and two, four'; this was to me a hateful sing-song; 'the burning of Troy,' and 'Creusa's shade and sad similitude,' were the choice spectacle

---

4. Augustine, *Confessions*, 1.3.14.

5. Augustine, *Confessions*, 1.4.20.

6. Augustine, *Confessions*, 1.4.23.

7. Augustine, *Confessions*, 1.5.27.

8. Augustine, *Confessions*, 1.3.17.

9. A catechumen is a person who is taught the Christian faith in preparation for baptism.

10. Augustine, *Confessions*, 1.2.12.

of my vanity."[11] Augustine also confessed to having committed the sin of thievery, greed, and pride, expressing itself in a desire for pre-eminence.[12] An adequate summary of his perception of his sinfulness is seen in the following quote, "Only sin was my own, when I sought joy, glory, and truth not in him but in things he made, in myself and other creatures, thus sliding off toward pain, dejection, and error."[13] He believed the reason for his willingness to sin was a love of the things of this world. Money, worldly honours, relationships are all things that God has given to humanity for their pleasure, but excessive love of these things leads to neglect of God who is the only true source of delight.[14] Augustine would eventually come to know that true lasting joy is not found in the things of this world, but in God and God alone.

Augustine's parents, with the help of Rominianus, a family friend, managed to save enough money to send him to the University in Madaura, but a short time later he went to Carthage, the capital of Roman Africa to study law, literature, and philosophy. His course of study prepared him for several possible occupations: a lawyer, a rhetorician, or a civil servant within the imperial government.[15] As Augustine passed from childhood into early manhood, he abandoned the Christian faith that his mother Monica taught to him. In fact, as a young man of sixteen, he added new sins to his ever-growing list. He wrote,

> During my sixteenth year of my age, when I surrendered with ready hand all rule over my self, turning it over to mad cravings condoned by our debased humanity but condemned by your law. My family did not care to divert me from my mad course toward marriage. They cared only that I might acquire rhetoric and sway others with my words.[16]

He noted that his father was willing to make burdensome sacrifices for the sake of his education, but had no concern for his son's relationship to God. All that mattered in the mind of his father was to establish his son in a good and lucrative career. His father even delighted in the fact that his son was now beginning to explore the lustful activities of youth. His

---

11. Augustine, *Confessions*, 1.4.22

12. Augustine, *Confessions*, 1.5.30.

13. Augustine, *Confessions*, 1.5.31.

14. Augustine, *Confessions*, 2.2.10.

15. Walker, *History of the Christian Church*, 198.

16. Augustine, *Confessions*, 2.1.4.

mother, on the other hand, was grieved and fearful for her son who was moving further away from God and slipping deeper into sin.[17]

Augustine continued his childhood practice of stealing, indicating that he stole for no other reason than the pleasure of stealing. He did not need the items he stole but stole because he "wanted the sin."[18] Augustine told a story to illustrate his point,

> There was a pear-tree near our vineyard, laden with fruit not enticing either in appearance or in taste. In dead night, after prolonging our pranks in the streets, as was our noxious custom, we malicious young punks steered our way to the tree, shook down its fruit and carted it off, a huge load we did not want to eat ourselves but to throw before swine—or if we ate some of it, that was not our motive. Simply what was not allowed allured us.[19]

He loved sin because it was sin. The act of stealing was desirable in and of itself. "To be lured by what was not allowed, just because it was not allowed."[20] He also took extra delight when he sinned in the company of others.[21]

Augustine spent two years in Carthage, and when living there, he cultivated a love for stage plays, while at the same time he studied philosophy. He found a book written by Cicero and read a section entitled *Hortensius*, which kindled within his heart a desire for the wisdom of God. As a result, he determined that he would commit himself to a study of the Bible but initially was not impressed with what he considered to be the lowly nature of Scripture when compared to other forms of literature. He wrote,

> I can say now is not what I felt then, as I looked at Scripture. It seemed trivial next to Cicero's majesty. My own loftiness was unfitted for its humility. My gaze reached no inner meanings. One must become a child to grow up again with the Scripture, and I was above such childishness. Pride made me swell to a big man in my own eyes."[22]

---

17. Augustine, *Confessions*, 2.1.5-7.

18. Augustine, *Confessions*, 2.2.9.

19. Augustine, *Confessions*, 2.2.9.

20. Augustine, *Confessions*, 2.2.14.

21. Augustine, *Confessions*, 2.2.16, 17.

22. Augustine, *Confessions*, 3.3.9.

One area in which Augustine had a particular struggle was sexual desire. Desiring to love and be loved he gave himself over to physical pleasure. He wrote, "Sweet as were loving and being loved, sweeter still was the taste of the loved one's body. I found the springs of pure love with the dregs of lust, muddying its clarity from the depths of my sexual drive."[23] In an attempt to satisfy these longings, he met a young woman, fell in love, and then moved in with her. He lived with this woman for seventeen years. Augustine remained faithful to this relationship but saw a distinct difference between it and true marriage. He wrote, "My life with her taught me the difference between the restraint of the marriage pledge, formed for the sake of offspring, and a lustful sexual arrangement, where any children born were unintended (though bound to be loved if born)."[24] In 372 they had a boy named Adeodatus, in whom Augustine took great delight.

In 373, Augustine joined the Manichaeans and spent nine years as both a student and a teacher. He joined them for three reasons. First, he believed he would find true wisdom among them, a wisdom that was based on logic and not revelation. Second, their claim to be true followers of Christ, and third, their apparent solution to the problem of evil.[25] When he was twenty-nine years of age, a famous Manichaean bishop called Faustus came to Carthage, so Augustine, who had been reading the philosophers, went to the bishop and questioned him on many topics. Although Faustus had a high reputation, Augustine, who had read widely on many subjects, was not impressed with him. He found that the philosophers were more effective at explaining the mysteries of the universe than Faustus, and as a result of this meeting, Augustine became disillusioned with the Manichaeans. After Augustine's conversion, he referred to Faustus as "the devil's chosen snare,"[26] and Manichaeanism as "a false and blaspheming religion."[27]

Augustine left Carthage and moved to Rome, not to seek more money for his lecturing, although that was desirable to him, but because the students in Rome were more serious in their studies than those at Carthage, who would sometimes disrupt classes. While in Rome, he

23. Augustine, *Confessions*, 3.1.1.

24. Augustine, *Confessions*, 4.1.2.

25. *Encyclopedia of Ancient Christianity*, 292.

26. Augustine, *Confessions*, 5.2.3.

27. Augustine, *Confessions*, 8.4.17.

continued to live with the Manichaeans for a while, but their hold on his mind was already broken. After becoming a Christian, Augustine recognized that it was the hand of God that led him to Rome, for the sake of his salvation.[28]

A request was sent to Rome from Milan seeking a court rhetorician. Augustine immediately applied for the position, in part because the students at Rome often failed to pay him the money they owed for his teaching.[29] His application was accepted, and he left Rome in a state carriage for Milan in 384. He was eventually joined by his two good friends, Alypius and Nebridius. At the time Augustine did not realize the significance of this change, for he was destined to meet the famed Christian bishop of Milan, Ambrose. When he first began listening to Ambrose, he was not overly interested in the content of his sermons, but the eloquence displayed in their delivery.[30] Augustine described the preaching of Ambrose as "lavish food," "gladdening oil" and "wine of sober intoxication."[31] Although this was his confessed motive in listening, he acknowledged that some of the content managed to lodge itself in his mind and in time began to affect his thinking. He became a "learner" in the Catholic Church, and slowly he began to embrace the Christian faith. He described himself at this stage of his life as being "loosened from error, but not fastened to truth."[32]

It was while he was in Milan that his praying mother, Monica came to live with him. Augustine acknowledged the value of his mother's prayers in his conversion and praised his mother's faithfulness in this matter. He wrote,

> Yet "from your heights you stretched your hand out over me," and drew my soul up out of this dark abyss, since my mother, your servant, was crying more abundant tears than mothers would cry for a dead son. She knew that I was dead…you heard her, Lord, and heeded her tears…[33] Her prayers were steadily making their way to you, while you left me for a time to toss and re-toss in the dark.[34]

28. Augustine, *Confessions*, 5.5.14

29. Augustine, *Confessions*, 5.6.22.

30. Augustine, *Confessions*, 5.7.24

31. Augustine, *Confessions*, 5.7.23

32. Augustine, *Confessions*, 6.1.1

33. Augustine, *Confessions*, 3.6.19.

34. Augustine, *Confessions*, 3.6.20.

Her prayers and tears for Augustine were so frequent that Ambrose, the bishop, was compelled to say to her, "The son of such tears as you are shedding will never be lost."[35]

Augustine struggled for a long time, in part because he was afraid of being led astray again. He was blinded to the truth for nine years with the Manicheans, and he was not willing to commit quickly to another religious group. He described it in this way, "I was leery of a good physician after dealing with a bad one. So it was with my soul's illness, which needed curing by belief, though I fought off the cure for fear of believing again in falsehoods."[36] He spent many hours speaking with Ambrose who patiently addressed Augustine's concerns, skillfully guiding him toward a true understanding of the Christian faith.

While in Milan, Augustine and his friends decided to start a monastery in which they could live their lives detached from the world and its troubles, giving themselves over entirely to the philosophical life. The venture, however, collapsed before it began.[37] In part, it failed because some of the men already had wives, and others were planning on getting married.

During this time, Augustine, urged on by others, became engaged to a younger woman, who was still two years away from marrying age. Because of this engagement, Augustine was compelled to send his mistress away, since she was not considered a suitable choice for a wife. His mistress, whom he loved very much, was as he put it, "torn out of my side."[38] Augustine was devastated by the breaking of this relationship. He wrote, "My heart, to which she had been grafted, was lacerated, wounded, shedding blood."[39] She left her son with him, went back to Africa, and vowed that she would remain chaste for the remainder of her life. Augustine, although wanting to live a chaste life, was not so successful, his lust leading him to take another mistress shortly after the departure of the first one. Augustine struggled between his love of lust and his desire to serve God. He recalled his youthful struggle when he wrote, "I used to pray to you for chastity, saying, "Give me chastity and self-control, but

35. Augustine, *Confessions*, 3.6.21.

36. Augustine, *Confessions*, 6.2.6.

37. Augustine, *Confessions*, 6.6.24.

38. Augustine, *Confessions*, 6.6.25.

39. Augustine, *Confessions*, 6.6.25.

not just yet." I was afraid you would hear me too soon, heal me too soon, from my sick urges, which I wanted intensified rather than terminated."[40]

Augustine was moving one step at a time toward his conversion to Christ, tormented in his soul with a growing consciousness of sin, increasing doubts concerning all that he believed to be true, relentlessly seeking for the truth; he would soon embrace the Christian faith with his entire soul. Initially, Augustine began reading books written by the Platonists, which helped to untangle some of his previous beliefs about God and the universe. He began to view God differently, not as a material being, but as an immaterial one, yet he still strived to understand the full truth about God. He described his pre-conversion struggle as follows,

> To my amazement, I could not maintain the love I genuinely felt for you (and not for some vain simulacrum of you), since I was alternately raised up to you by your beauty and rushed down from you by my weight. I moaned as I hit bottom. My weight was fleshly habit. But I still remembered you. I knew clearly whom I should hold fast to, but I was not yet one who could hold fast.[41]

Augustine's mind was opening to the true nature of God, not only through his reading of the Platonists[42], which he later acknowledged as being the means by which God prepared his mind to accept Scripture[43] but also by meditating on nature. And yet, even the glimpses he received of God quickly faded away as he was drawn back into the darkness of this world. The tormented ebb and flow of his spiritual life at this time is highlighted in his words, "I had caught the fragrance of a feast I could not consume."[44]

On one occasion an important official of the emperor's court paid a visit to Augustine and his friend Alypius. The original purpose of the visit was to request something of Augustine, but the conversation moved very quickly to spiritual things. The official was a Christian and noticing a copy of the scriptures on a table next to where they were sitting, he began to tell them the story of Antony, the Egyptian monk who forsook

40. Augustine, *Confessions*, 8.4.17.

41. Augustine, *Confessions*, 7.4.23.

42. Augustine described the philosophers' writings as "writings haunted in all kinds of ways by God and his Word." Augustine, *Confessions*, 8.2.3.

43. Augustine, *Confessions*, 7.4.26.

44. Augustine, *Confessions*, 7.4.23.

the things of this world for a home in the desert. As he unfolded the story, Augustine was convicted in his heart as he considered the worldly and selfish life he had lived up to that point. He was disgusted with himself as he mentally reviewed the last twelve years of his life: his pursuit of worldly fame, his lack of self-control, and his relentless pursuit of physical pleasure. Enraged with his stupidity, he realized he had no more excuses. He must commit to Christ. Bewildered by the anxious state of Augustine's mind, his friend Alypius followed him into a spacious and secluded household garden where Augustine began to tear at his hair, pound his head, hug his knees and make other disturbing bodily motions. He was tormented over his hesitation to serve the Lord even though he desired to serve him in his heart. Augustine wrote:

> So sick was I, so tortured, as I reviled myself more bitterly than ever, churning and chafing in my chains, not broken free of them entirely, held more loosely now but still held, as you were working in my hidden places, with your fierce pity wielding the double whip of fear and shame to prevent my relapse, to prevent the loosening and lighter bond that still held me from strengthening its grip, to grapple me again more tightly than before. My inner self was urging me: Now is the time! Now! With those words I was moving to a resolution, I was almost there—but was not there."[45]

He continued to struggle, eventually pulling away from Alypius so that he could be alone, free to weep unhindered by his friend's presence. He fell to the ground under a fig tree and cried out,

> How much more, Lord, how much more will this go on? Will you be forever angry, Lord, and never cease? Pay no further heed, I beg, to my entrenched vices. I felt still in the grip of those vices, and I blubbered pitiably: How long, how long—on the morrow is it, always tomorrow? Why never now? Why does this very hour not end all my vileness?"[46]

Without realizing it at the time, this was the moment of his deliverance, the chains of bondage he so often referred to would finally be smashed; his sins would be forgiven, new life would be granted to him, and his heart would be set free. As Augustine continued to weep he heard a child chanting the words, "take and read, take and read." Believing that

45. Augustine, *Confessions*, 8.5.25.
46. Augustine, *Confessions*, 8.5.27.

God was prompting him, he opened the scriptures and read the first verses his eyes fell upon, "Give up indulgence and drunkenness, give up lust and obscenity, give up strife and rivalries, and clothe yourself in Jesus Christ the Lord, leaving no further allowance for fleshly desires."[47] He said that immediately light began to flow into his heart bringing new assurance.[48] He described this as a ripping away of his chains moment.[49]

Augustine's friend Alypius wanted to see what he read and when he turned to the passage he read a few more lines, was encouraged in his own heart, and determined that he too would give his life to God. They both immediately went to speak with Augustine's mother Monica, whose heart was filled with joy at the news. She immediately broke out into an overflowing flood of praise to God for the wondrous work He had done in the heart of her son. Finally, after many years of tearful prayers, God had answered her prayers in a remarkable and wondrous way. From this point on Augustine gave up all pursuit of earthly gain, he retired from teaching rhetoric and abandoned his pursuit of marriage. Ambrose baptized him on Easter Sunday 387, along with his son Adeodatus, who was sixteen years of age.

After his conversion and baptism, Augustine, his mother, and companions left for Ostia, but his mother died while en route—she was fifty-six years of age. Her death was a great emotional blow to Augustine. He was thirty-three years old when she died and he and his friends abandoned their plan to go to Ostia, and instead went back to Rome. In 388, after spending eight to ten months in Rome, they went back to Africa, where Augustine sold his properties in Tagaste, gave most of his money to the poor, and then decided to live a quiet, monastic life of reflection with his son and some friends. Sadly, his son died in 389.

In 391 he went to Hippo in North Africa, where the Christian community forced him to accept the priesthood. In 395/396 he was appointed as co-bishop and in 397 he became the sole bishop of Hippo and would remain in that role till his death in 430.

47. Rom 13:13–14.

48. Augustine, *Confessions*, 8.5.29.

49. Augustine, *Confessions*, 8.1.1.

The Theological Disputes of Augustine

As the bishop of Hippo, Augustine immersed himself in his pastoral duties. He was a diligent writer who addressed many of the theological and practical issues of his day. He preached regularly, taught baptismal candidates, responded to letters, participated in church councils, and was able to bring about reconciliation between the Tertullianists and the Montanists with the Catholic Church. Augustine was particularly patient when dealing with heretics, in large part because he had been a heretic for many years and was patiently dealt with by his mother and Christian teachers like Ambrose.[50] Although Augustine wrote on a large number of topics, there were three main theological controversies that he sought to refute: Manichaeism, Donatism, and Pelagianism.

Manichaeism

After becoming the bishop of Hippo, Augustine first committed himself to the refutation of Manichaeism. Because he was once a Manichaean and was responsible for leading others into its fold, he felt a deep sense of responsibility to expose the false teaching of this sect.[51] Manichaeism is named after its founder, Mani who was born on April 14, 216 AD in Parthia. As a child, he allegedly received revelations from God instructing him to become a messenger of light and salvation. As such, he became the founder of a new religion called Manichaeism. Manichaeism was a syncretistic religious philosophy that included elements from Christianity, Judaism, Buddhism, Gnosticism, Zoroastrianism, and other eastern religions. It was a dualistic religion that sought to address the question, "Why does evil exist? The system was based on a belief in the primordial separation of light and darkness, good and evil which was understood to be the separation of spirit and matter. Light, good, and spirit made up the kingdom of light, whereas darkness, evil, and matter made up the kingdom of darkness. In the beginning, these two kingdoms were totally separated from one another, but at some point they came into conflict, resulting in a mixing of light and darkness, good and evil. The present world in which we live was created out of this struggle and consequently, all matter contains elements of light and darkness. Everything that is

---

50. Aquilina, *Fathers of the Church*, 247.

51. Gonzalez, *Story of Christianity*, 213.

good in this world can be attributed to the light and everything that is evil can be attributed to the darkness. This battle between light and darkness led to the creation of both Adam and Eve who are composed of both elements. In fact, they represent a small-scale version of the struggle between good and evil. Adam and Eve are not the creation of a good God but represent an attempt to keep light trapped in the material world. Salvation for the human being is to be freed from the material prison in which the light is confined. According to Manichaeism, Jesus was sent into the world by the kingdom of light to tell mankind how to be saved. While Jesus was sent to bring the knowledge of salvation to the world, Mani believed that his message was incomplete and that the full message had been revealed specifically to Mani himself. He rejected the orthodox belief that God became man because a being from the kingdom of light would never clothe himself with a material body. Like Gnosticism, Manichaeism taught that salvation was the deliverance of the soul from the material body and that only followers of the religion could bring this about. The elect, as they were called, lived ascetic lifestyles seeking to be involved as little as possible with matter, to free up as much light as they could. When the elect died, they were released from their material body enabling them to move in the direction of the kingdom of light. Those who were not of the elect were reincarnated as the elect, making them suitable for eventual salvation. The ultimate purpose in this was to move back to the original primordial state of complete separation of the kingdom of light and the kingdom of darkness. However, it would not be precisely the same because some light would be forever confined to the kingdom of darkness.[52]

Because of his immersion in Manichaean thinking, Augustine was uniquely qualified to defend the Christian faith against its false doctrine. He came to believe that their teaching was the teaching of demons and so he used his pen to expose their heresies.[53] His purpose in writing was not to intellectually crush those caught in the web of Manichaean deceit but to see them delivered from the teaching of this heretical sect.[54] He prayed that God would give him a calm and composed mind as he addressed the various errors.[55] One of the questions that Augustine addressed

---

52. Coyle, "Mani and Manicheism," 661–65.

53. Augustine, *Confessions*, 2.4.10.

54. Augustine, *Of the Morals of the Catholic Church*, 4:6.1.

55. Augustine, "Against the Epistle of Manichaeus," NPNF 1.1.

was the role of the will in decision making and its relation to evil. The Manichaeans taught that everything was preordained and that human beings were not free to choose but were moved by an innate necessity to act in a certain way. Augustine combatted this error by emphasizing the freedom of the human will. He argued that while it is true that human decisions are influenced by our circumstances, they are not determined by an innate necessity to act in a certain way.[56] He taught that the will is free enough to make choices for which a person is responsible, but not free enough to make choices that are without sin.[57] His teaching on free will enabled Augustine to answer the question about the origin of evil. If God is the creator of all things, did God create evil? Augustine said no. When God created man he created him good, but with the ability to fall away. Evil is not found in the essence of man, "but to negation or loss."[58] It is the corruption of that which is good.[59] Augustine argued that the human will was created by God and is therefore good. The ability to make decisions was a part of God's good creation, but it also meant that the will was capable of choosing between good and evil. Men and fallen angels exercised their freedom of will when they sinned against God which resulted in the introduction of evil, which is the loss or perversion of that which is good. Augustine concluded that evil finds its origin in the will of man, and angels, not God.[60]

Manichaeism taught Augustine that evil had a material existence.[61] They taught him that all things were made of a physical substance and that evil had its own unique material body.[62] Augustine eventually came to understand that evil is not a physical entity and has no existence in and of itself. He wrote, "I did not realize that evil does not exist of itself, but is a lack of good—short of the point where the lack erases existence altogether."[63] He came to define evil as a turning away from that which is of the highest good.[64] Evil is not part of creation but is the absence of good. It is the corruption of nature, not nature itself.

56. Gonzalez, *Story of Christianity*, 213.

57. Brown, *Heresies*, 205.

58. Augustine, "Of the Morals of the Manichaeans," 4:4.6.

59. Augustine, "Against the Epistle of Manichaeus," 4:35.39.

60. Gonzalez, *Story of Christianity*, 213.

61. Augustine, *Confessions*, 5.6.20.

62. Augustine, *Confessions*, 7.2.7.

63. Augustine, *Confessions*, 2.4.12.

64. Augustine, *Confessions*, 7.4.22.

As a Manichaean, he was also taught that God was a material being of immense size and magnificence.[65] He wrote, "If I tried to imagine God, I could think of nothing better than some vast material stuff, since it seemed to me that all reality had to be material—which was now my main and almost only source of imprisoning error."[66] While he didn't see God as taking on the form of a person he did view him as having some corporeal substance that resided in a specific location or was dispersed either throughout or outside the world.[67] After becoming a Christian, he began to see God as the creator and sustainer of the material world, not a piece of that material world.[68]

Donatism

From 303 to 305 the church suffered under the persecution of Emperor Diocletian. During this persecution, Christians were ordered to hand the scriptures over to the authorities or be punished for their refusal. Christians responded in three different ways to this order. First, some Christians and bishops willingly gave the scriptures to the authorities. Second, others refused to do so and suffered greatly for their defiance. Third, others handed over portions of manuscripts. After the persecution ended, the question was asked, "What should be done with the bishops who turned the scriptures over to the authorities? Some Christians believed the guilty bishops were "traitors" to the gospel and should be permanently removed from office, while others argued that it was not the personal purity of the bishop that gave him authority, but his ordination as a bishop. Those who argued that the bishops should be removed from office were known as Donatists, named after their leader Donatist who served as their bishop in Carthage from 313–55.

The division between the Catholic Church and the Donatists grew quickly and reconciliation seemed unlikely. After a series of often vehement exchanges between the two groups, emperor Constantine came out in support of the "traitors" and passed very strict laws against the Donatists, resulting in attacks upon some Donatist churches. In 321 Constantine changed his mind and abandoned any attempts at coercion,

65. Augustine, *Confessions*, 4.6.30.

66. Augustine, *Confessions*, 5.6.19.

67. Augustine, *Confessions*, 7.1.1.

68. Augustine, *Confessions*, 7.4.21.

most likely because of the growing influence of the Donatist church.[69] With this new found freedom, the Donatists spread rapidly throughout the Empire. They formed their own episcopal office in Rome in 320. In 330 they took over the leading church at Constantinople and in 336 Donatus called a council in Carthage that brought together 270 bishops. The Donatists were the dominant expression of the Christian faith in Africa for much of the fourth century.[70]

The Donatists were not a heretical body of Christians, but they believed that the Catholic Church was corrupt, not only because they allowed compromised bishops to remain in the ministry but also because of the growing relationship the church had with political authorities. Many Donatists believed that the Catholic Church was no longer a true church and should be rejected outright. They argued that ordinations performed by compromised bishops were not valid. They also rejected Catholic baptism as illegitimate and required people who joined them to be rebaptized.[71]

By 390 the Donatist church was at the summit of its power and influence, but the tide would soon turn against them. As a Catholic bishop, Augustine was unhappy with the influence of the Donatists in Hippo and throughout the empire. He was one of the few theologians with the intellectual ability to successfully debate with the Donatists and he turned all his intellectual strength against them. He disagreed with the Donatist's demand that the church and her leadership must be pure to administer the sacraments. Augustine believed that the church was a mixed body of believers and unbelievers and would remain so until the second coming of Jesus Christ, which is a central theme in his book *The City of God*. He sees support for his view in two biblical parables: The parable of the net,[72] and the parable of the weeds.[73] In the parable of the net, the net catches fish of many different types—both good and bad. The fish were then separated, the good ones were kept and the bad ones were thrown away. The fish represent believers and unbelievers who live together and will not be separated until the final day of judgement. In the parable of the weeds, both the weeds and the wheat grow together in the same field. The wheat

---

69. Dowley, ed., *History of Christianity*, 196.

70. *Encyclopedia of Ancient Christianity*, 736.

71. Walker, *History of the Christian Church*, 202.

72. Matt 13:47–50.

73. Matt 13:24–30.

represents believers and the weeds represent unbelievers. Both the wheat and the weeds are to be left to grow together until harvest time, which represents the Second coming of Jesus Christ. Augustine interpreted the field in which the weeds and the wheat grow as representing the church. Until the final day, the church will never be an entirely pure body and we should not expect it to be. Nor should we attempt to remove the "weeds" from the church but leave them alone until Jesus comes again to separate the wheat from the weeds.[74] According to Augustine, because the church is a mixed body, and even true Christians are sinners, the presence of sin in the church is not a sufficient reason for schism.[75]

Augustine also argued that the efficaciousness of any church ordinance was not dependent on the purity of the one administering it, otherwise, Christians would live in a constant state of doubt about the legitimacy of their own baptism. He did however argue that the ordinances of the church were only efficacious if they were performed by an ordained representative of the church.[76] This became the dominant view of the western church and was also held by most of the Protestant reformers, except for the more radical separatist groups of the Reformation.[77]

Augustine was unable to defeat the Donatists on intellectual grounds, so he encouraged the Roman authorities to get more directly involved in putting down the Donatist movement. Augustine quoted (out of context), Luke 14:23, "compel them to come in," as biblical support to justify calling upon the civil authorities to settle a church matter. Although he did not support the death penalty, he did support strict punishments enacted against the Donatists. He believed that as a Catholic Christian, the emperor was obligated to intervene for the sake of the salvation of those who lived outside the Catholic fold. The Roman emperor Honorius who ruled from 393–423 banned the Donatist church from Africa and confiscated all of their property. The conference of Carthage in May, 411 condemned the Donatists, and from that point on they began to lose ground to the Catholic Church. Several Donatist communities eventually reunited with the Catholic Church, and while there were some minor revivals of Donatism, they would never regain their prior preeminence and

---

74. McGrath, *Historical Theology*, 75.

75. McGrath, *Historical Theology*, 76.

76. Woodbridge, *Great Leaders of the Christian Church*, 90.

77. McGrath, *Historical Theology*, 77.

eventually disappeared with the rise of Islam and the Islamic takeover of North Africa in the seventh century AD.[78]

Pelagianism

The Pelagian controversy took place in the fourth century between Augustine and a British monk named Pelagius. We know very little about the early life of Pelagius. We know neither the date of his birth nor the date of his death. Early sources tell us that he was a learned man who spoke both Greek and Latin. In 405 while in Rome, he heard the words of Augustine, "I have no hope at all, then, but in your pity for me. Granting what you require, require whatever you will."[79] He was not impressed with the emphasis on the need of divine grace in one's life to live in obedience to God's commands, so Pelagius began to write and preach against Augustine's views.

The Pelagian controversy has been described as "a struggle for the very foundations of Christianity."[80] Pelagius taught the total freedom of the human will and thus denied the sovereignty of God in salvation. He believed that "All men are ruled by their own will,"[81] and that he acts without any assistance from God.[82] In his own strength, man is capable of obeying God's commands. In fact, God only issued commands that can be obeyed.[83] When we sin, it is a voluntary act and not due to a sinful nature inherited from Adam. He believed that Adam's sin was his own and was not handed down through his descendants.[84] Babies are born without sin and are capable of choosing to live a sinless life. God in no way assists us in our performance of moral duties, but only provides moral guidance. The central principle of Pelagianism is the belief that human beings are capable of living up to all that righteousness requires, that is, a man can live a life that is pleasing to God in his own strength.[85]

78. Walker, *History of the Christian Church*, 203.

79. Augustine, *Confessions*, 10.4.40.

80. Warfield, "Introductory Essay," NPNF, 4:xiv.

81. Augustine, *On the Proceedings of Pelagius*, NPNF, 5:5.

82. Augustine, *On the Proceedings of Pelagius*, NPNF, Chapter 7.

83. Pelagius, *Letter to Demitrius*, NPNF, 16.

84. Brown, *Heresies*, 201.

85. B.B.Warfield, "Introductory Essay," NPNF, 4:xiv.

One might ask whether or not Christianity is even necessary if the doctrines of Pelagius are true. If there is no original sin, and the will of man is not corrupt, what need is there for a Saviour? If a man can live a sinless life in his own strength, Jesus could be relegated to being nothing more than a good example to follow.[86] The substitutionary death of Christ is not a necessary part of Pelagian thinking. This insidious doctrine needed to be confronted and defeated, so Augustine took it upon himself to defend orthodox doctrine against it.

Unlike Pelagius, Augustine taught that human beings are conceived and born in sin and have an inward desire toward evil. Augustine taught that when Adam was created, he was created good, but with the ability to sin. Adam was the only one who truly possessed a will that was capable of choosing between good and evil. Sadly, Adam misused his free will and sinned against God, which destroyed the possibility of fellowship with God. As a result of Adam's sin, it was now impossible for him to live a life without sin. His nature became corrupt and this corrupt nature was handed on to all his progeny.[87] Because of their corrupt nature, a person cannot obey the commandments of God and do not possess the power to live a holy life. Augustine did not deny that humans still possessed a will, but argued that human wills are enslaved because of sin. He provided a helpful illustration of this,

> Consider a pair of scales, with two balance pans. One balance pan represents good, and the other evil. If the pans are properly balanced, the arguments in favour of doing good or doing evil could be weighed, and a proper conclusion drawn. The parallel with the human free will is obvious: we weigh up the arguments in favour of doing good and evil, and act accordingly. But what, asks Augustine, if the balance pans are loaded? What happens if someone puts several heavy weights in the balance pan on the side of evil? The scales will still work, but they are seriously biased towards making an evil decision.[88]

Although the sinner is free to choose between various options, he is no longer free to not sin. A fallen human being will always choose sin.

Augustine also argued that salvation is a gift of God, and cannot be secured through human merit. He often quoted John 15:5: "...for apart

86. Brown, *Heresies*, 202.

87. Brown, *Heresies*, 202–3.

88. McGrath, *Historical Theology*, 80.

from me you can do nothing." The nature of man is sinful and without the transforming power of the Holy Spirit, he will never choose God because it is impossible for him to do anything apart from God's grace in his life. God shows mercy to the elect by giving the grace necessary to believe but metes out justice to the non-elect by passing over them and leaving them in their sin. Our salvation is based not upon our own works, but solely upon the sacrificial death and resurrection of Jesus Christ.

Although the controversy raged on for several years, Pelagianism was eventually rejected by the church. It was condemned at the Council of Carthage in 418 as well as the Council of Ephesus in 431. Despite its condemnation, Pelagianism in various forms has continued throughout the history of the church. Even in Augustine's day, some struggled with his emphasis on grace. Many of the monastic communities suspected that his teaching on grace undermined the life of prayer to which they were devoted. Many also saw it as removing human responsibility. This resulted in the development of semi-Pelagianism which sought to provide a middle-of-the-road position. Semi-Pelagianism taught that the initial act of faith in God was an act of the will unassisted by divine grace, but that divine grace was needed once a man exercised his faith in God. Augustine took exception to this idea arguing instead that grace was necessary at every stage of a sinful man's pursuit of God. The will must be transformed by the Holy Spirit before a man will ever reach out to God in faith.[89]

While there were many attempts to snuff out both Pelagianism and Semi-Pelagianism, they continue to influence the thinking of both Christians and non-Christians alike. Pelagianism can be seen as the undergirding philosophy in modern humanism with its belief in the inherent power and goodness of humanity. Semi-Pelagianism or Arminianism is alive and well in Wesleyan, free will Baptist, Pentecostal, and other Christian denominations. The influence of Augustine is also felt throughout the global Christian community. The theology of the Protestant Reformation was predominately Augustinian and continues to provide the foundation for the theology of many Reformed, Baptist, Presbyterian, and other Christian denominations throughout the world.

89. Hinson, *Early Church*, 338.

Discussion Questions

1. What does Augustine's life story teach us about God's grace and love toward sinners?

2. Do you agree with Augustine's view that humans have a will free enough to make choices for which they are responsible, but not free enough to make choices that are without sin? Why or why not? How would you support your answer with Scripture?

3. Regarding Augustine's approach to Donatists, how would you respond to Augustine's view that because the church is a mixed body of believers and nonbelievers, including Christians that sin, that the presence of sin in the church is not sufficient reason for schism?

4. Explain the differences between the views of Pelagius and Augustine concerning human will.

5. What are the basic beliefs of semi-Pelagianism? How would you refute semi-Pelagian doctrine?

Chapter 16

Patrick (c.389–c.461/492)

"APOSTLE TO THE IRISH"

In 54 BC, Julius Caesar (dictator from 49–44 BC) was the first Roman who attempted to conquer Britain and bring it under the umbrella of the Roman Empire. He failed in this effort, and it would not be until 43 AD that emperor Claudius managed to turn it into an imperial province under Roman authority. Roman rule in Britain would last for three hundred and sixty-seven years, providing stability to the region. Although much of Britain was brought under Roman control, the Picts in the north (modern-day Scotland) would not submit to the Romans. In 122 AD, emperor Hadrian began constructing the wall, known as Hadrian's Wall, to protect Roman Britain from the northern tribes. The wall marked the most northern border of the empire.

In the final decades of the fourth century and the early years of the fifth century, the Barbarians[1] became a severe threat on the Roman empire's northern border of the Danube. The Vandals and the Alans came from Gaul and settled in the unprotected provinces of Spain. The Franks began to cross the Rhine into Roman territory with little opposition. Rome was in full retreat, and on August 24, 410, the Visigoth, Alaric, sacked the city of Rome. Although he left after three days, the western Roman Empire was in an irreversible state of decline. The city of Rome was sacked a second time in 455 by the Vandals. In 476, the last western

1. Barbarian was a derogatory name to describe anyone who lived outside the Roman Empire. It was first used by the Greeks when referring to people that lived beyond their territory. The word Barbarian refers to the incomprehensible language of a foreigner. It sounded like they were babbling to the Greek and Roman ear. They were viewed as an uncultured, and savage people.

Roman emperor, Romulus Augustulus, was deposed by the Germanic barbarian king, Odoacer.[2] By the end of the fifth century, the western Roman empire had fallen[3] and was replaced with independent kingdoms of Barbarian tribal groups.[4]

The decline of the empire was devastating for Roman Britain. For several decades leading up to the final withdrawal of Rome from Britain, the various pagan tribal groups became increasingly bold in their attacks. In 410, the last Roman legions left the island, and the emperor, Honorius (393–423), told the Britains they were on their own and should not expect any further help from the empire. It was not long before Britain was overrun by Angles, Saxons, and Jukes—Viking invaders from Denmark.[5]

The Irish also became a thorn in the flesh to the people of Roman Britain. They were never part of the Roman empire, and with the decline and ultimate fall of Roman Britain, Irish raiders came across the water to capture unsuspecting people and carry them off as slaves to Ireland. The early fifth century was a time of violence, fear, instability, and suffering in Britain. It was into this changing, tumultuous, cruel, and disintegrating world that Patrick was born.

Patrick was born into a Christian family of moderate means sometime around 389 AD in Roman Britain. His father Calpurnius, served as a deacon in the church and was a local magistrate. His grandfather, Potitus, was a priest. His mother's name was Concessa. As a young man, Patrick appears to have lived a carefree and non-religious life. He did not heed the teaching of the priests and was more interested in sports than in academic pursuits.[6] He confessed that at sixteen years of age, he did not know God.[7] This changed, however, when he experienced a very dramatic and life-disrupting event.

When Patrick was sixteen years of age, he, along with thousands of other Britains, were captured by a band of pirates and sold into slavery in Ireland. He spent six years in captivity serving as a herdsman (c.405–411). Patrick believed that this culling of the British was a deserved punishment

2. Mathisen, *Ancient Roman Civilization*, 467–68.

3. The Eastern Byzantine Empire would continue for another thousand years.

4. Mathisen, *Ancient Roman Civilization*, 472.

5. Mathisen, *Ancient Roman Civilization*, 467.

6. St. Secundinus, "Hymn on St. Patrick," *Works of St. Patrick*, 4.

7. "Patrick's Confession," *Works of St. Patrick*, 1.

from God because of their rebellion against God's commands.[8] While a captive in Ireland, God began to move in his heart, bringing about a religious conversion. Patrick wrote that he,

> lived in death and unbelief until I was severely chastised and really humiliated, by hunger and nakedness, and that daily…I did not go to Ireland of my own accord, not until I had nearly perished; but this was rather for my good, for thus was I purged by the Lord; and He made me fit so that I might be now what was once far from me.[9]

Further to this, he wrote, "I must not, however, hide God's gift which He bestowed upon me in the land of my captivity; because then I earnestly sought Him, and there I found Him, and He saved me from all evil."[10] While in captivity, despite the harsh weather he endured while working outdoors, he started praying multiple times, both day and night, with great fervor. At some point, while praying one night, God spoke to Patrick, saying, "It is well that you fast, soon you will go to your own country." A short time later, he heard the words, "See, your ship is ready."[11] In response to these words, Patrick fled and, after a long and arduous journey, made his way back to Britain. Upon returning, he went to live with his family. Having grown more serious about spiritual things, he continued his education which had been interrupted because of his time in exile. The six-year gap in his education deeply affected Patrick's view of his own abilities, and he struggled with insecurity for the rest of his life. An example of this insecurity is seen in his following words,

> As a youth, nay, almost as a boy not able to speak, I was taken captive, before I knew what to pursue and what to avoid. Hence to-day I blush and fear exceedingly to reveal my lack of education; for I am unable to tell my story to those versed in the art of concise writing—in such a way, I mean, as my spirit and mind long to do, and so that the sense of my words expresses what I feel.[12]

He also wanted to write but was hesitant because of his lack of education. He wrote, "I had long had it in mind to write, but up to now I

8. "Patrick's Confession," *Works of St. Patrick*, 1.

9. "Patrick's Confession," *Works of St. Patrick*, 27, 28.

10. "Patrick's Confession," *Works of St. Patrick*, 33.

11. "Patrick's Confession," *Works of St. Patrick*, 17.

12. "Patrick's Confession," *Works of St. Patrick*, 10.

have hesitated. I was afraid lest I should fall under the judgment of men's tongues because I am not as well read as others."[13] Despite this handicap, he felt compelled to speak about all that God had done for him.

One night, while dreaming, Patrick heard a voice saying, "We ask thee, boy, come and walk among us once more."[14] From this point on, there was a burning desire set aflame in the heart of Patrick for the Irish people. Even though many sought to persuade him of the folly of going back to Ireland, he was resolute in the call to preach the gospel. He wrote, "I am prepared to give even my life without hesitation and most gladly for His name, and it is there that I wish to spend it until I die, if the Lord, would grant it to me."[15] Elsewhere he wrote, "I never had any reason except the Gospel and its promises why I should ever return to the people from whom once before I barely escaped."[16] And so, with a fire in his heart to serve the Lord and an unshakable belief in the gospel, he prepared to go back to Ireland, this time, not as a slave to the Irish, but a freed slave of Jesus Christ. Patrick said, "I am a servant in Christ to a foreign nation for the unspeakable glory of life everlasting which is in Christ Jesus our Lord."[17]

The Ireland in which Patrick preached the gospel was untouched by the influence of Roman culture. The people of Britain, Scotland, Ireland, and western Europe were known by the Greeks as the Celts as early as 500 BC. Some of these people groups also referred to themselves as Celts at this time.[18] The Celts did not represent a single and unified people group but included many tribes that shared a similar culture and a common Indo-European Celtic language.[19] Each tribe had a specific marked-out portion of land that included forests and wilderness. They functioned within a tribal system in which the extended family was of paramount importance. There were no cities, but there was a great abundance of farms and farmland. Many of the farms in Britain today are located on ancient Celtic sites. When Julius Caesar first invaded Britain, he was impressed with the large population and the numerous cattle and farms.

13. "Patrick's Confession," *Works of St. Patrick,* 9.

14. "Patrick's Confession," *Works of St. Patrick,* 23.

15. "Patrick's Confession," *Works of St. Patrick,* 37.

16. "Patrick's Confession," *Works of St. Patrick,* 61.

17. *Letter to the Soldiers of Coroticus,* 2.10.

18. Mathisen, *Ancient Roman Civilization,* 7.

19. Mathisen, *Ancient Roman Civilization,* 8.

The Celts were polytheistic. The names of three hundred and seventy-three gods and goddesses are known, many of which would have probably represented deities connected with a particular tribe. Twenty of these names are mentioned more frequently and probably represent the principal gods of the larger community of Celts spread across Europe.[20]

The religion of Ireland was that of the Druids. The Druids were both male and female and held incredible power over the people.[21] They were more than just religious leaders. They also preserved the community's culture and lore (teachings) and had authority over every tribal chief. They were the educated class who filled the many intellectual and leadership positions in society: functions like "philosopher, judge, teacher, historian, poet, musician, physician, astronomer, prophet, political adviser or counselor," and sometimes even kings.[22] The colleges of the Druids were famous throughout Europe, and the program of study was long and rigorous. A candidate had to study from twelve to twenty years, and the course of study included memorizing the oral tradition of the people.[23] Sadly none of these oral traditions have been written down, and our understanding of the Druid religion is limited.

The first missionary to Ireland was Palladius (408–431- c. 457/461). He left Ireland only a few months into his mission because of fierce opposition from the Druids who likely feared losing their position of influence amongst the Irish people. According to Patrick, Palladius' mission was a failure. Nevertheless, there were a few Christians in Ireland when Patrick arrived.

Patrick landed in Ireland a few years later (c.432), and over several decades of relentless work, he successfully spread the gospel throughout much of the country. Although Patrick was exposed to many dangers and his life was threatened several times, his missionary efforts were blessed. He saw massive numbers of people converted, and he baptized thousands of souls. He wrote,

> Hence, how did it come to pass in Ireland that those who never
> had a knowledge of God, but until now always worshipped idols
> and things impure, have now been made a people of the Lord,

20. Ellis, *Druids,* 114.

21. Ellis, *Druids,* 21.

22. Ellis, *Druids,* 14.

23. Ellis, *Druids,* 13, 14.

and are called sons of God, that the sons and daughters of the kings of the Irish are seen to be monks and virgins of Christ?[24]

He also oversaw the ordination of large numbers of clergy.[25] His love for the people of Ireland is clearly seen in his writings. He wrote:

> I went to you and everywhere for your sake in many dangers, even to the farthest districts, beyond which there lived nobody and where nobody had ever come to baptize, or to ordain clergy, or to confirm the people. With the grace of the Lord, I did everything lovingly and gladly for your salvation.[26]

These kinds of comments are sprinkled throughout his confession.

Patrick was certainly skilled in the art of diplomacy, as evidenced by his ability to move and preach freely throughout the country. As he traveled about, he would give presents to the different tribal kings and pay the expenses of their children who traveled with him.[27] He would also pay money to the local administrators in the districts that he frequently visited.[28] It appears that his method of evangelism was to focus on the leaders, believing that the people would quickly embrace the faith of their princes.

Patrick was fearless in his defense of the church in Ireland. He wrote, "Daily I expect murder, fraud, or captivity, or whatever it may; *but I fear none of these things.*"[29] On one occasion, he was compelled to speak out against the violence committed against some new converts. The day after a group of converts was baptized, Coroticus, a British chieftain, and his soldiers attacked them, savagely slaughtering them. Those not killed were kidnapped, taken to Britain, and sold to the pagan Scots and Picts. In response, Patrick wrote a scathing letter of rebuke to Coroticus, calling him to repent of his heinous crimes against the church. According to one tradition, having spent about thirty years as a missionary to the Irish people, Patrick died at Saul in Ulster on March 17, 461. Other traditions place his death around 492.

The church established by Patrick had a couple of distinguishing marks. First, it was evangelistic. The Irish church continued to prosper

24. "Patrick's Confession," *Works of St. Patrick*, 41.

25. "Patrick's Confession," *Works of St. Patrick*, 50.

26. "Patrick's Confession," *Works of St. Patrick*, 51.

27. "Patrick's Confession," *Works of St. Patrick*, 51.

28. "Patrick's Confession," *Works of St. Patrick*, 53.

29. "Patrick's Confession," *Works of St. Patrick*, 55.

after Patrick's death, becoming a place of great learning and missionary endeavor. For hundreds of years, young men from England and other countries went to Ireland to study at Irish schools. In 565, the Irishman Columba, along with a dozen young men, established a monastery on the island of Iona, just off the shores of Scotland. From that location, they successfully preached the gospel to Picts. Other Irish missionaries preached the gospel in France, Switzerland, Italy, and other European countries.

Second, asceticism and the monastic life were encouraged and practiced. In chapter twelve, we saw that Basil's monasteries functioned in cooperation with the broader church community. The local bishop, not the abbot, possessed supreme authority in the monastery. Patrick established a de-centralized form of church government. The abbot, not the local bishop, had ultimate authority in the church, and the abbots appointed men to the office of bishop. This form of church government continued for more than two centuries. In the mid-sixth century, several important monasteries were established in Ireland at Derry, Clonard, Durrow, Bangor, Clonmacnoise, and Clonfert.[30]

Discussion Questions

1. What do you think are the reasons for Patrick's missionary success?

2. What does Patrick's life experience teach us about God's providence in our own lives?

30. Ferguson, *Church History*, 1:354.

Chapter 17

Leo the Great (c.390–461 AD)

"Majesty took on humility, strength weakness, eternity mortality: and for the paying off of the debt belonging to our condition inviolable nature was united with passible nature, so that, as suited the needs of our case, one and the same Mediator between God and men, the Man Christ Jesus, could both die with the one and not die with the other. Thus in the whole and perfect nature of the true man was true God born, complete in what was His own, complete in what was ours."—Leo the Great

Leo, also known as Leo the Great, lived during a time of great upheaval. The western Roman empire was in its final years, and the Barbarians were overrunning the land. There was ecclesiastical confusion in the church, with few men of the character and strength needed for strong leadership in these tumultuous times. A notable exception was Leo I, bishop of Rome. A gifted preacher, theologian, administrator, and negotiator, Leo I took a leading role in rebuilding Europe from the ashes of the western Roman empire. He is a key figure in understanding the transition between the Roman world and the rise of Christendom.

Little is known about Leo's early years. He was born sometime around 390, but his birthplace is unknown. He served as archdeacon in the 420's and 430's in the church in Rome, and he was elected the bishop of Rome while he was traveling on church business. He served in this role from 440–461.

The influence of Leo on the church is undeniable. Yet, this influence was rightly said to be "partly for good and partly for bad."[1] Leo is prob-

---

1. Schaff and Wace, eds., "Introduction," NPNF, 12:v.

218

ably most famous for negotiating peace with Attila the Hun (406–453) in 452. If not for his negotiating ability, Rome may have been destroyed by the Huns. Leo also contributed to the rise of the Roman Catholic papacy. Many historians identify Leo as the first pope, and even those who disagree must acknowledge that Leo led the way in establishing the doctrinal basis for the papacy. His most significant and positive contribution to the church is theological. Leo was instrumental in combatting the false teaching of both Nestorianism and Eutychianism on the nature of Christ. His doctrinal formula on the nature of Christ is accepted as the orthodox position in the church.

Attila the Hun

Attila, king of the Huns, established a vast empire in western Asia and eastern Europe in the fifth century AD. In 451, he began an invasion of western Europe, and in 452, Attila led his armies into Italy, capturing the city of Aquileia. After taking the city, there was nothing that stood between him and the city of Rome. Emperor Valentinian III sent Leo with two other envoys to negotiate peace with Attila. Nothing is known about the conversation between them, but it must have been an extraordinary discussion. Following his meeting with Leo, Attila agreed not to attack Rome, turned his armies to the north, and died shortly thereafter in 453. We will never know what Leo said to convince this great warlord to turn back, but we can certainly conclude that Leo was an exceptional negotiator and singlehandedly saved Rome from the wrath of the Huns. Unfortunately, in 455, the Vandals sacked the city of Rome. Leo negotiated with the Vandal leader, Genseric (also known as Gaiseric), and while he could not prevent the Vandals from taking Rome, he managed to keep them from burning the city and destroying the churches. Leo's success in negotiating with these foreign invaders would undoubtedly have increased his prestige and authority in the city of Rome.

The Nature of Christ

Leo defended an orthodox Christology in the face of heretical views on the nature of Christ. There were three important councils during the life of Leo, the Council of Ephesus in 431 (the Third Ecumenical Council), the second Council of Ephesus in 449, and the Council of Chalcedon (the fourth Ecumenical Council) in 451.

The Council of Ephesus in 431 was the third ecumenical council, called by the Roman emperor Theodosius II (408–50) and presided over by Cyril (c.378–444), bishop of Alexandria from 412–44. More than two hundred bishops gathered to settle what is known as the Nestorian controversy.

Nestorius was born c.381 and was appointed as Bishop of Constantinople in 428. While he was bishop, he began to make his views on the nature of Christ more publicly known. He strongly objected to referring to Mary as the mother of God (Theotokos), saying that, at best, Mary can be said to be the mother of the man Jesus. He believed that applying the term to Mary led to a misunderstanding of the relationship between the human and divine nature of Christ.[2] Attempting to protect the nature of Christ from the errors of Apollinarianism[3] and Arianism, Nestorius sought to preserve the distinctions between the humanity and deity of Christ. However, it appears that he went too far. According to Leo, Nestorius denied that there was any union between the deity and the humanity of Jesus at his conception. The Son of God did not become the Son of man but only "linked himself with created man."[4] Nestorius was accused of teaching that the deity and humanity of Christ represent two separate, distinct natures, and thus two distinct persons, two Christs, and two Sons. He argued that the Logos indwelt the human man Jesus, which made Jesus a God-bearing man. Nestorius denied this accusation claiming instead that he believed in the unity of Jesus Christ.[5]

The Council of Ephesus opened on June 22, 431. After much discussion, it ruled against Nestorius, removed him from his position as Archbishop of Constantinople, and excommunicated him from the church. His doctrines were condemned, and the orthodox doctrine of the Nicene Creed was affirmed. The council emphasized the true personal unity of Christ, declared Mary the mother of God (Theotokos), and also renewed the condemnation of Pelagianism. Whether or not Nestorius was a heretic is a question on which scholars are divided. Some believe that his enemies misrepresented his teaching, and his condemnation was more political than theological.[6] Nevertheless, the church rejected the Christological doctrine that was identified with his name.

2. Gonzalez, *History of Christian Thought*, 354.

3. See Appendix 1.

4. "Sermon 28.5," NPNF 12:143.

5. "Nestorius—Nestorianism," *Encyclopedia of Ancient Christianity*, 2:907.

6. Gonzalez, *History of Christian Thought*, 360.

The second council of Ephesus, in 449, was not one of the four great ecumenical councils but was nonetheless an important gathering. There were one hundred and thirty bishops in attendance, and they gathered to examine the teaching of a monk named Eutyches. Leo was unable to attend the council personally but sent three emissaries to represent his views. Eutyches (c.378–454) was the leader of a large monastery in Constantinople and was thus a very influential man. Although he opposed Nestorianism, he was guilty of another heresy. He argued that before the Incarnation, Jesus Christ had two natures, one human and one divine. After the Incarnation, the two natures were mixed, forming one new nature. He also denied that the body of Jesus Christ was fully human. He argued that Jesus' body was not of the same substance as our bodies.[7]

Eutyches was condemned at an earlier local council held in Constantinople in 448 and was consequently removed from the priesthood and the administration of the monastery. He wrote a letter to Leo[8] arguing that he was wrongly treated and the accusations against him were false. He affirmed his belief in the Nicene Creed and called upon Leo to act in his defense. The Council of Ephesus in 449 was called to investigate the issue further. Leo provided a written response to the topic at hand to be read during the council. The council was a raucous affair, and it had difficulty conducting any business, mainly because a large number of unruly monks interrupted the proceedings. Leo's letter was not read, but Eutyches was allowed to publicly defend his position, which was accepted as orthodox by the council members. He was brought back into fellowship with the church and was reinstated to his position as Abbot of the monastery. There was a great deal of outrage at the proceedings, and it came to be known as "the robber council of Ephesus."[9]

The Council of Chalcedon (fourth ecumenical council) was called by Marcian, emperor of the east from 450–57, in 451, and was held in the city of Chalcedon. It was called in part to repair the damage done by the second council of Ephesus. Five to six hundred bishops gathered to address the Eutychian heresy. Many consider it the most important of the early ecumenical councils because it dealt effectively with the Christological controversy that plagued the church. It precisely defined the relationship between the human and divine nature of Christ, and its definition is

7. "Letter 26," *A Second One from Flavian to Leo*, 37.

8. "Letter 21," *From Eutyches to Leo*, 32–34.

9. NPNF "Introduction," 12:viii.

still accepted as orthodox in the church.[10] Leo played a crucial role in the success of the council.

Leo's letter, that was not read at the Council of Ephesus, was read out at the Council of Chalcedon. It is probably his most significant letter and is commonly known as "the Tome."[11] In response to Eutyches' denial of the full humanity of Jesus, Leo emphasized that Jesus "took our nature on Him and made it His own." He also wrote, "For though the Holy Spirit imparted fertility to the Virgin, yet a real body was received from her body." When speaking about the relationship between the deity and humanity of Jesus, Leo wrote, "For both natures retain their own proper character without loss; and as the form of God did not do away with the form of a slave, so the form of a slave did not impair the form of God." As one reads through his letter, Leo's understanding of the relationship between the deity and humanity of Christ becomes increasingly clear:

> For it must again and again be repeated that one and the same is truly Son of God and truly son of man, God in that "in the beginning was the Word, and the Word was with GOD, and the Word was God;" man in that "the Word became flesh and dwelt in us." God in that "all things were made by Him, and without Him was nothing made:" man in that "he was made of a woman, made under the law."[12]

Leo's statement of faith is rooted in the Apostle's Creed and the Nicene Creed. He declared this to be the belief of the true body of Christ. He wrote:

> The whole body of the faithful confess that they *believe in God the Father Almighty, and in Jesus Christ, His only Son, our Lord, who was born of the Holy Spirit and the Virgin Mary.* By which three statements the devices of almost all heretics are overthrown. For not only is God believed to be both Almighty and the Father, but the Son is shown to be coeternal with Him, differing in nothing from the Father because He is God from God, Almighty from Almighty, and being born from the Eternal one is co-eternal with Him; not later in point of time, not lower in power, not unlike in glory, not divided in essence: but at the same time the

10. Need, *Truly Divine and Truly Human*, 93.

11. "Letter 28," 38–43.

12. "Letter 28.4," 41.

only begotten of the eternal Father was born eternal of the Holy
Spirit and the Virgin Mary.[13]

After articulating the orthodox position on the nature of Christ,
the council condemned Eutychus for teaching that the LORD had two
natures before the incarnation but only one after the fact. Leo criticized
the council of Ephesus of 449 for their failure to recognize the danger
of Eutychus' opinions. He believed that most heresies are rooted in an
unwillingness to accept the two natures of Christ in one person.[14] He
recognized many falsehoods, but he singled out Nestorianism and Eutychianism as being particularly dangerous and encouraged people to
avoid them.[15]

The Council of Chalcedon produced the following Creed:

> We then, following the holy Fathers, all with one consent, teach
> men to confess one and the same Son, our Lord Jesus Christ, the
> same perfect in Godhead and also perfect in manhood; truly
> God and truly man, of a reasonable [rational] soul and body;
> consubstantial [coessential] with the Father according to the
> Godhead, and consubstantial with us according to the Man-
> hood; in all things like unto us, without sin; begotten before all
> ages of the Father according to the Godhead, and in these latter
> days, for us and for our salvation, born of the Virgin Mary, the
> Mother of God, according to the Manhood; one and the same
> Christ, Son, Lord, Only-begotten, to be acknowledged in two
> natures; inconfusedly, unchangeably, indivisibly, inseparably;
> the distinction of natures being by no means taken away by the
> union, but rather the property of each nature being preserved,
> and concurring in one Person and one Subsistence, not parted
> or divided into two persons, but one and the same Son, and only
> begotten God the Word, the Lord Jesus Christ, as the prophets
> from the beginning [have declared] concerning him, and the
> Lord Jesus Christ himself has taught us; and the Creed of the
> holy Fathers has handed down to us.[16]

The Creed incorporated the Nicene and the Constantinopolitan
Creeds into its definition. The council did not believe they were rewrit-
ing or replacing the earlier creeds but were affirming their truthfulness.

13. "Letter 28.2," 39.

14. "Sermon 28.4," 142.

15. "Sermon 28.5," 143.

16. Schaff, Trans. *Creeds of Christendom*, 2:62–63.

Although it did not silence debate on the relationship between the humanity and deity of Christ, it has remained the orthodox statement of faith in the Roman Catholic and Protestant churches to the present day.[17] Many churches in the east, including Coptic, Syrian, Ethiopian, and Armenian, rejected the Chalcedon statement.[18]

The Rise of the Papacy

Leo promoted the primacy of the Roman church and the authority of the pope of Rome. The term pope means "father" and was used when referring to any esteemed bishop in the early centuries of the church. In the western church, it eventually came to be used exclusively for the bishop of Rome. Leo was instrumental in this development along with the centralization of church government with ultimate authority placed in the hands of the bishop of Rome. When Leo was the bishop of Rome in the fifth century, he did not have the universal authority the pope would eventually possess in the Roman Catholic Church. He did, however, believe that he possessed that authority and promoted his belief throughout the church. From the beginning of his ministry, we catch a glimpse of his view of the Roman bishopric. When Leo was elected bishop of Rome, he preached on the day of his ordination. He referred to himself as the successor of Peter, appointed to stand at the church's helm.[19] He said that the office of Peter was perpetual and established by Jesus Christ himself.[20] He quoted Matthew 16:16–19 (a main Roman Catholic text to this day) in support of his belief that the bishop of Rome is the successor of Peter.

Leo wrote many letters to bishops in which he continued to assert this authority over them. He wrote in his letter to Dioscorus, bishop of Alexandria, and argued that Mark would not have made decisions apart from the will of Peter in Rome.

> For since the most blessed Peter received the headship of the Apostles from the LORD, and the church of Rome still abides by His institutions, it is wicked to believe that His holy disciple

---

17. Need, *Truly Divine and Truly Human*, 99–100.

18. Need, *Truly Divine and Truly Human*, 108.

19. "Sermon 2.2," 116.

20. "Sermon 3.2," 117.

Mark,[21] who was the first to govern the church of Alexandria, formed his decrees on a different line of tradition.[22]

He also wrote a letter to the Bishops of the Province of Vienne in which he said:

> He has placed the principal charge on the blessed Peter, chief of all the Apostles; and from him as from the Head wishes His gifts to flow to all the body: so that any one who dares to secede from Peter's solid rock may understand that he has no part or lot in the divine mystery.[23]

He wrote in the same letter:

> The Apostolic See, such is the reverence in which it is held, has times out of number been referred to and consulted by the priests of your province as well as others, and in the various matters of appeal, as the old usage demanded, it has reversed or confirmed decisions: and in this way "the unity of the spirit in the bond of peace" has been kept.[24]

The council at Chalcedon gave a precise definition of the nature of Christ for the church, but it also helped to promote the authority of the papacy. After reading Leo's letter (the Tome), the bishops cried out, "This is the faith of the fathers, this is the faith of the Apostles. So we all believe, thus the orthodox believe. Anathema to him who does not thus believe. Peter has spoken thus through Leo…"[25] In doing so, the bishops strengthened the idea that the bishop of Rome possessed the authority of the apostle Peter to speak on behalf of the church, and thus the Papacy was established.

Discussion Questions

1. How much authority, if any, do the early ecumenical councils have in the church today?

21. It is believed that Mark, the disciple of Peter, was the first to preach the gospel in Alexandria.

22. "Letter 9.1," *To Dioscorus, Bishop of Alexandria*, 7.

23. "Letter 10.1," *To the Bishops of the Province of Vienne*, 8.

24. "Letter 10.2," 9.

25. NPNF, "Seven Ecumenical Councils," 14:259.

2. Describe the importance of having a precise definition of the relationship between the humanity and the deity of Jesus Christ?

3. Does the papacy have any biblical support?

4. Should churches in our time hold ecumenical councils to address significant theological issues? Who would call the councils, and what authority would they have over churches?

Conclusion

THE FIRST FIVE HUNDRED years of the Christian church were years of ongoing growth. Peter preached on the day of Pentecost with incredible results. We read, "But many of those who had heard the word believed, and the number of the men came to about five thousand."[1] We also read statements like, "And the Lord added to their number day by day those who were being saved,"[2] and "more than ever believers were added to the Lord, multitudes of both men and women."[3] Also, "For he [Barnabas] was a good man, full of the Holy Spirit and of faith. And a great many people were added to the Lord."[4] Although we are not given exact numbers, there were tens of thousands of believers when Paul was martyred in c.68 AD. The population of the Roman Empire in 300 AD was approximately seventy million people. While it is impossible to know exactly how many Christians there were at this time, it is estimated that at least ten percent of the Roman population were professing believers, approximately seven million people, and it could have been significantly more. The numbers of professing Christians grew rapidly after Emperor Constantine legalized and favoured Christianity in 313 AD. This growth accelerated further when Emperor Theodosius declared Christianity the official religion of the Roman Empire in 380. This increase has continued to the present day, where there are approximately 2.3 billion professing Christians worldwide.

While the church was growing numerically, it was under constant attack both externally and internally. Satan's two-pronged approach to destroy the church has always been to stir up persecution against

1. Acts 4:4.

2. Acts 2:47.

3. Acts 5:14.

4. Acts 11:24.

Christians and to introduce false teaching into the church. This is certainly what we see in the early centuries of the church. The church was persecuted by the Jewish establishment and then by the Romans. By far, the more significant threat to the future stability of the church was the rise of false teachers. The early councils were called to address the myriad of opinions on the doctrine of God, the nature of Jesus Christ, and the Holy Spirit, along with other secondary doctrines. The struggle to formulate the creeds[5] that came to be accepted as the orthodox expression of the Christian faith was long and hard. The struggle to defend these early expressions of Christianity continues to the present day.

As the church moved further away from its inception on the day of Pentecost, many doctrinal compromises were made, and aberrant liturgical practices were introduced into the church's worship.[6] Many of these find their origin in pagan rituals. For example, the first Christians did not use candles and incense in Christian worship because of their association with paganism.[7] Over time, these things were Christianized and were a regular feature in Christian worship.

The growing adoration of Mary in the early church finds its origin in pagan religion. Artemis was worshiped at Ephesus, and many believe that this worship was transferred over to Mary as people left paganism and entered the church. Other scholars identify Mary with the Egyptian goddess Isis who was worshipped throughout the Roman Empire. Isis was referred to as "the Great Virgin" and "Mother of the God." When paganism was outlawed in the latter fourth century, many pagans who converted to Christianity would naturally transfer their affection over to Mary.[8] This affection turned into exaltation and eventually led to the official acceptance of the immaculate conception of Mary in 1854 and her miraculous assumption to heaven in 1950. What started as a recognition of her privileged position as the mother of our Lord eventually led to the belief that Mary held an exalted place in heaven and that prayers could be offered directly to her. By 590 AD, Mary was considered "queen of the army of saints,"[9] held the leading position of all the saints, and had a cen-

---

5. The Nicene and Chalcedonian creeds in particular.

6. Schaff, *History of the Christian Church*, 3:93, 376.

7. Dowley, *Eerdmans' Handbook*, 132.

8. Dowley, *Eerdmans' Handbook*, 132.

9. Schaff, *History of the Christian Church*, 3:409.

tral place in the worship of the church.[10] Cyril of Alexandria (c.376-444) heaped extravagant words of praise on Mary when he wrote, "She was the crown of virginity, the indestructible temple of God, the dwelling place of the Holy Trinity, the paradise of the second Adam, the bridge from God to man, the loom of the incarnation, the sceptre of orthodoxy; through her the Trinity is glorified and adored, the devil and demons are put to flight, the nations converted, and the fallen creature raise to heaven."[11] With these kinds of accolades, it is no wonder that Mary took a central place in Roman Catholic worship.

Another superstition that took hold of the church is the cult of the saints and the martyrs. Famous Christians, particularly those martyred for the faith, were held in high regard in the church and were given the title saint to distinguish them from ordinary Christians.[12] Chapels and church buildings were erected over their burial sites, festivals were held on the day of their death, and these festival days were incorporated into the Christian calendar. The bones, teeth, hair, etc., of the saints were preserved and venerated. It was believed that these relics possessed the powers of healing, and eventually, the church charged money if people wanted to see them and receive their benefits. The commercial trade of relics became a huge problem, and in 381, church officials ordered that the sale of relics be terminated.[13] This order did not put an end to the market, and the buying and selling of relics grew in magnitude over the centuries, eventually becoming an exceptionally lucrative trade for the church. Although the saints were not to be worshiped, by the end of the sixth century, the church encouraged prayers to be offered to the saints who it was believed would intercede with God on their behalf. Many scholars believe that the cult of the saints and the martyrs was the Christianisation of the polytheism of the pagan world. The saints replaced the pagan gods, and the chapels and churches built in honour of the saints took the place of the pagan temples.[14]

The power of the bishop of Rome continued to grow until, in the later sixth century, the spiritual and temporal authority of the papacy and

10. Cairns, *Christianity Through the Centuries*, 174.

11. Schaff, *History of the Christian Church*, 3:421.

12. The word "saint" in the New Testament is used of all Christians and is not a designation for a special class of holy Christians. To be a Christian is to be a saint (Rom 1:7; 1 Cor 1:2; 2 Cor 1:1).

13. Cairns, *Christianity Through the Centuries*, 175.

14. Dowley, *Eerdmans' Handbook*, 132.

his superior position over the other bishops was accepted by most Christians in the west. His power continued to grow in the western church to the point where the pope claimed sovereignty over the monarchs of Europe. Until the present day, the pope of Rome is considered the head of the Roman Catholic Church, although his influence over the governments of Europe has been greatly diminished.[15]

We also see the development of the sacramental system in the fifth and sixth centuries. By the end of the sixth century, the seven sacraments of the Roman Catholic church[16] were firmly embedded in the church's worship. Many in the church came to believe that the sacraments could only be administered by the priest if they were to be spiritually efficacious. This belief resulted in a growing distinction between the clergy and the laity.[17]

As the church transitioned from its early Roman period to what is known as the Middle Ages (c.500 to 1400–1500 AD), the centrality of Mary in worship; the cult of the saints and the martyrs; universal papal authority over both church and state; the sale of relics, and the sacerdotal system, including the doctrine of transubstantiation became the theological and liturgical foundation for the church. The monastic system should be included, which continued to develop and spread throughout Europe.

By the beginning of the Middle Ages, the Roman Catholic Church was developing rapidly, reaching the zenith of its power during these thousand years. The church in the Middle Ages had control over virtually every aspect of a person's life, from the cradle to the grave. People were born into the world of Roman Catholic Church, lived under its teaching, and died in the arms of the Roman church.

By 500 AD, the church had moved far away from the simplicity of its worship in the first and second centuries. This drift away from the earlier years of the church would continue throughout the Middle Ages until an inevitable reaction against the doctrinal and political corruption of the medieval church took place. The Protestant Reformation of the sixteenth century sought to re-establish the church on the foundation and authority of the Bible and to preach the simplicity of the gospel message that

15. The Eastern Orthodox Church has never accepted the pope in Rome as the head of the church.

16. The seven Roman Catholic Sacraments are: Baptism; the Lord's Supper; ordination; confirmation; Penance; anointing the sick (formerly known as extreme unction); and marriage.

17. Cairns, *Christianity Through the Centuries*, 172–73.

a man is saved by grace alone, through faith alone, in the sufficiency of the sacrifice of Jesus Christ alone, plus nothing. The Reformation sought to purge the church of the many false doctrines that had developed over the centuries and make the church's worship more Christ-centered and biblically-based. But that is a story for another time.

FALSE TEACHING IN THE EARLY CHURCH

"But false prophets also arose among the people, just as there will be false teachers among you, who will secretly bring in destructive heresies, even denying the Master who bought them, bringing upon themselves swift destruction. And many will follow their sensuality, and because of them the way of truth will be blasphemed. And in their greed they will exploit you with false words. Their condemnation from long ago is not idle, and their destruction is not asleep."

—2 PETER 2:1–3

THIS GLOSSARY PROVIDES DEFINITIONS of many of the major theological deviations in the early church. It is important to note that some of the doctrinal errors in the church were of greater importance than others. Some are rightly called heresies, while others may be erroneous but not necessarily heretical. Arianism, for example, is heretical because it denies the deity of Jesus Christ and the triune nature of God. In contrast, Novatianism may be an extreme reaction to those who denied Christ in times of persecution but is not heresy. Both the major and minor theological divisions are put together here in one place.

Ebionism: Ebionism was mainly a Jewish heresy and was never widely adopted by Gentile believers. It was strongest in the latter half of the first century and continued several decades into the second. The Ebionites were a sect of Judaizing Christians who taught the necessity of obeying the Old Testament law to obtain salvation (although they did reject animal sacrifice as an extra-biblical addition to the scriptures). While affirming that Jesus was a man anointed by the Spirit of God, they denied the deity of Jesus Christ. Jesus was the son of Joseph and Mary, and there was nothing unique about his birth. Jesus was only a human prophet in a long line of prophets. They also rejected the apostle Paul's teaching that Jesus had fulfilled the law on behalf of others, arguing instead that Jesus set an example of law obedience that we are all required to follow.[1] They denied that we are saved by faith alone, but also through obedience to every detail of the law.[2]

Gnosticism: Gnosticism included various ideas taken from several different sources, including Christianity. The mixing of Christian doctrine with the teachings of Gnosticism resulted in a confused Gnostic version of Christianity which became a significant threat to the doctrinal stability of the church. Presenting itself as an alternative way of salvation, it appealed to the minds of many people. The Gnostics taught that all matter is evil and that salvation is found in deliverance from the body, which was viewed as a prison house for the soul. One needed to obtain true knowledge or gnosis if he was to be delivered from this prison-house. The problem is that human beings are unable, in their imprisoned state, to discover this knowledge on their own. It was, therefore, necessary for a messenger to come from the spiritual world and reveal that knowledge to us. For the Christian Gnostic, Jesus was that messenger. Gnosticism has an intense dislike or even hatred of the material world, which led to a denial of the basic tenants of the Christian faith. Several key doctrines were threatened by Gnostic teaching: The sovereignty and goodness of God; the goodness of creation; the inspiration of the Old Testament scriptures, the incarnation, the virgin birth, the vicarious death of Christ, justification by faith alone, the resurrection of Christ, and the future resurrection of believers. In other words, the Gnostics denied the very gospel itself and threatened to rip the heart out of the Christian faith.[3]

Docetism: The word Docetism is derived from the Greek word δοκέω which means "to seem or appear." The Docetists believed that Jesus was

---

1. Gonzalez, *History of Christian Thought* 122–26.

2. Eusebius, CH 3.27.

3. For a good summary of Gnosticism see Gonzalez, *History of Christian Thought*, 1:126–41.

God; however, they denied that he was human but only appeared or seemed to be human. Docetism was a natural outgrowth of Gnostic belief with its insistence that matter (including human flesh) was evil and its denial that God would ever take on a human body.

Montanism: Montanus, the founder of Montanism (a name given to his movement by those who opposed him), emerged In Phrygia sometime between 155–160 AD. He claimed that he was chosen by God and given new revelation, along with two prophetesses, Maximilla and Priscilla, who followed him. He also claimed to be the embodiment of the Holy Spirit promised in John 14:26, "But the Helper, the Holy Spirit, whom the Father will send in my name, he will teach you all things and bring to your remembrance all that I have said to you" (ESV). He also declared that because the Holy Spirit spoke through him, he was above the authority of Scripture.[4] Montanus believed that a new dispensation and prophetic movement had begun with his ministry. He thought he was living in the final days and predicted that the world would end immediately after his death. Montanism promoted a rigorous lifestyle where marriage, although allowed, was frowned upon, and widows and widowers were not permitted to remarry. Extreme fasting and almsgiving were required, and martyrdom was encouraged while running away in times of persecution was forbidden. Montanism taught that the New Jerusalem in Revelation 21 would come down from heaven to Pepuza, Phrygia and that all Christians should be in Pepuza at the Second Coming of Jesus Christ.[5] The movement also emphasized speaking in tongues. Some object to Montanism being included under a list of false teaching because it was theologically orthodox, for the most part. Some early church teachers did not favour condemning the Montanists despite acknowledging their aberrant beliefs and behaviors. Nevertheless, Montanism threatened both the stability of the emerging structure of the Christian Church and the finality of revelation given in Jesus Christ.[6]

Manichaeism: Manichaeism was a third-century Gnostic movement founded by Mani, who was born in 216 AD. In 240, he began teaching his radical offshoot of Gnosticism. He had a dualistic view of the world,

4. *Encyclopedia of Ancient Christianity*, 2:834.

5. *Encyclopedia of Ancient Christianity*, 2:833.

6. Gonzalez, *History of Christian Thought*, 1:143.

believing that light and darkness were in constant conflict with one another. He taught that Satan stole light particles from the world of light and implanted them into people's minds. Salvation involved the releasing of these particles of light imprisoned in men's souls. Jesus, Buddha, the Prophets, and Mani himself, had come to help people in this task. Extreme asceticism was adopted as a means of accomplishing this feat.[7]

Modalism: Modalism is a Trinitarian heresy that propounds the belief that God the Father, God the Son, and God the Holy Spirit are one and the same divine person. Although modalism does not deny the deity of Christ, it denies his distinct personhood. The Son and the Spirit were considered modes in which God revealed himself. In the same way, an actor may play three different roles by holding three different masks over his face at various points in the performance, so God sometimes presented himself as Father and at other times as the Son or the Holy Spirit.

Patripassianism: Patripassianism is a doctrine that teaches that the Father suffered in Christ while on the cross. This teaching is a logical progression from modalism which denied any distinction between the three persons of the Trinity. It is a form of Monarchianism and is also known as Sabellianism.[8]

Monarchianism/Adoptionism: Monarchianism was a theological movement in the second and third centuries. It taught that Jesus became Christ at His baptism and was adopted by the Father after His death. There were two distinct Monarchianism groups:

The Adoptionist or "dynamic' Monarchians" taught that Jesus was God in that the power of God was upon him as a human being. When he was born of the Virgin Mary, he was only a man but more holy than other men. Because of his holy life, the divine spirit came upon him at his baptism, which resulted in his deification. Some adoptionists taught that Jesus was deified at his baptism, while others said it was after his resurrection.

7. *Dictionary of the Christian Church*, 1027.
8. *Dictionary of the Christian Church*, 1233.

The Modalist Monarchians or Sabellians said that the differences between the persons of the godhead were only "modes" or "operations."[9]

Novatianism: While Novatianism is not technically a heresy, it resulted in a great division in the early church. Novatius refused to give communion to believers who had denied their faith, offered sacrifices to the emperor, or handed over scriptures to be burned during the persecution of emperor Decius in 250.

Donatism: Followers of Donatus Magnus refused to accept Christians who handed the scriptures over to the secular authorities and did not recognize bishops ordained by a church leader who had handed over the scriptures during the Diocletian persecution (303–5).

Arianism: Arianism denied the deity of Christ and the triune nature of God.

Eusebianism: Eusebianism is a Christological heresy also called "Semi-arianism." Christ is of similar essence with the Father but is subordinate to Him. Their Christology was mid-way between full-blown Arianism and orthodoxy.

Macedonianism: Macedonianism is a trinitarian heresy also called "Pneumatomachianism." Macedonius was a priest in Constantinople around 335 and became the bishop in the city in 344. He was a controversial figure who held to the Homoiousios position (that Christ was of "like or similar substance" with the Father, but not of the "same" substance) in the Christological debates. While not a true Arian, he did not believe that the Father and the Son shared in the same divine essence. Around 360, Marcedonius, along with other Homoiousians, denied the deity of the Holy Spirit. While some believed the Holy Spirit to be a creature, others were less clear in their definitions while still denying him full divine status.[10] Athanasius and other supporters of the Nicene Creed and the Trinity referred to them as Pneumatomachoi, but they eventually became known as "Macedonians."[11]

---

9. *Dictionary of the Christian Church*, 1102.

10. *Encyclopedia of Ancient Christianity*, 2:649.

11. *Encyclopedia of Ancient Christianity*, 3:237.

Pneumatomachism: Pneumatomachianism is a fourth-century heresy that denied the full deity of the Holy Spirit. A conservative branch accepted the consubstantiality (of same substance or essence) of the Son with the Father while rejecting the divinity of the Spirit. The more radical Pneumatomachians also denied the consubstantiality of the Son. Pneumatomachianism was condemned at the council of Constantinople in 381.[12]

Apollinarianism: Apollinarianism, named after its founder Apollinaris, is a Christological heresy that represents an early attempt to work out the relationship between the deity and humanity of Christ. Apollinaris was born at Laodicea around 315 AD, eventually becoming the bishop of Laodicea. He supported the Nicene Creed, affirmed the deity of Christ, and believed that the Son was of the same essence as the Father. In an attempt to protect the deity of Christ, Apollinaris was in danger of obliterating his humanity. At the heart of the issue is the rejection of the idea that Jesus possessed a human personality. While he affirmed that Jesus had a human body, he argued that he did not have a human spirit (mind) but only the mind of the divine Word (logos). If Jesus lacked a human spirit, he would not have had human intelligence and thus could not be truly human. While he did believe that God was made flesh, he argued that the humanity of Christ was made divine and that there was no real distinction between the deity and the humanity of Christ. The problem with this view is its failure to appreciate the full humanity of Jesus Christ. If Christ is not fully human, how can he secure salvation for all mankind? If Christ was to provide redemption for fallen humanity, there had to be a point of connection between God and man. Jesus had to experience suffering in a human body and spirit to reconcile man to God.[13]

Nestorianism: Nestorianism was a Christological error that taught that the humanity and deity of Jesus Christ were two separate and distinct natures.

Eutychianism: Eutychianism was a Christological heresy that taught that Jesus was neither fully human nor fully divine but a mixture of both natures. Eutychianism is a form of Monophysitism.

---

12. *Dictionary of the Christian Church*, 1303.
13. Brown, *Heresies*, 162–65.

<u>Monophysitism</u>: Monophysitism is the belief that Jesus Christ possessed only one nature. In the incarnation, the human and the divine union resulted in a single nature. Jesus was God with human attributes. It was declared a heresy in 451 at the fourth church council in Chalcedon.[14]

<u>Monothelitism</u>: Monothelitism is a Christological heresy. It taught that Christ had a divine will but no human will. This view stripped the human nature of Christ of its human attributes, making it "impersonal and lifeless."[15] The Maronite Church in Syria holds to this view today. It was a title used after the Council of Chalcedon (451) as a designation for those who rejected the council's definition of Christ as being one person 'in two Natures.'

<u>Pelagianism</u>: Pelagius believed in the total freedom of human will and denied the sovereignty of God in salvation. He taught that Adam's sin was his own and was not inherited by his descendants. He defined grace as the natural abilities God has given to man. Grace reveals what God requires but does not assist us in performing our moral duties. Grace only provided moral guidance but did nothing for the inner life or actions of man. He believed that man is justified and accepted by God based on human merit. The Council of Ephesus in 431 declared Pelagianism as heretical.

14. *Dictionary of the Christian Church*, 1104.

15. Brown, *Heresies*, 187.

Further Reading

Earle E. Cairns. *Christianity Through the Centuries*. Grand Rapids, MI: Zondervan, 1996.

Eamon Duffy. *Saints and Sinners: A History of the Popes*. New Haven, CT: Yale University Press, 2006.

John Fea. *Why Study History?* Grand Rapids, MI: Baker Academic, 2013.

John Ferguson. *The Religions of the Roman Empire*. New York: Cornell University Press, 1970.

Mark Galli and Ted Olsen, eds. *131 Christians Everyone Should Know*. Nashville, TN: Broadman & Holman, 2000.

Michael A.G. Haykin. *Rediscovering the Church Fathers: Who They Were And How They Shaped The Church*. Wheaton, IL: Crossway, 2011.

James S. Jeffers. *The Greco-Roman World of the New Testament Era*. Downers Grove, IL: InterVarsity, 1999.

Diarmaid MacCulloch. *A History of Christianity: The First Three Thousand Years*. London: Penguin, 2009.

H. J. Rose. *Religion in Greece and Rome*. New York: Harper and Brothers, 1959.

Bibliography

Aquilina, Mike. *The Fathers of the Church*. Huntington, Indiana: Our Sunday Visitor, Inc., 2013.

Athanasius. *On the Incarnation*. Yonkers, NY: St. Vladimir's Seminary Press, 2011.

———. *The Life of St. Antony*. In *Ancient Christian Writers*, Vol.10. New York: Newman, 1950.

Augustine. *Confessions*. Translated by Garry Wills. New York: Penguin, 2002.

Baker. B., trans. *The Life of Saint Paul of Thebes*. The Lives of the Great Desert Fathers. Florence. AZ: Sagon, 2019.

Barrow, R.H. *The Romans*. London: Penguin, 1949.

Basil the Great. *On Social Justice*. Popular Patristics Series, Vol. 38. Translated by C. Paul Schroeder. Crestwood, NY: St. Vladimir's Seminary Press, 2009.

Bright, William. *The Age of the Fathers*, Vol. 1. New York: AMS, 1970.

Brown, O.J. *Heresies: Heresy and Orthodoxy In The History Of the Church*. Peabody, MA: Hendrickson Publishers, 1984.

Burn, A.R. *The Pelican History of Greece*. London: Penguin, 1965.

Cairns, Earle E. *Christianity Through the Centuries*. Grand Rapids: Zondervan, 1967.

Chrysostom, John. *On the Priesthood*. Translated by Graham Neville. Crestwood, New York: St. Vladimir's Seminary Press, 1977.

Coyle, J.K. "Mani and Maniceheism." In *Encyclopedia of Ancient Christianity*, edited by Angelo Di Berardino, 661-665. 3 vols. Downers Grove, IL: IVP Academic, 1994-2013.

Cyprian. *The Letters of St. Cyprian*. In Ancient Christian Writers, Vol. 43. Translated by G.W. Clarke. New York, N.Y.: Newman Press, 1984.

———. *The Lapsed, The Unity of the Catholic Church*. Ancient Christian Writers, Vol. 25. Translated by Maurice Benvenot. New York, NY: The Newman Press, 1956.

Dictionary of the Christian Church. Edited by F.L. Cross and E.A. Livingstone. Peabody, MA: Hendrickson Publishers. 1997.

Dictionary of Major Biblical Interpreters. Edited by Donald K. McKim. Downers Grove: InterVarsity, 2007.

Doleac, Miles. *In the Footsteps of Alexander*. London: Amber, 2014.

Dowley, Tim, ed. *Eerdmans' Handbook to The History of Christianity*. Hertfordshire, UK: Lion, 1977.

———. ed. *The History of Christianity*. Grand Rapids: Eerdmans, 196.

Ellis, Peter Berresford. *The Druids*. London: Constable, 2002.

Encyclopedia of Ancient Christianity. 3 vols. Edited by Angelo Di Berardino. Downers Grove, IL: IVP Academic, 1994-2013.

Encyclopedia of the Ancient Roman Empire. Edited by Carlos Gomez. London: Amber, 2019.

Esler, Philip F. *The Early Christian World.* London and New York: Routledge, 2000.

Eusebius. *The Church History.* Translated by Paul L. Maier. Grand Rapids, MI: Kregel, 2007.

———. *History of the Church.* Edited by Betty Radice. London: Penguin, 1965.

Everitt, Anthony. *The Rise of Rome.* New York: Random House, 2012.

Ferguson, Everett. *Backgrounds of Early Christianity.* Grand Rapids: Eerdmans, 2003. Kindle.

———. *Church History, Vol.1. From Christ to Pre-Reformation.* Grand Rapids, Michigan: Zondervan, 2005.

Gomez Carlos. *The Encyclopedia of the Ancient Roman Empire.* London: Amber, 2019.

Gonzalez, Justo L. *The Story of Christianity.* Peabody, MA: Prince, 1984.

———. *A History of Christian Thought.* Nashville: Abingdon, 1987.

Haykin, Michael A.G. *Rediscovering the Church Fathers.* Wheaton, IL: Crossway, 2011.

Hinson, E. Glenn. *The Early Church, Origins to the Dawn of the Middle Ages.* Nashville: Abingdon, 1996.

Hunt, John. *Concise Church History.* Chattanooga, TN: AMG, 2008.

Irenaeus. *Against the Heresies.* Ancient Christian Writers 64. Translated by Dominic J, Unger. New York: Paulist, 2012.

Jerome. *The Letters of St. Jerome.* Vol.1. Translated by Charles Christopher Mierow. New York: Newman, 1963.

Josephus. *The Complete Works.* Translated by William Whiston. Nashville: Thomas Nelson, 1998.

———. *The Essential Writings.* Translated by Paul L. Maier. Grand Rapids: Kregel, 1988.

Kalmin, Richard. "The Miracle of the Septuagint in Ancient Rabbinic and Christian Literature." In *"Follow the Wise:" Studies in Jewish History and Culture in Honor of Lee I. Levine,* edited by Zeev Weiss, Oded Irshai & Jodi Magness, 241–54. Winona Lake, IN: Eisenbrauns, 2010.

Kazhdan, Alexander P., ed. *Oxford Dictionary of Byzantium.* 3 vols. Oxford: Oxford University Press, 1991.

Kelly, J.N.D. *Early Christian Doctrines.* Peabody, MA: Prince, 1978.

Kleist, James A., trans. *The Epistle to Diognetus.* Ancient Christian Writers, Vol.6. New York: Newman, 1948.

Lightfoot, J.B. *The Apostolic Fathers.* Grand Rapids: Baker, 1987.

The Lives of the Great Desert Fathers. Translated by B. Baker. Florence, AZ: Sagom, 2019.

Malingrey, A.M. *John Chrysostom. Encyclopedia of Ancient Christianity.* 2 vols. Edited by Angelo Di Berardino. Downers Grove, IL: IVP Academic, 2014.

March, Jenny. *The Penguin Book of Classical Myths.* London, UK: Penguin, 2008.

Mathisen, Ralph. W. *Ancient Roman Civilization.* New York: Oxford University Press, 2019.

McGrath, Alister, ed. *The Christian Theology Reader.* Oxford, UK: Blackwell, 1995.

———. *Historical Theology.* Oxford, UK: Blackwell, 1998.

McKim, Donald K., ed. *Dictionary of Major Biblical Interpreters.* Nottingham, UK: InterVarsity, 2007.

Need, Stephen W. *Truly Divine and Truly Human.* Peabody, MA.: Hendrikson, 2008.

O'Loughlin, Thomas. *The Didache.* Grand Rapids, MI: Baker Academic, 2010.

Orthodox Wiki. "Nicene-Constantinopolitan Creed." https://orthodoxwiki.org/Nicene-Constantinopolitan_Creed.

Oxford Dictionary of Byzantium. 3 vols. Edited by Alexander P. Kazhdan. Oxford: Oxford University Press, 1991.

Palladius. *Dialogue on the Life of St. John Chrysostom.* Ancient Christian Writers 45. Translated by Robert T. Meyer. New York: Newman, 1985.

Patrick. *The Works of St. Patrick.* Ancient Christian Writers 17. Translated by Ludwig Bieler. New York: Paulist, 1953.

Percival, H. R. "The Canons of the 318 Holy Fathers Assembled in the City of Nice, in Bithynia." In *The Seven Ecumenical Councils,* edited by P. Schaff and H. Wace, 19–20. New York: Charles Scribner's Sons, 1900.

Petterson, Alvyn. *Athanasius.* Harrisburg, PA: Morehouse, 1999.

Pliny. *The Letters of The Younger Pliny.* Translated by Betty Radice. Middlesex, UK: Penguin, 1969.

Polycarp. *Epistles to the Philippians.* Ancient Christian Writers, Vol. 6. New York: Newman, 1948.

Roberts, J.M and O.A. Westad. *The History of the World.* Oxford: Oxford University Press, 2013.

Rogers, Nigel. *Roman Empire.* Leicestershire: Hermes House, 2011.

Sciortino, Elisabetta Segala Ida. *DOMVS AVREA,* Milan: Electa, 1999.

Schaff, Philip. *History of the Christian Church.* 7 vols. Peabody, MA: Hendrickson, 2006.

———. *Nicene and Post-Nicene Fathers.* Peabody, MA: Hendrickson, 2004.

———. *The Creeds of Christendom.* 3 vols. Grand Rapids: Baker, 2007.

Sheldon, Henry. *History of the Christian Church.* Volume 1. Peabody, MA: Hendrickson, 1994.

Shelly, Bruce, L. *Church History in Plain Language.* Nashville: Thomas Nelson, 1995.

Silvas, A. *The Rule of St. Basil in Latin and English*: Revised critical edition. Collegeville, MN: Liturgical, 2013.

Smith, A. Michael. *Basil the Great.* Great Leaders of the Christian Church. Edited by John Woodbridge. Chicago: Moody, 1988.

Socrates. "Ecclesiastical History." In *Nicene and Post-Nicene Fathers,* vol. 2, edited by Philip Schaff. Peabody, MA: Hendrickson, 2004.

Sozomenus. "The Ecclesiastical History of Sozomen." In *Nicene and Post-Nicene Fathers,* vol. 2, edited by Philip Schaff, 239–427. Peabody, MA: Hendrickson, 2004.

Speros, Vryonis, Jr. *Byzantium and Europe.* London, UK: Thames and Hudson, 1967.

Suetonius. *The Twelve Caesars.* Translated by Robert Graves. London: Penguin Random House, 2007.

Tacitus. *The Agricola and The Germania.* Translated by H. Mattingly. London: Penguin Books, 1988.

———. *The Annals of Imperial Rome.* Translated by Michael Grant. London: Penguin, 1989.

Theodoret. *The Ecclesiastical History of Theodoret. Nicene and Post-Nicene Fathers,* vol. 3. Edited by Philip Shaff. Peabody, MA: Hendrickson, 2004.

Tuck, Steven. *A History of Roman Art.* West Sussex: Wiley-Blackwell, 2015.

Walker, Williston, Richard A. Norris, David W. Lotz, Robert T. Handy. *A History of the Christian Church.* New York: Charles Scribner's Sons, 1918.

Warfield, Benjamin. "Revelation and Inspiration," In *The Works of Benjamin B. Warfield.* Vol.1. New York: Oxford University Press, 1932.

Welsh, Frank. *The History of the World*. London: Quercus, 2011.

Whitmarsh, Tim. *Battling the Gods: Atheism in the Ancient World*. New York: Penguin Random House, 2015.

Wilkins, Paige, T., M. J. and R. P. Martin. *Worship, Theology and Ministry in the Early Church: Essays in Honor of Ralph P. Martin*. Sheffield: Sheffield Academic Press, 1992.

William Bright. *The Age of the Fathers*. 2 vols. New York: AMS, 1970.

Woodbridge, John D. *Great Leaders of the Christian Church*. Chicago: Moody, 1988.

Wylen, Steven M. *Jews In The Time Of Jesus, An Introduction*. Mahwah, NJ: Paulist, 2008.

Young, Frances M. *From Nicaea to Chalcedon*. London: SCM, 1983.